Citizens of Europe?

Citizens of Europe?

The Emergence of a Mass European Identity

Michael Bruter

Lecturer in European Politics and Political Science,
London School of Economics and Political Science

First published in 2005 by
PALGRAVE MACMILLAN
Houndmills, Basingstoke, Hampshire RG21 6XS and
175 Fifth Avenue, New York, N.Y. 10010
Companies and representatives throughout the world.

PALGRAVE MACMILLAN is the global academic imprint of the Palgrave Macmillan division of St. Martin's Press, LLC and of Palgrave Macmillan Ltd. Macmillan® is a registered trademark in the United States, United Kingdom and other countries. Palgrave is a registered trademark in the European Union and other countries.

ISBN-13: 978–1–4039–3239–6 hardback
ISBN-10: 1–4039–3239–5 hardback

This book is printed on paper suitable for recycling and made from fully managed and sustained forest sources.

A catalogue record for this book is available from the British Library.

Library of Congress Cataloging-in-Publication Data
Bruter, Michael, 1975–
    Citizens of Europe? : the emergence of a mass European identity / Michael Bruter.
        p. cm.
    Includes bibliographical references and index.
    ISBN 1–4039–3239–5 (cloth)
        1. Nationalism – European Union countries. 2. National characteristics, European. 3. Group identity – European Union countries. 4. Political culture – European Union countries. I. Title.
JN40.B78 2005
155.8′94′090511—dc22   2005047291

10 9 8 7 6 5 4 3 2 1
14 13 12 11 10 09 08 07 06 05

Printed and bound in Great Britain by
Antony Rowe Ltd, Chippenham and Eastbourne

Contents

Appendices   179

List of Tables and Figures

Tables

Figures

Acknowledgements

Under the pretence of thanking those who truly deserve it, acknowledgements often are an excuse for the overworked and frustrated author to tell plenty of irrelevant things about his 'life and experience' of writing a time and energy-consuming work! This one will be no exception and I apologise for it, but I genuinely owe a lot to the outstanding and amazing people, whose invaluable help I have been lucky enough to receive. Needless to say that I remain wholly responsible, however, for all the flaws and imperfections of this book ...

A 'finished' research forces one to measure the discrepancy between the original idealistic hopes for a seminal piece and the actual final product, with its imperfections, shortcomings, and disappointments. However, any (hopefully) remaining strength in the book is largely due to the following ...

I could not have proceeded to do my primary research without the two grants I obtained from the Reitmeyer Fund (Hartford) and the Economic and Social Research Council.

My thanks to all those who have provided invaluable comments on my work, in particular – and in no specific order – Thomas Risse (Frei Universitat Berlin), Lauren McLaren (University of Nottingham), the ever so bubbly Ulrike Meinhof (University of Southampton), Richard Herrmann (University of Ohio), Robert Erikson (Columbia University), Susan Scarrow (University of Houston), Ray Duch (University of Houston), Gail McElroy (Trinity College Dublin), my colleagues at the London School of Economics and Political Science for their advice.

I could not explain how indebted I am to – and how proud I am to know – the three great scholars whom I consider my three mentors. Cees van der Eijk (University of Amsterdam), for his extreme kindness and availability, and the extreme cleverness of any advice he has ever given me; Mark Franklin (Trinity College Hartford), whom the words 'supervisor' and 'mentor' hardly do justice to. His trust and his invaluably intelligent help, have assumed over the years, more different forms than I thought possible; and finally Ed Page (LSE), to whom I owe a significant part of my taste for research and of my career, but first and foremost, with his family, a proper friend, whose bacon and sausage sandwiches or Hull City football outings simply make life so much better! ...

I want to thank my family: father Jean, mother Sylvia, and grandparents David, Haim, Mathilde, Amelie, for having always been here.

Finally, this first book is co-dedicated to the two most important persons in my life at the moment: to Sarah, my Princess, love, and Sweetheart, and to my brother, Jonathan, to whom I feel always closer, and the best person I know on earth.

Plan of the Book: Summary of the Chapters

Chapter 1: What is Identity?

The main question

What is identity, what is so peculiar about studying a 'European identity', and what is the object of this book?

The themes addressed

In this first chapter, I am mostly concerned with the conceptual framework of the study and with explaining why I believe it is interesting to figure out whether such a thing as a European identity has emerged over the past 30 years, how it connects with the other components of citizens' identities, and whether or not it changes over time. The first part of the chapter is largely dedicated to conceptual puzzles and the state of our knowledge on European identity: I talk about the concepts of identity and political identity. I examine the contributions of various disciplines to the study of European identity, such as political science, history, sociology, social psychology, anthropology, and even philosophy and geography. What do we know about what is Europe? About the way different identities can co-exist or contradict each other? About what people mean when they say 'I feel French' (or European, or Black)? This helps us to identify four major caveats in our current knowledge on European identity:

- As yet, we do not really know what people mean when they say that they feel European.
- We do not really know why some people feel more European than other.
- We have contradictory findings about whether or not a mass European identity has emerged over the past 30 years.
- We have contradictory theories about whether an individual's political identity can evolve over time and whether institutions and the media can influence them.

These four questions and paradoxes are precisely the ones this book will answer. The end of the chapter outlines how I intend to manage this, using a framework in which identities are assumed to be multiple, and political identities made of two main components, a 'civic' one and a 'cultural' one.

Chapter 2: The Model and Research Design: Institutions? Media? And the Development of a Mass European Identity

The main question

What is this book doing? Testing the impact of news and symbols of Europe on citizens' identity and the emergence of a mass European identity between 1970 and 2000.

The themes addressed

This chapter explains the model of the book and the methods used to test it. In short, I want to answer two big questions, at two different levels. First, I want to know if a mass European identity has emerged over the past 30 years in Europe, if it concerns equally all the member states of the European Union, and what it has meant for citizens' other identities. Second, I want to know how this has happened and this implies looking at individuals rather than masses. Why do some citizens feel more European than other? Do they all feel European in the same way? What is the impact of what people hear and read on Europe on their European identity, and what has been the impact of the many symbols of European integration the European Union has generated in order to try and make people feel more European? Here, I also describe the methods I use to answer these questions. They include (1) a time-series analysis of the evolution of a mass European identity across countries since 1970, with very novel results; (2) a comparative experiment assessing the effect of news and symbols of Europe on citizens' European identity in these countries: United Kingdom, France, and the Netherlands; (3) a series of focus group discussions on what it 'means' for people to be European. This mixture of qualitative and quantitative new data is quite unprecedented in the literature on this topic.

Chapter 3: Institutions and the Formation of Mass Identities in New Political Communities – Four 'Lessons From The Past' (United Kingdom, Austria, Israel, and the United States of America)

The main question

What do we know about the way institutions and the media have tried to either encourage or impede the formation of a mass identity in new communities, and of what makes this work or not?

The themes addressed

This chapter simply looks at the development of new political identities in the United States, the United Kingdom, Austria, and Israel. I look at the pre-existing situation, the initiative taken by the media and political institutions to try and encourage or impede the formation of new political identities, and the results, over time, in terms of identity formation. This opens the way to analyse the case of the European Union in the next chapter.

Chapter 4: With Aforethought? Institutions, Symbols, and the Quest for a New Identity in Europe

The main question

How have European institutions tried to mould a European identity through the use of symbols and a change in the focus of European integration?

The themes addressed

In this chapter, I first look at the evolution of European integration, from an international co-operation project in the 1950s to a policy-making project in the 1960s, an institutionally consolidated system in the 1970s, and a system trying to foster its own identity and citizenship in the 1980s and 1990s. I then consider the various symbols of European integration generated by the European Union and the meanings it tried to attach to them: flag, passport, names, Euro notes, day of Europe, etc. I propose a typology of these symbols, a study of the context of their choice and design. I differentiate between 'community' and 'union' symbols, with a civic or a cultural stance. I show how the type of symbols selected has clearly evolved over time and what expectations were formulated in terms of identity formation.

Chapter 5: Who Feels European? Measurement of European Identity and Differences Across Individuals

The main question

How to measure European identity and its civic and cultural components, and what can we learn about who feels 'more' (or differently) European than whom? ...

The themes addressed

This chapter proposes a totally new way to measure European identity, based on its sub-division into 'spontaneous', 'civic', and 'cultural' components. I define a series of brand new questions asked of my respondents in a survey and aimed at measuring their relative levels of general, civic, and cultural European identity. The results are then used to look at individual differences according to basic variables such as the gender, age, or political opinions of the respondents. I find, for example, that left-wing and centrist people are more likely to feel attached to an EU 'civic' community, while right-wing voters are more sensitive to perceptions of a European 'cultural' identity and European shared heritage. I also find that the people who feel closer to their town and country also tend to feel closer to Europe and not the contrary, and that while civic European identity has a positive impact on the likeliness of citizens to support further European integration, this is not the case of cultural identity.

Chapter 6: News, Symbols, and European Identity

The main question

What is the influence of symbols of Europe and news on Europe on citizens' European identity?

The themes addressed

This chapter gives the main answers to the first 'big' question of the book: can institutions and the media influence citizens' political identities (and, in this case, European identity)? It is the first time this question is tested so directly and empirically, and the findings are very interesting. First, I show that both symbols of Europe and the connotations of the news people read influence their European identity. Second, I show that while news has a predominant effect on 'civic' identity, symbols have a predominant effect on 'cultural' identity. This has tremendous effects, not least in explaining the differences in levels of European identity across countries and individuals, and across generations.

Chapter 7: 1970–2000 – The Emergence of a Mass European Identity

The main question

Has a mass European identity emerged between 1970 and 2000 across the European Union member-States?

The themes addressed

Based on the insight from the previous chapter and an innovative measurement of European identity, I present unprecedented evidence on the emergence of a mass European identity over the past 30 years. I also look at differences across countries, and explain them on the basis of the results of Chapter 6. The results are analysed in their historical context and with regards to media and institutions' attitudes in the various member-states.

Chapter 8: On What it Means to 'Be European': Making Citizens Talk About 'Europe' and 'Europeanness'

The main question

What do various citizens mean when they claim to feel (or not) European?

The themes addressed

Based on the results of Chapters 6 and 7, and on focus group discussion with over a hundred respondents, this chapter closes our discussion on whether or not a mass European identity has emerged in Europe over the past 30 years, and on whether institutions and the media have contributed to facilitate or impede it by analysing citizens' answers to various questions about what it actually means to be or feel European. The results of this qualitative part of the project are truly interesting, with citizens talking about their daily experience of Europe in terms of human communication, borders, and social and cultural change over the past 50 years. The findings are presented by organising the answers of citizens from three countries in these half an hour discussions, and using abundant quotes and extracts. The participants also tell us how they think the media inform them on Europe, and how they receive the many symbols of the European Union, hereby illustrating the differences between the intended meaning of top-down messages, and their constructed meaning in public perceptions.

Chapter 9: Conclusions: Institutions and the Emergence of a Mass European Identity – Lessons for the Future

Summary of the main findings, implications for public opinion attitudes towards further political integration, the legitimacy of the European project, enlargement, the socialisation of new generations in Europe, and questions which remain to be answered.

1
What is Identity?

Along the past fifty years, a new, unique, political project – European unification – has emerged to unite peoples and nations, which had historically appeared to embody the archetypal symbols of war and enmity. How citizens have been led to accept peace and co-operation with their traditional enemies is a question, which has struck many observers as being extremely challenging and paradoxical. Have European citizens accepted European unification only because they have accepted the idea that it was favourable to their economic development and without developing a new political identity or, because they have progressively acquired such a new European identity? Surely, if European citizens have gone on not identifying politically with the European integration and equated the European project with a pure economic concept, there must be an overwhelming majority of citizens opposed to any further unification. Indeed, now, unification is predominantly political, and opens itself to poorer countries at a cost for the wealthier ones. Moreover, many of the specific policies of the European Union have been depicted in highly negative terms by the mass media and large numbers of politicians. However, at the same time, support for European integration has not decreased dramatically, and the political and social aspects of integration generally find greater support than the economic ones.

What is it all about? (And why does it matter? ...)

A citizen's political identity can be defined as his sense of belonging to politically relevant human groups and political structures. It has long been understood by political theorists that the emergence of a corresponding political identity can be considered as the primary source of legitimisation of a political community. In *Du Contrat Social*, Rousseau

(1762) explains that citizens choose to give their political community its legitimacy, and its right to determine what is the 'general will' through a social contract. After the original 'explicit' contract, however, the social contract that links citizens to their State is maintained implicitly legitimate because citizens choose to *identify* themselves to their community. Without identity, it seems that there can be no true, durable, legitimacy attached to a political entity, no conscious acceptance of the power of the State and of its monopolistic right to use legitimate coercion (Weber, 1946). Every time a new political community has been created, therefore, the legitimacy of the contract that links it to its citizens and gives it its fundamental institutional acceptability requires the creation of a new political identity.

This book is concerned with the formation and development of new political identities in general and of a European identity in particular. Its whole purpose is to evaluate whether such a thing as a mass European identity has emerged since the launching of the European project and, if so, how, and thanks to what actors, this has happened. It looks at the state of citizens' identity in the 15 pre-2004 member-States of the European Union after decades of unification, institutional change, and slow socialisation, and sketches what may happen in the countries that have – and will – join the European Union since the unification of Europe. It will evaluate how people identify with their new European political community, what influences their sense of identification, and how this new identity has affected other components (e.g., national, regional, and local) of their identity structure. In other words, this book shows whether – and which – European citizens have started to identify with the new construct of a political Europe, and, also, whether political actions, messages, and symbolic initiatives may have stimulated or impeded such a political identification process with the new Europe.

The question is everything but trivial. Since the eighteenth century, the very legitimacy of modern liberal democratic states has relied on a combination of guaranteed democratic processes and underlying political identity. Indeed, while democratic suffrage and constitutions have been one of the main determinants of politically acceptable states since the late eighteenth century, the Wilson doctrine of 1919 has transformed into a principle of international right that State borders should be defined according to mass identity realities and that populations should ultimately have the right to choose the political communities they want to belong to. Little by little, throughout the past half-century, a clear evolution of the European project has taken place. The European Union has quite explicitly transformed from a primarily economic agreement to a deeply and quintessentially political construction. This new face of Europe makes it absolutely necessary to evaluate whether this move is only and purely the product of a unilateral, undemocratic, choice of the European political elite or whether it also corresponds to a new European 'social contract', and a real change in the political identities of European citizens. Therefore, if a predominantly political Europe suffers from the type of democratic deficit many commentators suspect it does, it is of utmost importance to know whether it can, at least, claim to rely on a progressive underlying mass identity as this would be, indeed, the main foundation of its very legitimacy.

Studying European identity: a challenge for political science

Traditionally, empirical political scientists have been more interested in the degree to which European citizens support European integration than in the extent to which they identify with the new political entity created (e.g., Inglehart, 1997, Gabel, 1994). Sometimes, scholars have even had to assume, for theoretical or practical purposes, that the latter is simply another expression of the former (Inglehart, 1997). By focusing *only* on the relative support of citizens for European integration, political scientists would run the risk of missing a fundamental and predominant link in their models of such a support. Models would end up explaining support for European integration without understanding the full depth and 'philosophical' significance such a support probably involves at this stage of the integration process. As a discipline, focusing on support without studying identity would mean that we would break a golden hierarchical assumption of the study of political behaviour: the idea that for every individual, his beliefs influence his attitudes, which, in turn, influence his actual behaviour (Hurwitz and Peffley, 1987, Feldman, 1988). Moreover, from a methodological perspective, ignoring the role of identity in models where support for European integration is endogenous might result in statistical bias when European identity, as an omitted variable, would also be endogenous. This is particularly bound to be the case when predictors of both variables are included and if there is – as there most obviously is – a causal link between European identity and support for integration. Therefore, within the framework of methodological individualism in the study of political behaviour, one must acknowledge that behaviour is never self-standing and that political identities in particular, as the most fundamental self-characterisation of individuals, will influence citizens' beliefs, attitudes and behaviours.

It was often claimed that the consolidation of the creation of an American State was directly caused by the successful and relatively rapid emergence of a mass American identity. From this historical point of view, such a success could be explained by common ideals, common interests, and a set of favourable political circumstances. But can we really study the emergence of a new political identity as a purely aggregate and 'coincidental' phenomenon? In this research, it is be hypothesised that the formation of a new identity is a political phenomenon that can be stimulated or impeded by elites and institutions. It is theorised that it can be successful or unsuccessful at both the individual and aggregate levels. It is considered that identity formation is a fundamental battle for political elites, and a question of individual and aggregate responsiveness to political symbols, images, experiences, and the actual achievements and failures of a political entity. It is, in other words, a potential result of intense political communication and persuasion.

This book does not satisfy itself with being purely theoretical or purely empirical. It has two main goals. First, it seeks to provide a renewed conceptual and theoretical framework for the analysis of political identities, that is, what they are, how they may or may not be formed, strengthened or threatened. Second, it provides an empirical analysis of the emergence of such an identity among European citizens first at the individual level, and then over the past 30 years at the aggregate level.

This first chapter is concerned with a discussion of the concept of identity, and how it can be studied. It makes a series of very important conceptual distinctions and assumptions without which no study of the emergence of a European identity itself would be possible. In this discussion, I propose a brief 'reader' of some of the main studies on political and European identities, and use the insights of political scientists, and also philosophers, social psychologists, sociologists, historians, anthropologists, and even discourse analysts, all traditionally keener on the study of identities than political scientists, and more concerned with the study of identities 'outside of language' than us.[1] Using their works, I shall first define identities, political identities, and the way they can be studied. I will then propose some theoretical distinctions on components of political identities and a theory of political identities and the way they are connected.

Two conceptions of mass identities: top-down and bottom-up perspectives

A first necessary distinction has to be made between two ways of studying identities. Depending on academic perspectives, theoretical assumptions, and research questions, two main perspectives for the study of identities in general and a European identity in particular have been used by scholars. The first can be defined as a 'top-down' perspective, and the second as 'bottom-up'. Let us consider the logic of the two perspectives with regards to the study of European identity, that is, in a way, the study of 'who is European'.

The first angle of research – or 'top-down' model – focuses on questions such as who *should* be considered European, what unites Europeans in terms of geography, politics, culture, and where the natural limits of 'Europe' are. Studying European identity from a top-down, 'objective', perspective has meant to try to understand what unifies Europe and Europeans in terms of cultural heritage, values, and the like and how to characterise Europe and a presumed European common heritage. This task has been undertaken by political scientists such as Ester, Halman, and de Moor (1993), who have investigated the degree of convergence of values in the EU countries across a 10-year time period. Similarly, social historians such as Wintle *et al.* (1996) have conducted extensive work on culture and identity in Europe, and particularly enriched the debate on the 'borders' of Europe both historically and contemporaneously. These insights add to the empirical research of Van Deth and Scarbrough (1995), Inglehart (1990, 1997), Dalton (1996), and Duchesne and Frognier (1995). A more theoretical approach to the questions of what is Europe, who are Europeans, what is European citizenship, and what are the grounds of a European identity has also been taken by Howe (1995), Meehan (1993), Guild (1996), and Waever (1995). Finally, the institutional identity of the European Union and its social meaning, in terms of images of identity and community, have been mostly studied by sociologists and anthropologists such as Shore (1993), Shore and Black (1992), and Abeles, Bellier, and McDonald (1993).

In contrast to this approach, the second tradition of social science research to which this book clearly belongs takes a behavioural 'bottom-up' perspective and tries to answer questions such as: who 'feels' European (using an individual level perspective)? Why do some citizens identify with Europe while others do not? What do people 'mean' when they say that they feel European? From the point of view of the political scientist, this question involves serious theoretical, conceptual and empirical problems. Indeed, the basic question addressed here is how to define, conceptually, a European identity? Bruter (2003) has argued that we should differentiate between two aspects of political identities, a 'cultural' one and a 'civic' one. This typology, which is further developed here, has been adopted, since then, by a certain number of researchers on political identities such as Risse (2004) or Meinhof (2003).

Citizenship and identity

While this book focuses on the political (and particularly European) identity of individuals and how institutions and the media can influence it, it is important to remember that some scholars (perhaps somehow idealistically) have occasionally held the belief that an absolute coincidence could ultimately exist between the way citizens relate to their political systems (identity) and the way the political system tries to include its population (i.e., by determining the attributes of their citizenship). In other words, the borders of a single territory could – and should – be matched with a unified state, citizenship, and political identity.

Identity and citizenship are, in a way, the two mirrored components of the relationship between the institutional and human foundations of a political community. In this sense, defining the fundamental basis of political identities implies the formulation of assumptions regarding what constitutes and unites a nation and defines a citizenship. The nation consists of this human component of a political community, while the fundamental basis of citizenship in a corresponding political system shows how the political system will identify those who belong to it, their specific rights, and their particular duties.[2] Altogether, while the notion of European identity has only received scholarly attention in recent years, the study of a European (Union) citizenship has already made great progress over the past two decades. The body of literatures on citizenship and on identity are as distinct as the concepts they are dedicated to, and it is not the object of this book to rewrite a new theory of EU citizenship, but rather, to understand how EU citizens *feel*. However, because the two approaches paint a symmetric march of a European political system towards its people, and of a European Union people towards its political system, it is important to underline the contribution of the study of the latter in defining the potentials arisen, and difficulties faced, when trying to give a new depth and width to the emerging EU citizenship.

Authors such as Wiener (1998) have gone a long way in trying to understand what constituted the specificity of a EU citizenship as opposed to its national equivalent. Similarly, Mokre, Weiss, Bauböck *et al.* (2003) have looked at the 'national' tie of European Union citizenship (as opposed to the possible territorial and direct sense it could have assumed), making it an extension of national citizenships rather than a cross-cutting supra-European one. This could have expected implications on the nature of European identity and its relationship with national identities, to the extent that EU citizenship itself has been largely built as a supplemental citizenship.

The consequences of this supplemental identity may be all the more important since the European Union, even after the 2004 enlargement, does not match the borders of a European culture and civilisation (most of the Balkans, South Eastern, and Eastern Europe are not included alongside Norway, Switzerland, and number of small Western European states from Monaco to Iceland whilst the rest of Western and Central Europes are included).

Moreover, while the most 'traditional' attributes and privileges of citizenship used to include the right to vote, to do one's military service, and to work in the civil service of one's country, in the context of the European Union, the practical benefits of citizenship – beyond the right to vote in European Parliament elections and the right to work (with some functional exceptions) in the civil service of any of the member-States – partly vary according to whether one's country belongs to such entities as the Eurozone or the Schengen area. In this sense, European citizenship and identity might be expected to present themselves in an extreme variety of shades and nuances. At the same time, however, the constructivist aspect of EU citizenship may also have an impact on the predicted strength and sustainability of a EU citizenship based on a legal status rather than an *ex ante* cultural demand.

As this volume intends to study the emergence of a European identity from a bottom-up perspective, normative questions, and objective analyses of whether there is theoretically enough 'ground', in objective terms, for a European common identity to have emerged (a question posed, for example, in more general terms, by Miller, 2000, or Kymlicka, 1995) will not be of interest here, except in some extremely specific and marginal respects.

Indeed, instead, the choice of a bottom-up perspective, which relies on citizens' own perceptions of their individual identities, implies a need to answer further (and no less complicated) questions such as the link between European and other identities. This question, briefly explored empirically by Licata (2000) and Bruter (2003) has raised tremendous debate in the literature and in the 'popular press' alike, with number of commentators still conceiving national and European identities are naturally in tension both in terms of psychological identification and political allegiance. Our interest is almost exclusively focused on what makes people *feel* European, and how the European population has grown to feel European from the origins of the European project to the dawn of the third millennium. The notion of identity having been limited to its subjective perspective for the purpose of this book, let us now consider, some of the debates that have surrounded this extraordinarily 'intimate' concept which relates, in its subjective form, what people are to how they perceive their own self.

Cross-disciplinary perspectives on identity: self, belonging, and out-groups[3]

Before it became an area of interest for historians, sociologists or political scientists, the notion of 'identity' was extensively studied by philosophers and psychologists. In psychology, the concept of identity is what bridges the gap between the self and the outside world, the idea that while individuals are unique and independent, their perceptions of themselves can only be constructed in relation, sympathy, or opposition to elements of the outside world (Mummendey and Waldzus, 2004). Identity is therefore understood as a network of feelings of belonging to and exclusion from human subgroups: belonging to a gender group, a given age group, a family, religion, race, community, nation, etc. The unique superposition of groups a human being feels attached to constitutes its individual and unique 'identity' together with the definition of what constitutes the out-group (Mummendey and Waldzus, 2004, Wodak, 2004). The definition of an identity in psychological terms is obviously a mixture of real connections or differences and prejudices, the latter being necessary to enrich the world with one's own knowledge and certitudes, whether 'objectively' true or false (Mummendey and Waldzus, 2004).

Because of this presence of clear subjective elements in the definition of one's identity and the out-groups it is defined against, according to psychologists, we can only first understand identities at the individual level and using the traditional framework of methodological individualism. This implies that to understand the development of a mass European identity, one must analyse how the identity structure of individuals varies, how an individual identity is either formed in the stages of early socialisation, or bent later in an individual's life to incorporate further elements of reference. If one fails to take into account that identity is first and foremost an individual characteristic, the array of research questions linked to identity formation becomes much narrower, and their answers less flexible. Studied from a societal perspective, as done by many sociologists such as Bourdieu (1991) and Leca (1992), identities become fixed, rigid, categories that only evolve through generational replacement and environmental evolution. From an individual perspective, however, changes in mass identities present all the ambiguities and complexities of veritable 'realignments' with the wide variety of theoretical and analytical explanations that can be attached to them.

The concept of identity realignment

In terms of analyses of electoral behaviour, 'realignments' – turning points when the patterns of partisan identification of the electorate sharply transform – have always led to serious theoretical controversies. Campbell, Converse, Miller and Stokes (1960), Butler and Stokes (1974) and others have tried to survey the various possible theoretical patterns of realignments and face them with real situations, contrasting aggregate-level and individual level-generated changes, conversion, and replacement, and so on. Comparing the emergence of a new mass identity to an 'identity realignment' may sound a bit audacious at first. However, when one considers the questions raised by the study of the emergence of a new political identity – such as a European identity – the realignment approach seems to be relatively logical or relevant.

In *The American Voter*, Campbell, Converse, Miller and Stokes (1960) define realignments as changes in mass party *identification*. Their very keenness on anchoring the study of voting behaviour in terms of psychological identification – and therefore identity – should encourage us, in turn, to perceive the question of the emergence of a new mass political identity as a matter of true and fundamental realignment. The traditional hierarchy used in political science orders beliefs, attitudes, and behaviours. It is clear that while party identification, despite its name, could be predominantly classified as an attitude, focusing on an identity realignment, that is on the evolution of a political belief or even what comes 'before' beliefs, would add a new dimension to the existing studies on realignments. It would help us greatly, as a discipline, to understand better the more general concept of realignment at a deeper and further level than the traditional but rather narrow borders inherited from the very valuable works of Campbell, Converse, Miller and Stokes, Butler and Stokes, and many others.

Personal, social, and political identities

In the sociological and psychological literatures, it has become quite traditional to separate materially two forms of identities. According to Breakwell (2004), it is possible to distinguish between the personal and social identities of an individual. Personal identity is made of a network of references to family belonging, upbringing, personal and cultural characteristics. Personal identity therefore appears to be a form of identification directly centred on the individual and extending towards the rest of the world. The individual identifies his world 'inductively' from his own self, defining the various yardsticks of his identity. That is to say that personal identity is, in essence, the affective definition of one's 'friends' and 'support' in a world far too wide for an individual. In contrast, social identity is a set of references to pre-existing social groups, feelings of belonging to characteristics that 'make a difference' in the society in which the individual lives. These can include gender, race, social class or category, sexual orientation among other possible social identity features, which have been most often studied by social scientists of all sorts. Social identity, therefore, starts from a group socially expected to matter and that is found to include or match, 'deductively', the individual.

For many sociologists, studying the 'political' identity of individuals is a mere extension of what is known as their 'social identity'. This assumption, often found in the literature implies that political identity should be considered predominantly as a feature of social difference or distinction rather than a deeper cultural sense of belonging to a given community. In short, to make a parallel with one of the most traditional conceptual distinctions used by political scientists, political identity is understood by this body of literature to be a matter of status or citizenship, rather than a deeper personal constitutive identity.

The conceptual perspective taken by this study, however, seeks to invalidate this quite common assumption. It intends to put forward the claim that instead of being a mere sub-category of social identities, political identities are a form of identity in their own right, which can be reduced neither to a social component nor to a personal component of identity but, instead, involves both. The argument underpinning this theory is that far from being a 'pure' question of status – as social identities are, indeed, defined by Bourdieu (1991), political identities involve an affective dimension, like any element of a personal identity. This affective dimension is most evident when people cry when 'their' team wins the football World Cup, 'their' astronauts are the first to land on the moon, or 'their' soldiers die at war. No social identity would be expected to provoke such reactions, while personal circles of identity, such as family, would. For most purposes, and in most cases, the distinction may seem to be meaningless. It will, however, have an impact on the way political identities can be studied. Taking them as a form of status would not be enough because political identities involve a whole 'philosophical' position of individuals towards the imaginary institution of the social contract, towards democracy, community, society, and relationships between human beings altogether. It is, therefore, impossible to ignore the importance of both social and personal elements in political identities both in absolute terms, and when it will be attempted to measure them.

Defining 'civic' and 'cultural' components of political identities[4]

As shown earlier, the distinction between social and personal identities seems, therefore, fairly pointless when it comes to studying the emergence of a new political identity. In contrast, this book largely relies on a new and fundamental distinction between two hypothesised components of political identities, which I call civic and cultural. This theoretical and empirical distinction largely underlines the two components of identity I mentioned in the introduction: identification with a political group and with a political structure. I now explain the theoretical foundations and implications of the distinction between the civic and cultural components of political identities in general and a European identity in particular.

Conceptually, political identities have been the subject of heavy theoretical and ideological quarrels between political scientists. Three main perspectives have been used since the eighteenth century to characterise the foundations of the legitimacy of political communities.

The first, derived from the French Enlightenment and the 1789 Revolution, links the legitimacy of political communities to the very existence of political institutions that are implicitly accepted by society through a social contract (Rousseau, 1762). Following their lead, Habermas (1992) suggests that institutions altogether have the power to create a citizenship that will be strong enough to generate a feeling of bonding between the members of a community and sufficient allegiance to the political system.

The second, developed by German political thinkers such as Fichte (1845) and Herder (1913), links the legitimacy of political communities to a corresponding 'nation', defined by a common culture (and principally, for Fichte and Herder, a common language). At the same time, several contemporary philosophers also question the likelihood that a common citizenship can be sustainable without unifying 'national' cultural attributes such as a common culture and language (Miller, 2000, Kymlicka, 1995, Taylor, 2004) or, in the context of a multicultural society, without a clear definition of how ethnic cultures will participate in the shared national identity (Parekh *et al.*, 2000).

Finally, the third conception, formalised by Renan in 1870, modernises the original universalistic theory of the French Revolution, and associates the legitimacy of the State institutions to the existence of a 'common desire to live together' of its citizens. At the aggregate level, dealing with the top-down 'reality' of citizenship, Leca (1992) and Deloye (1997) find that citizenship is generally based on a mixture of these ideal-typical perspectives of national rationales. It is also clear, however, that specific countries have emphasised, to different extents, the various aspects of national definitions and their consequences. The French revolutionary perspective led to a clear universalism of the Revolution, intended, in the early 1790s, to extend to the rest of Europe and led to the development of theories of a cross-national interest of the 'citizens of Revolutionary Europe' (Bernstein and Milza, 1994). At the same time, the German culturalist conception led Fichte to propose maps of the German nation that 'democratically' included almost half of Europe, from Austria to Belgium, from Sweden to Ukraine, and from Poland to Switzerland through Hungary, Alsace, and the Italian Veneto! (Fichte, 1845). Needless to say that many of the so-defined 'Germans' concerned did not share the German identity claimed by Fichte for them.

From these three theories, I derive two interpretations of the notion of identity of individual citizens to existing political communities. The first, a '*cultural*' perspective, would analyse political identities as the sense of belonging an individual citizen feels towards a particular political group. This group can be perceived by him to be defined by a certain culture, social similarities, values, religion, ethics or even ethnicity. The second, a '*civic*' perspective, would see political identities as the identification of citizens with a political structure, such as a State, which can be defined as the set of institutions, rights, and rules that preside over the political life of a community. To some extent, in order to relate – in an over-simplified way – this conceptual discussion with two of the main notions used in political science, the first, cultural, perspective links political identities to the idea of a 'nation', and the second, civic one, to the idea of a 'State'.

Rather than assuming that political identities are one or the other, the contention made here is that the two components of political identities exist in parallel in citizens' minds and should simply be differentiated conceptually and empirically whenever possible. A given citizen may have a stronger civic or cultural European identity, and differences may well be systematic across individuals, countries, or time periods.

Of course, the 'cultural' and 'civic' components of most political identities are almost impossible (and would not necessarily appear to many as very useful) to distinguish because in many cases, the dominant 'State' and 'Nation' of reference are super-imposed. Even in cases of countries where regionalist and separatist tendencies are strong (see the studies of Lipset and Rokkan, 1967, or Seiler, 1998 on that question), differentiating between cultural and civic identities might only be possible for peripheral, minoritarian groups. For example, in Britain, many Scots would think of themselves as having a dual Scottish/British identity. For most Englishmen, however, Englishness and Britishness will be considered as implicitly or explicitly similar. Europe, however, presents a completely different pattern. Indeed, while conceiving Europe as a cultural identity presumably implies a reference to Europe as a continent or civilisation that stretches from the Atlantic to the Ural, conceiving Europe as a 'civic' identity would imply a reference to the European Union, which covers well under half of it. In these particular circumstances, the political entity referred to in the hypothesis of a European civic identity does not match the cultural entity as yet. This makes tests for the differences between the two types of identities and their relative strengths – even for the 'centre' – much easier to perform than in any other existing case, and more interesting when it comes to the study of the political significance of further enlargements of the European Union on local as well as Western European public opinions.

Identity and identification

Another major theoretical debate in the literature on identity formation that we need to consider is the distinction between the 'recognition' of a pre-existing identity and the active 'identification' of an individual with a new identity group (Laclau *et al.*, 1994). This debate refers to a major conceptual opposition of the causal sequence of identity formation and, also, on the need for objective markers of identity, that is of the relation between the 'top-down' and 'bottom-up' approaches distinguished earlier. Believers in the 'identity recognition' theory assume the pre-existing relevance of a multitude of patterns of 'actual' identity of individuals with human sub-groups. Individuals are perceived to be truly – although latently – defined by such characteristics as their gender, race, religion, sexual orientation, country, or town, which influence their status, beliefs, and attitudes (Hurwitz and Peffley, 1987, Feldman, 1988). The maturation of their individual identity leads them to 'recognise' or 'acknowledge' the relevance of these characteristics of their identity and its impact on who they are and how they think and live.

On the contrary, theories of identification suggest that all patterns of 'actual' identity that could be used to describe an individual are indeed irrelevant as long as this individual does not think of them as parts of his own, constructed, identity. Identities refer largely, as explained by Anderson (1991) to 'imagined communities'. Here again, the difference between the two theories could be caricaturally characterised by the distinction between two approaches that define identity as the relevance of real world elements for an individual, and the relevance of individuals for elements (groups) of the real world respectively. The theoretical impact of the debate is far from negligible. Indeed, it modifies the focus of the dependent variable of interest and the way analytical puzzles can and should be formulated by political science research. For defenders of the 'identity recognition' approach, the main dependent variable of interest is generally not the individual identity perceptions of human beings but the 'true' category of identification. Indeed, in the theoretical framework that is then conceived, the acknowledgement of various aspects of identity depends largely on the nature of the true category itself, its visibility, its social acceptability, social relevance, and more generally the macro-level social images attached to a given human category. Identities must then be studied primarily at the aggregate level, and primarily through the true category they are attached to rather than as self-standing subjective feelings of belonging. Individual differences of identification become mostly interesting through the different images of the true category they translate, the reasons of the recognition or non-recognition of the identity by various individuals, and the gap between the true category and the various subjective images it generates (Wodak, 2004).

Thinking of identity as an identification process, however, implies the necessity to consider identity formation as a purely mental phenomenon largely independent from any true category of actual shared characteristics it might relate to. The 'truth' about identification categories becomes absolutely irrelevant since only the unique individual subjective images a human being attaches to a group matter. In fact, there is no unique category of reference for all identifiers to, say, Europe, but as many perceptions of the category of reference as there are individual identifiers. When identity formation is conceived in terms of identification, it becomes a matter of structural image formation (Castoriadis, 1975), that is, the projection of the self on an imaginary category and not, as in the previous case, the attachment of the self to a true pre-existing ad hoc category. In other words, while the first theory implies the internalisation by the respondent of objective categories, the second one implies the opportunistic extrapolation of individual characteristics of the subject.

Here again, the conceptual perspective of the book must be made very clear. The idea that there is a 'true' shared European heritage, based on the diffusion of the Greek, Roman, and Judeo-Christian traditions seems to make some sense, but it is of no interest to us here. As explained earlier, a large amount of historical and sociological literature has been dedicated to what Europe is in 'real' terms, and I do not intend to build on that by any means. While the very concept of cultural identity implies that an individual perceives the group to have a certain shared heritage, and while it would be most interesting to know whether Europeans perceive this shared heritage to rely mostly on common values, ethnicity, religion, democratic principles, and others or why different individuals interpret this common baggage differently, it is, simply, not a task for this book except very marginally in the chapter dedicated to the analysis of focus group discussions of what Europe is perceived to 'mean' for citizens.

Multiple identities and theories of identity connections

Studying the emergence of a new identity implies very fundamental questions on the possible evolution of an identity. Many authors have considered identities to be totally fixed and the sheer result of early socialisation. Nevertheless, considering that an adult individual may, over time, feel more or less European hypothesises the possibility of identity evolution, and, indirectly, of multiple identities as the emergence of a new identity in an individual is unlikely to condemn the other, pre-existing components of his identity. If a citizen may identify, at the same time, with several communities, will there necessarily be a hierarchy between these different identities? Can this hierarchy change? How can it be modelled? Risse (2004) tries to answer this question with the 'Russian doll' and 'marble cake models'.

Up to the nineteenth century, most political thinkers believed that individuals could only have some allegiance to one given State (e.g., Petöfi, 1871). If one believes in this theory, then we should consider different identities as opposed in principle and therefore incompatible in so far as they are 'positive' identities. In the case of European identity, this is the idea defended by sociologists like Japperson who therefore consider European identity as an elite phenomenon, and, for all practical purposes, an 'anti-identity' that really measures cosmopolitanism.

To some extent this is also the implicit definition that seems to be used by Inglehart (e.g., 1990) in all his works on that question.

Later on, however, the introduction of new State organisations such as federalism, confederalism and decentralisation, reinforced not only the idea that several hierarchical levels of government were compatible, but also that they were possible in a democratic context where multiple allegiances would therefore be required of citizens. In the context of European integration, this even led to the formulation of the ideal of subsidiarity, that is, a system where each decision, depending on its nature and whose life it will influence, is taken at the lowest possible level of government.

The subsidiarity principle has an equivalent in terms of theory of identities. It is the theory that claims that several identities can coexist, but that they are additive and based on territorial proximity. In other words, the coexistence of identities can be summarised as a form of concentric model as shown in Figure 1.1. A citizen will 'naturally' feel closer to people from his own city than to people who are from the same region but another city, closer to people from the same region than to people from another region but the same country, closer to people from

Figure 1.1   A concentric theory of political identities

Notes: The level of identity with a community is the inverse of the distance between the individual and the corresponding circle. Because communities are included in one another, identity feelings are therefore additive. That is, identity level with country = identity level with Europe + supplementary identity.

the same country than to Europeans from another country, etc. The relative strengths of each additional level of proximity (region in addition to nation, town in addition to region, etc.) are then graphically represented by the relative width of each additional circle (Figure 1.2). However, the absolute size of each new circle is also of interest since we can consider that some citizens might be, by personality, strong identifiers, with large circles at all levels while others might be weak identifiers with all circles being small and meaningless. The emergence of a new

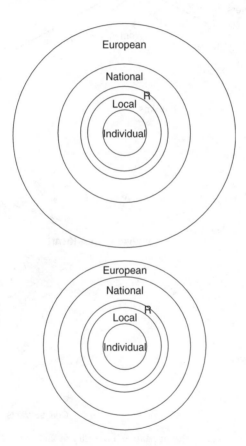

Figure 1.2   Relative strength of territorial identity circles: the example of strong and weak European identities

Notes: The two diagrams represent the territorial identity patterns of two imaginary individuals. All circles are equal, except the two 'European identity' circles. This circle is much wider for the first individual, meaning a much 'looser' identity. The circle is much narrower for the second respondent, which means that his European identity is much stronger.

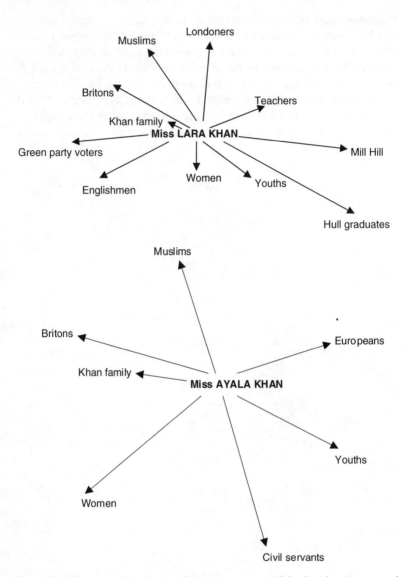

Figure 1.3 Measuring identity in relative proximity models: the identity maps of the (imaginary) sisters Lara and Ayala Khan

Notes: The cases are, obviously, totally imaginary. All the identity links that are perceived as relevant by the subject are represented. The closer the group to the individual, the stronger the identity link. The 'maps' vary in terms of numbers, global strength, and hierarchy of the identity links.

European identity will have been symbolised by the addition of a new exterior circle without necessarily modifying in any way the other existing circles. On the contrary, the other circles might not have stayed the same, with any change having been dependent or independent from the emergence and possible progress of a new European circle.

To reintegrate this model in the more global 'map' of all political and non-political identities, that is, in a model where all identities are not territorially organised, we can represent the complex identity map of an individual as a star-shaped network of identity feelings still centred on the individual. This model is shown in Figure 1.3. Here, the relative strength of an identity feeling is inversely measured by the distance between the individual and the community of interest. The 'closer' a dot to the centre of the map, the stronger the identity. Additivity has to be abandoned in this more global map because of the impossibility of comparing or adding up some utterly different identity links, such as familial and political. Here again, however, we may suspect maps to be different in their shapes from each other. This will not only be because of the relative position of each identification group and their number, but also because some individuals might be strong identifiers in need of a lot of close-by yardsticks while others might be weak identifiers.

Many political scientists rely implicitly on models of identity opposition when studying European identity. The design of the first few questions on identity in Eurobarometer, for example, as designed by Inglehart, asked respondents whether they felt mostly (their nationality, for example British) *or* European. It does not seem particularly logical to us to *assume* any theory about the relationship between different political identities. The model of identity complementarity that I have just proposed and intend to use as the basis of my theory leaves room for any form of internal organisation and relation between identities. The questions derived from this theory of identities will allow us to show – instead of to assume – whether national and European identities, for example, are opposed or, on the contrary, positively correlated, or, even more simply, totally uncorrelated. The questions built on the assumption that identities are opposed do not leave room for any such test.

Summary of the conceptual framework of the study

The concept of identity and the difference between bottom-up and top-down approaches are, as seen, at the centre of some significant scientific controversies in the social sciences. In this context, this book chooses a clear and specific conceptual framework: to focus on individual identity feelings and the way they react to institutional and elite messages. Unlike most studies of identities, this research is based on the perspective of methodological individualism. It takes a behavioural, 'bottom-up' perspective and is not interested either in normative conclusions or in the study of objective commonalties between Europeans, or in the study of 'what is Europe' from an absolute philosophical or historical perspective. It is not another study of European citizenship either, but rather a study of how citizens perceive themselves politically in a context where institutions and the elites have clearly tried for the past few decades to tell them how they should perceive themselves. I defined the identity of an individual as the perception of him/herself in relation to the outside world and to the different relevant groups (s)he identifies in it. I showed that elements of identity could be ranked in three categories: personal (or affective) identities, social identities (or elements of status) and political identities, which do not fit in any of the two other categories and have both some affective and status-related components. I defined two possible components of political identities based on the existing literature on the relevance of States and nations. The first is a 'civic' component, and the second a 'cultural' component. These two dimensions complement the self-attributed and spontaneous 'general' identity of citizens. I posed that the emergence of both components is necessary to the legitimacy of a new institutional construction like the European Union, within a context of multiple identities that allows for the opposition, independence, or even positive correlation between various identities.

Plan of the book

This book is concerned with the emergence of a mass European identity and what has influenced it. It is also interested in its evolution at the individual and aggregate levels. It is structured in two main parts.

In this first part, I am interested in the theoretical model that is to be tested in Part II of this book. In this chapter, I have considered the concept of identity and defined the analytical framework of the study. The chapter reviewed the existing literature and theoretical debates surrounding the notions of identity and political identity, and proposed a new paradigm based on two – civic and cultural components – of a European identity, and within a context of compatible and mutually enriching multiple identities. Chapter 2 specifies the theoretical model that is tested throughout this book and the methods that are used to test it. It focuses on the mechanisms that may enable institutions such as political institutions and the mass media to influence citizens' identities. Chapter 3 complements this theoretical argument by examining four 'lessons from the past'. It proposes a comparative analytic narrative of identity formation in four countries: the United Kingdom, the United States, Austria, and Israel. Last Chapter of Part I, Chapter 4 examines the nature of the attempts made by institutions to foster a new European identity, by providing European citizens with a series of clearly identifiable symbols aimed at anchoring the very notion of Europeanness. In the second part of the book, I empirically test the model developed in part I at the individual and aggregate levels. I start by providing some empirical insight on the strength and nature of the European identity of individuals in three member-States of the European Union, based on the results of the survey conducted for the purpose of the project on which the book is based (Chapter 5). I then look at the impact of good and bad news on Europe and symbols of the European Union on individuals' levels of European identity (Chapter 6). The rest of the study proceeds to analyse how and to what extent a mass European identity has emerged at the aggregate level in the European Union between 1970 and 2000 (Chapter 7). Finally, I propose to analyse some qualitative evidence on what Europe and European identity mean to citizens, and how they perceive symbols of the Union and the way they are informed about Europe (Chapter 8). Chapter 9 provides a general discussion of the findings and conclusion for the book.

Part I

Theorising the Emergence of a European Identity

2
The Model and Research Design: Institutions? Media? And the Development of a Mass European Identity

Institutions, communication, and mass political identities

This book is concerned with the progressive emergence of a mass European identity. As outlined earlier, in conceptual terms, this work depends on an understanding of political identities that considers them mutually compatible at the individual level, and also susceptible to evolve over time. Analytically, however, the claims of my model go further. Indeed, in this book, I assert that political identities, if they transform over time, do not just evolve randomly but can be at least partly influenced by the messages sent by institutions to citizens.

In a way, the perception that institutions can influence political identities did not first originate from political science but from some of these institutions themselves. When Belgium demonstrated for its independence in the summer of 1830, it was a self-asserted nation without a common history, language, flag, or anthem. The people taking the streets of Brussels were marching holding a French flag, literally opposite to the desire of revolutionary leaders who certainly did not intend to escape the Dutch rule to fall back, once again, into the French area of influence. Young revolutionary leaders met urgently to find back a distinctive Belgian flag (they dug up the black, yellow, and red flag of Brabant, forgotten for centuries) and, one evening, in a bar, wrote in a few hours time a Belgian national anthem under the conduct of a junior revolutionary called Jenneval (Bruter, 2003). Following the success of their revolution, the independentists leaders were quite convinced that these new Belgian symbols, a new figurehead (the King) and a rather tight control of the national press would allow them to make sure that their new people 'felt' Belgian relatively quickly.

In fact, leaders of the twentieth century have been more strongly convinced than ever that institutions could influence the emergence and modification of political identities. From Nazi propagandists in the 1930s and 40s to the leaders of post-Communist new states such as Moldova in the 1990s, the emergence of almost every single new state, regime, or self-governed nation in the world has been accompanied by an institutional effort to strengthen the emergence, resistance, or reinforcement of a corresponding political identity.

In this chapter, the model of the book is explained, that is I specify how and why I suggest that institutions such as governments, EU institutions and the mass media may be able to influence the emergence and strengthening of new political identities in general and a European identity in particular.

A double claim, a double model

The book offers a double claim, a double model, and a double set of original findings. Indeed, as explained in Chapter 1, this volume studies in two steps (1) how institutions may influence the European identity feelings of individual citizens in what I have defined as the civic and cultural components of their European identity, and (2) how such an influence has, over time, resulted in the emergence of a new mass European identity. The double model is therefore a model of institutional influence over citizens' identities at the individual level, and a test of the emergence of a European identity over the past 30 years at the aggregate level, as a result of the media and institutional initiatives.

While describing the theory and framework of analysis of political identities in this book, I assessed how likely it seemed, both logically and theoretically that political identities could evolve. It was claimed that political identities have a cultural and a civic component, and that political identifications with different territorial levels of political communities are not exclusive, but, on the contrary, complementary. These assumptions are necessary to conceive the possible emergence of a mass European identity over the second half of the twentieth century. Following these preliminary enquiries, the first element of the theory is, therefore, that a mass European identity has emerged in addition to, and not against, the sub-European (particularly national, regional, and local) identities of European citizens. Second, using the existing literature on political identities, public opinion, and political attitudes, I explain why one could expect institutions, both political and civil, to influence the emergence of a European political identity. While talking about the possible impact of institutions on the emergence of a European identity, it is essential to explain why such an influence is possible, and also to identify the specific mechanisms that may allow political institutions and the mass media to have an impact on the political identity feelings of individuals. This chapter, where the theoretical model and hypotheses of the book are exposed, first looks at the general theory used to justify expectations of an institutional influence on identities. The following is a presentation of the three mechanisms of institutions' influence that will be tested in this book:

- First, the effect of symbols of European integration on an emerging European identity;
- Second, the effects of good and bad news on Europe on this emerging European identity;
- Third, the effect of the existence of European integration per se on the emergence of a mass European identity, or the impact of what is labelled in this book as the impact of 'institutional inertia'.

How can political institutions influence European identity?

The structuralist model

It has just been seen that in 1830, Belgian independentist leaders, who managed to overturn the Dutch occupation of Belgium and took power over their newly independent country expected to play a role, as a new set of political institutions, in the emergence and strengthening of a somewhat weak Belgian national identity. In particular, they thought that such 'physical' attributes of the new state as a flag and a national anthem would be indispensable to the emergence of this new mass identity.

Beyond the instinct of political leaders, I can theorise academically the expected impact of top-down symbols of a political system on the identity of the mass public using structuralist theory. Based on the work of Saussure (1974) in linguistics, Castoriadis (1975) explained that in structural terms, identity formation proceeds from the identification of individuals to the images they form of given social and political communities. In fact, the community itself is so broad, varied, heterogeneous, and hard to comprehend for any individual that any physical representation of it, be it its symbols, its leaders, its name, or its institutions, will be used by citizens and outsiders alike as a medium that can be characterised and, beyond it, can serve to characterise the community itself.

In itself, the structuralist model says more about the role of institutions as *objects* in the process of identification of citizens with a political community, than as conscious manipulators of these identities. However, it is not difficult to derive from Castoriadis's analysis that 'official' symbols of a community can be expected to channel and influence the images formed of the communities in citizens' minds and, therefore, the likeliness of their identifying with it. Moreover, the symbols used by political systems are always chosen with the hope that they transmit certain values and meanings that are consistent with the 'idea' of the community that institutions want to convey. As will be shown, for example, in the case of European integration, institutions chose symbols that were expected to convey some very specific – and often expressly defined – connotations related to the European project.

As has been the case in virtually any creation of a new political system, the symbols of the European Union have been meant to push forward positive, seducing perceptions of Europe to which people will identify. Therefore, these symbols can be expected to favour higher levels of European identity if they have been chosen cleverly. Another body of literature, however, which is derived from the behaviouralist trend, has come up with more specific findings regarding the impact of political communication, which must be looked at when assessing the likely effect of the messages of institutions (both political institutions and the mass media) to influence citizens' identities in general and the more specific emergence of a European identity.

Extending existing models of the impact of political communication on public opinion

Since the late 1960s, the influence of news on political behaviour has attracted more and more attention from political scientists. Iyengar's, Peter's and Kinder's (1982) experimental research has been one of the most influential in the analysis of political communication and the receptivity of citizens to TV programmes. Beyond the impact of news messages on political attitudes, Norris (1999) and Evans and Norris (1999) have shown that exposure to the messages of the mass media can also influence the party identification of individuals. The difference is noticeable. In reference to the work of Hurwitz and Peffley (1987), one can draw a hierarchy between political beliefs, political attitudes, and political behaviour (Figure 2.1). Showing that exposure to specific news can influence party identification opens the way to hypothesise that

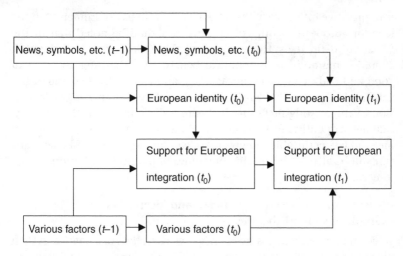

Figure 2.1   A model of European identity and support for European integration: theoretical justification for using a surrogate pre-test

Notes: Equations: Y = European identity, Y' = Support for integration, X = News, symbols, etc., and E = Various factors.

$$Y_1 = \beta_{11} Y_0 + \beta_{21} X_0 + \epsilon_1$$
$$Y_0 = \beta_{12} X_{-1} + \epsilon_2$$
$$Y'_0 = \beta_{13} Y_0 + \beta_{23} E_{-1} + \epsilon_3$$
$$Y'_1 = \beta_{14} Y_1 + \beta_{24} E_0 + \epsilon_4$$

political communication can influence citizens yet more fundamentally than previously shown by the literature. In other words, it makes it possible to claim that not only behaviour but also attitudes are influenced by media messages, and suggest that perhaps, deeper identities may be influenced by political communication as well.

So far, specialists of political communication have been mostly interested in the direct link between media and individuals/public opinion, in terms of the effectiveness of political communication and manipulation. However, their research also shows that political behaviours and attitudes are influenced by the specific successes and failures of political parties, candidates, or leaders. In other words, their findings point out to a combined effect of the actual news the media convey on the one hand, and the subjective messages they add on the other hand. The result is that political attitudes and behaviours are constantly changing according to citizens' perceptions of the successes and shortcomings of leaders.

In this work, it is hypothesised that the news on Europe – again, without arbitrating here between the role of substantive events and the interpretative influence of the media itself – also has an influence on the level of European identity of citizens. It should be noted that in the hierarchy defined by Hurwitz and Peffley (1987), political identities should come even before political beliefs. Hypothesising an effect of good and bad news on European integration on individual and aggregate levels of European identity is not, therefore, a simple, logical extension of the existing literature. It theoretically implies, on the contrary, that deeper political feelings such as identities, albeit stronger, more stable, and less permeable to news than 'weaker' attitudes and behaviours, can still be affected by specific outcomes of political institutions in the long run.

Is there a link between 'superficial' and 'deep'? The example of support theories

To claim that repeated positive or negative *perceptions* of a political system may ultimately influence citizens' *identities* goes down to claiming that in spite of their conceptual opposition, there is a path, a link, between superficial and deep categories of psychological reference. In other words, the repeated perception that the outcomes of a political system are good or bad, while fundamentally different from a high or low level of identification with this system may, in the long run, influence it.

Here, I base my argument upon the existing literature in a variety of research areas. Of particular interest, however, is the relationship between specific support and diffuse support or legitimacy (e.g., Gibson and Caldeira, 1995). Gibson and Caldeira, using Easton's conceptualisation, interpret diffuse support (their definition of legitimacy) as a 'reservoir of good will' that makes citizens accept specific decisions they do not support from given institutions. In that sense, diffuse support is differentiated from specific support, that is the attitudes of citizens towards any individual and specific outcome of the work of this institution (a policy decision, a law, etc.).

However, despite this important distinction, it seems logical to think that long series of publicly unsupported or unpopular decisions by a given institution may damage, in the long run, the diffuse support of that institution. My perspective on a new European identity is the same. As shown in Chapter 1, I think that the emergence of a European identity is probably what has led some citizens to support European integration even when they have not supported specific decisions of the European Union or when European integration has not been directly 'in their interest' either from an egocentric or from a socio-tropic perspective (McKuen, Erikson, Stimson, 1992). My residual operationalisation of European identity in the aggregate model is also directly derived from – and theoretically justified by – this perspective, and by the expected correlation between European identity and support for European integration in my individual level design.

Therefore, whilst perceptions of specific outcomes of European institutions will also influence citizens' attitudes towards Europe, that is, their support for European integration, I also hypothesise that long, systematic, series of perceived good or bad news on Europe will ultimately alter the level of European identity of individuals. This expectation is similar to the way long series of perceived good or bad decisions of an institution are expected to alter individuals' perceptions of the legitimacy of an institution in the context I just described.

Do 'time in' and 'experience' matter?

In addition to the serial 'qualitative' perceptions of European outcomes, however, I also need to use more general claims on the impact of socialisation and long-term participation in the European Union in the development of a mass European identity. My definition of the civic and cultural components of a European identity in Chapter 1 referred to the perception that the European Union is a relevant political system, granting citizens rights and duties that define their political self, and a perception of relative closeness to fellow Europeans as compared to non-Europeans regardless of what constitute their 'shared' heritage, baggage, or values, respectively. On that basis, it is not unreasonable to posit that institutions, by their very existence, and the level of interaction citizens have with them, will influence the level of European identity of Europeans.

The theory stating that experience of Europe and the European Union as an individual and as a country can be traced directly to theories of political socialisation. From Greenstein (1965) to Inglehart (1971), political psychologists and political scientists have long believed that political institutions alongside individual contexts could influence the political belief systems of individuals.

With regards to the European integration process itself too, many authors have taken for granted that there is such a thing as a learning process operated by both States and citizens over time. Some authors have even gone so far as to claim that radical differences may be found across the various 'generations' of European member-States (Hix, 2005) with the more ancient the members, the more pro-European the citizenry while Bruter (2003) suggests, instead, that the 'style' of integration at the time of entry explains the expectations – and therefore later assessment – of citizens on European integration, explaining why levels of support appear higher amongst those who joined in the 1950 and the 1980s than amongst those who joined in 1973 and 1995. Either way, time of belonging and the extent of membership certainly gives countries a certain 'experience' of the relevance of the European Union in their daily lives.

In similar ways, comparisons between elites and masses largely underline the importance of European experience in explaining the level of European identity of groups. In this sense, the work of Hooghe (1997) on the people who work in European institutions gives us an interesting insight on the effect of 'living Europe' every day on the emergence of a European elite's identity.

Therefore, the expected impact of the European experience on an individual may be understood as the individual level socialisation correcting the aggregate level institutional inertia of a country within the European Union – that is, the time the country has belonged to it. Indeed, it represents the impact of being exposed, this time, not to the general institutional reality itself but to its human reality through European family origins, life and travel in the rest of Europe, or, in the case of elites, exposure to the daily impact of European integration.

In a way, European institutions – in particular the European Commission and the European Parliament, have assumed the importance of this European experience and try to give more depth to its meaning, particularly since the mid-1980s. Indeed, since the Delors presidency of the European Commission – and in particular since the Single Act of 1987, the European Communities developed the project of a People's Europe, with efforts on human mobility, easiness of travel, students and youth exchange programmes, and workers mobility programmes. Through this, the European Union has openly stated its belief in the influence of European experience on the development of a European identity. The particular emphasis on programmes towards the youth shows the belief of European institutions that the emergence of a European identity will develop through the emergence of a new 'European culture' among those who never experienced a time of war and rigid opposition between Western European countries.

If exposure to Europe is all the more important than it shows the salience of European integration, then experiencing this salience in people's everyday life or knowing its cultural significance through mixed European family origins should reinforce individuals' European identity. I can therefore sub-divide my conception of European experience in several elements. On the one hand, some are purely cultural, such as having family origins in another European country, which is expected to give individuals the sense that there is some commonality between different European cultures, or speaking foreign languages, which make trans-European communication easier. On the other hand, some elements of European experience also have a civic aspect. Travelling to or living in another European country is a cultural experience to the extent that it allows citizens to experience another European culture and see similarities with their own, but it also allows citizens to experience what have changed directly due to European integration. These elements include no customs, no passport control within the Schengen area, and the effect of the common currency within the 12 countries of the Eurozone.

In parallel, the impact of institutional inertia must be understood primarily at the aggregate level. The theory of institutional inertia is indirectly linked to the French Revolutionary definition of the emergence of a national community that I described in Chapter 1. Indeed, the theory of the impact of institutional inertia on the emergence of a new political identity is that the very existence and survival of an institutionalised political community will, over time, naturally generate the progressive emergence of the related political identity.

Indeed, the common political institution creates a shared legal and political system, which consists of common laws, participation, political personnel, and so on. In other terms, institutionalisation generates, by definition, elements of a common political culture (Meehan, 1993, Laffan, 2004), which I expect, in turn to create a corresponding political identity. Like all models of political culture, I can expect a difference in the effect of institutional inertia on the European political, administrative, and social elite and among masses, as shown by Wodak (2004), and Hooghe (1997).

Indeed, as I show in Chapter 3, how to conceive the obvious emergence of a clear Austrian identity among the imperial elites and, later, mass population of all cultures in the nineteenth century, except by acknowledging some form of effect of institutional inertia? Obviously, this wasn't enough to guarantee a clear definitive cohesion of the empire, but as shown by Fejtö (1993), interpreting the collapse of the Austro-Hungarian empire as a national and ethnic explosion would be historically very questionable and problematic. Some form of Austro-Hungarian identity did clearly exist prior to the major collapse of the 1910s and the collapse of the imperial must be primarily understood as the collapse of a political system.

Hypotheses of the book

Based on these theoretical and analytical considerations, I am now in a position to specify how I expect institutions to impact, directly and indirectly, at the individual and aggregate levels, the emergence of a new European identity. In particular, I can derive from the last few pages three major mechanisms of institutional influence on an emerging European identity:

- Good and bad news on Europe and European integration;
- Symbols of Europe and the European Union;
- European experience, in the form of institutional inertia, or individual cultural characteristics.

Good news, bad news, and European identity

In the first part of this chapter, we saw that political communication and assessment of 'news' on Europe might be expected to have an impact on an emerging European identity. The next problem becomes, of course, to evaluate directly and globally what leads to perceptions of achievements and failures of Europe. Such perceptions undoubtedly depend on individuals, the context, the type of media one is in contact with, one's definition of what would constitute a success or a downside, whether I limit myself to news on European integration or try to add news on Europe, and so on. Moreover, it would be impossible to assess one's perception of good or bad news on European integration without taking into account the obvious risk of endogeneity of individuals' assessments. Indeed, as mentioned as a criticism of the study of the influence of parties' records on party identification, one's perception of the record of European integration will be partly dependent upon the a priori European identity of a given citizen.

It is, therefore, important to refine further my typology of what should be included in the likely 'good' and 'bad' news on Europe that citizens may be exposed to. Conceptually, I can define perceived good news on Europe for a citizen as news that will stimulate a favourable assessment of European integration by this individual. Similarly, perceived 'bad news' is what will be assessed negatively by an individual.

A first distinction must then be drawn between two theoretical possibilities. On the one hand, there may be 'intrinsically' good and bad news on European integration that will be perceived as such by all Europeans. On the other hand, I might expect that in some other cases, perceptions of good and bad news will be dependent upon personal circumstances and characteristics of individuals. In order to understand what will be perceived as good or bad news by individuals, it is very important to understand how individuals will assess news on European integration.

Specialists of the analysis of political behaviour have dedicated extensive work on political evaluation and assessment by citizens. Most of the literature has been concerned with the assessment of parties' and candidates' records and with the evaluation of the economic situation of a country. Several analytical categorisations have been identified in particular, several of which are of interest to us in evaluating what Europeans will perceive to be good and bad news on Europe.

The first distinction has focused on the difference between retrospective and prospective assessment (McKuen, Erikson, Stimson, 1989). This means that citizens can evaluate either the 'record' of a country or candidate per se at the time of interview, or make predictions as to the likely situation in the near or medium range future, as a predictable consequence of the policy, situation, or political leader considered. Given the recent and futuristic character of European integration, this retrospective vs prospective distinction turns out to be extremely relevant in my study of European identity. Indeed, while McKuen, Erikson, and Stimson are mostly interested in the 'general tendency' of the debate and show that prospective assessment is dominant over retrospective, I may derive from their dichotomy that, both or either retrospective and prospective news on what European integration has done and will be doing may have an effect on the stimulation of citizens' European identity. This might result in different appreciation of what constitutes 'good' and 'bad' news, and even in different impact of news on individuals' levels of European identity.

A second major distinction is that between egocentric and socio-tropic political evaluations, used in the analysis of the assessment of existing policies (Stimson, McKuen, Erikson, 1992). An evaluation is egocentric when an individual assesses a policy with regards to its influence on his own, personal circumstances. The evaluation is socio-tropic when the evaluation is made with regards to the effects of the policy on society as a whole.

In the specific context of the assessment of the achievements and failures of European integration, however, between these two traditional categories, it seems important to propose a third, intermediary category that could be called a '*socio-centric*' evaluation. I call 'socio-centric' the evaluation of European integration or any of its aspects with regards to its impact on any sub-European group, and particularly on a given nation or region. This is opposed to Europe as a whole (socio-tropic evaluation, in all its 'universalistic' spirit) or a given individual or restricted interest group (egocentric evaluation). This distinction is all the more necessary since European integration is, obviously, far from having put an end to the importance of national interest, as regularly shown by European negotiations in sensitive areas such as agriculture or regional development funding and detailed by many political scientists. At the same time, it cannot be substituted for the 'most' socio-tropic concern of citizens since the welfare of Europe as a whole (or indeed, sometimes, humanity) is also clearly present in many people's minds when they support European integration. This is clearly shown by mass public opinion surveys such as Eurobarometer (when one compares answers to questions on national benefits from EU membership with general questions on support for European integration) and by the literature (Duchesne and Frognier, 1995). Given those two distinctions, I define conceptually four types of good (bad) news on European integration that I call *socio-tropic, socio-centric, categorical, and egocentric*:

- Good news for all Europeans (socio-tropic): these may first be news about elements of improvement of the life of all citizens such as news showing general economic and social progress, or news on the adoption of unanimously accepted legal dispositions. They can also be news about successes of the European Union when in competition with the rest of the world, for example successes in economic and commercial competition with other countries, diplomatic successes of the European Union, et caetera.
- Good news for citizens from a sub-European specific geographic area (socio-centric): a given country or region will get more from the European Union through transfer revenues (e.g., structural funds), indirect economic and industrial benefits (new factories as a result of European co-operation ...), political success in negotiations within inter-national European institutions such as the Council, and so on.
- Good news for a cross-national social sub-group, whose interests are taken care of by the European Union (categorical): students (e.g., through improvement of exchange programmes), women (anti-discrimination measures), minorities and so on.
- News idiosyncratically perceived as good by a given individual for any reason (egocentric).

Bearing these categories and the theoretical background mentioned earlier, in mind, I can formulate hypothesis 1, on the hypothesised influence of good and bad news on European identity. The hypothesis reads as follows:

Hypothesis 1: The exposure of European citizens to news on the achievements or failures of European integration will influence their level of European identity.

Giving Europe a face: institutions, symbols, and European identity

The second aspect of my theory of the influence of top-down communication, based on strcuturalist models, relates to the impact of symbols of European integration. As shown in Chapter 4, European institutions have provided the European Union (and before it the Council of Europe, European Community of Steel and Coal [ECSC], European Economic Community [EEC] and European Community [EC] with many quasi 'statal' and 'national' symbols. European institutions have quite clearly recognised directly and indirectly that they have expected such symbols to stimulate and reinforce a mass European identity among European citizens. This clearly appears in several documents such as the guidelines distributed by the European Commission to its external service (Bruter, 1999). From these explanations and the theory developed earlier in this chapter, I can come up with hypothesis 2, which reads as follows:

Hypothesis 2: Exposure to symbols of European integration stimulates the development of a European identity by individual European citizens.

Does socialisation create identity? Experience, institutional inertia, and the emerging European identity

Finally, I outlined the theoretical reasons that suggest to us that both the time a country, as a whole has been part of the European project, and the individual experience of individual citizens should have an effect on their level of European identity. I mentioned earlier that the impact of institutional inertia was likely to be higher on the elites than on the mass public. I also suggested that institutional inertia may naturally primarily stimulate the emergence of some form of 'civic' identity rather than some 'cultural' one, since the identification is literally to common institutions, rules and policy outputs, while individuals' experience may have a stronger cultural identity effect.

I also showed that, if cultural identity will only be expected by most political scientists to correspond to some imagined or existing underlying common culture, it is clear that civic identity will *necessarily* correspond to belonging to a common political and institutional context and, therefore, to institutional survival. The hypotheses on the impact of institutional inertia (defined as the duration for which a country has belonged to the European Union) and individual experience and socialisation on identity is fundamentally based upon a relation between *time* of survival and identity, and a relation between the relevance of European integration for an individual and his level of European identity. On this basis, I can formulate the third hypothesis of my model on the hypothesised impact of institutions on the emergence of a European identity as follows:

Hypothesis 3: The survival and increasing political significance of the European Union as an institutionalised political system reinforces a mass European identity. This effect will be combined with the individual experience and socialisation of individual citizens, in particular the degree to which their cultural background makes them spontaneously conceive the existence of a European shared baggage or heritage, and their direct exposure to the reality of their EU citizenship. It will result in the progressive emergence of a consolidating mass European identity across the member-States between the 1970s and the beginning of the third millennium (and will continue to grow afterwards).

The model

I can now summarise the model proposed of the institutional impact on the emergence of a mass European identity over time. The model can be formulated in two different ways at the individual and aggregate level.

At the individual level, the research question concerns the level of European identity of individual citizens at a given time. It is modelled according to their exposure to good and bad news on European integration, to symbols of European integration, to their European experience, and to the salience and durability of European integration for the primary political system (State) to which they belong. The model is summarised by Figure 2.1.

At the aggregate level, the question of interest is how a mass European identity has emerged and evolved over time. Here again, the independent variables of interest will be the diffusion of symbols of European integration, good and bad news on European integration over time, and institutional inertia. The model is summarised, this time, by Figure 2.2.

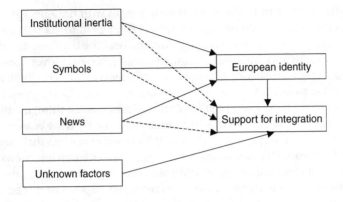

→ Known effect from European identity model

--→ Unknown link: risk of bias in identity model if not null.

Figure 2.2 Test-model of support for European integration

The methods

The individual level and aggregate level models are obviously directly connected as, in part, the possible emergence of a mass European identity over time can only be explained to the extent that I understand better how identities in general and a European identity in particular may evolve and be influenced by institutions at the individual level. The relationship between the two, however, is reinforced by the methodological arsenal used in this book, which is expected to bridge the gap between the individual level and aggregate level models.

The individual level model will be primarily tested using an experimental design. The survey-based experiment was administered in three countries (the United Kingdom, France, and the Netherlands) on a total sample of about 210 respondents. The experimental design, described in detail in Chapter 5, allows a tailor-made measurement of the dependent variable, as conceptualised in Chapter 1, and separated in its cultural and civic components. The experiment also enables us to proceed to a refined analysis of the effect of good and bad news on Europe and exposure to symbols of European integration on the level of European identity of individuals. At the same time, the questionnaire-based design leads to a test of the effect of European experience on European identity, albeit with a non-representative sample.

The second part of the analysis, which deals with the aggregate level, uses the series of Eurobarometer surveys from 1970 to 2000. It assesses the emergence of a mass European identity over the last three decades of the twentieth century, and compares this emergence over time and across countries, hence providing social scientists with findings never available so far.

Finally, to these two quantitative techniques, I add a third, qualitative methodology, which enables us to understand better what citizens actually *mean* by 'Europe' and by their own Europeanness when they claim to feel European. This part is based on a series of focus group interviews conducted in three countries, and will show, among other things, the relevance of the civic/cultural distinction made in Chapter 1 of this book.

The juxtaposition of the three methods has many advantages. First of all, the three methodological approaches enable us to answer a series of connected questions, which no single method could have addressed on its own. Second, the methods proposed, in their combination, have the important quality of counter-balancing each other's shortcomings. First, the measurement of the dependent variable in the aggregate model is much rougher, because of the lack of good direct measures of European identity in the series, but it is validated by the measurement of the experiment. At the same time, the experimental sample is, of course non-representative (which is fine for experimental designs as shown by Norris, 1999), and the design is obviously artificial and could be charged, like any experiment, with having problems of external validity. However, if its results are confirmed by the analysis of the Eurobarometer series, then their generalisation will immediately gain a much higher credibility. Finally, while the two quantitative techniques do not fully sort out the question of what Europe and identity actually *mean* to citizens, this is partly achieved by the qualitative section of my enquiry, that is, the focus group interviews of citizens from three countries of the European Union, which, again, would be very limited if its findings were not backed by the experimental and time-series components of the analysis.

3
Institutions and the Formation of Mass Identities in New Political Communities – Four 'Lessons From The Past' (United Kingdom, Austria, Israel, and the United States of America)

In Chapter 1, I defined some of the key concepts and analytical distinctions that are used throughout this book. Competing theories of identity formation, competing models of inter-connection between multiple identities, and the distinction between civic and cultural components of identity are among the many major conceptual elements that can be illustrated with reference to the emergence and evolution of mass political identities in various old and recent political communities. In this chapter, four case studies will be analysed in order to illustrate some of these conceptual and theoretical elements that were proposed earlier and to show how new political communities have always tried, in their own way, to foster the emergence of a corresponding mass political identity. The four countries presented in this chapter, the United Kingdom, the United States, Austria, and Israel have been selected because they represent a diversity of political situations in which the formation of a new mass identity did not seem to be obvious either culturally or politically.

The progressive unification of the United Kingdom followed – quite lately – the emergence of unified communities in England and Scotland and the changes of status of Wales and Ireland. The unification of England and Scotland occurred only in 1707 and lasted less than three centuries before the transformation of the territorial organisation of the country into an unprecedented system: that of devolution, which is different in essence from federalism (Burgess, 2000) and confederalism while showing a rupture with the traditional centralised British state. This analytic narrative (Bates *et al.*, 1997) of mass identity formation in the United Kingdom will first focus on the emergence of a new – predominantly civic – 'UK identity' in parallel with existing sub-State identities, particularly in Ireland, Scotland and Wales. I will then consider the theory of complementarity – rather than opposition – of identification with different territorial levels.

The United States constitutes, at first sight, a completely different case of mass political identity. There, I consider a structure that was meant to emerge, first and foremost, as a virtually 'pure' political and civic project, in which citizenship has tried to be explicitly untied to any specific *ex ante* cultural unity. The United States has also been characterised by one of the highest rates of absorption of non-national newcomers in the community throughout the nineteenth century. These two features obviously imply particular challenges in terms of mass identity formation, preservation, and evolution. Here, the narrative is, therefore, mostly concerned with the development of a mass civic identity and the creation of a 'shared heritage' (Wintle, 1996) making, probably, the most extensive use of symbols of identity of all democratic countries.

The third example, modern Austria, is a particularly interesting example to the extent that it has been recognised by several political scientists as one of 'failed' identity formation. Ever since the emergence of the republic of Austria in 1919, after the breakdown of the old multi-cultural Austro-Hungarian empire, modern Austria has appeared to be a country searching for its mass identity in vain (Wodak, 1995). Often feeling culturally indistinct or unbounded, refusing to identify with a weak and long-dependent political system (Austria remained, in practical terms, an 'occupied' country until 1955), I study how Austrians have tried to form images of Austria with which to identify, in spite of major difficulties.

The last example considered in this comparative analytical narrative, and the newest of the four states studied, is the case of Israel. With the triumph of the Zionist ideology that re-transformed Jewish identity into a clear national claim since the 1870s and particularly after 1896, Israel was finally officially founded in 1948. It has been based on a cultural community that became less clearly delineated with increasing secularisation, and the immigration of citizens of numerous different ethnic and cultural origins, so that Israel is probably one of the most interesting examples of mass political identity formation and evolution. In the first place, in this specific narrative, I am particularly interested in the distinction and relationship between civic and cultural identities in Israel. I also focus on the long-term impact of good and bad news on identity feelings in a country the history of which has been one of the most complicated and controversial, within its own society, of the whole developed world.

State formation and identity evolution in the United Kingdom

If 'England' is one of the oldest countries in the world, the United Kingdom, conceived as a multi-national – and, according to the Parekh report of 2001, multi-cultural – State in its current form, stands out as one of the relatively recent political constructions in European history. After unifying Wales and England with the treaties of 1536 and 1543, the historic union between England and Scotland took place in 1707. The kingdom took a more global shape in 1800 with the Union Act, which added Ireland to it (Colley, 1992). Following the Home Rule Act of 1914 and the foundation of an independent Republic of Ireland in 1921, the country was redefined as the 'United Kingdom of Great Britain and Northern Ireland' in 1927. Its strongly unitary constitution was put to an end in 1998 when devolution was granted to Scotland and Wales, while the situation of Northern Ireland is constantly evolving towards even greater autonomy.

Almost since the first days of its unification, the United Kingdom has been one of the most striking cases of unbalanced identity construction. The double process of historical absorption of formerly independent entities, and devolution of power as well as the deep economic, social, and political fractures that reinforced the heterogeneity of the country have made it very difficult from the start for institutions to help consolidating a global national identity. The result is an imbalance between the status of England and the other components of the Kingdom in identity terms. On the one hand, Scotland, Northern Ireland, and Wales, have clearly developed distinct (and some would say dominant) national identities even at times of clear civic cohesion of the Kingdom. On the other hand, the English have progressively identified – and mostly equated – their senses of 'Britishness' and 'Englishness' (Colley, 1992, Paxman, 1999). In sporting events, the British and English flags are often used almost interchangeably by supporters, and in surveys and interviews, scholars and survey companies are often faced with respondents describing alternatively or equivalently their nationality as English and/or British. In fact, according to Pattie, Seyd, and Whiteley

(2004), 57 per cent of the British population chose 'English' as their first level of attachment, but at the same time, according to the data of the national statistics office, 48 per cent of Englishmen claim to feel British while this proportion is much lower in Scotland (27%) or Wales (35%).

Thinking of Weber's model of evolution of the State and its various stages of power legitimisation (Weber, 1946), political identification in England, as in most monarchies, probably started with a sense of loyalty and identification with the main symbol of State authority, the monarch. Before being an alliance between two States, the twinning of England and Scotland emerged as a personal alliance between monarchs. In a similar way, the Union acts linking Wales to England were preceded by the traditional conferring of the crown of Wales to the eldest son of the King of England since 1301. Apart from their shared head of state and political fate, no specific common cultural, historical or linguistic heritage was here to link Wales and England a priori. As shown by Thiesse-Morse (1999), the emergence of a British 'national' identity can, therefore, not be spontaneously conceived on the grounds of a specific common heritage. On the contrary, it has been based on a commonality of political institutions and the emergence of shared symbols of sovereignty: a common flag, motto, and the like (Bruter, 1998). Later on, socially recognised symbols of British identity started to adapt to perceived external threats. Currently, in a context of progressing European integration, driving on the left-hand side and the non-metric system (in the 1990s, following a European directive, the metric reference system was imposed for weights in general trade but has, since, largely co-existed with the imperial system) have assumed the role of new symbols of Britishness against a presumed European de-culturalisation. Following the Maastricht treaty and project of a monetary union, the Pound Sterling also became a symbol of British identity in the eyes of some predominantly eurosceptic political parties (such as UK Independence Party [UKIP] and the Conservatives) and mass media (particularly tabloids). The fact that the Pound Sterling, exactly like the Euro, is a currency which is shared by different people while assuming different physical representations (e.g., in England and Scotland) renders the symbolic role conferred to it by some British politicians particularly paradoxical and nonetheless interesting. As an anecdote, it can be noted that while the imperial weighting system is often flagged by Euro-sceptics as another threatened and secular symbol of Britishness, it was no earlier than the mid-nineteenth century, that England chose to adopt the pounds/ounces system, instead of the metric scale that had been in use since the eighteenth century, that many nationalist intellectuals protested against the abandonment of the metric system, perceived as an ultimate 'symbol of British identity'!

Given this situation, two clear features of the evolution of a mass identity in the United Kingdom should be noted in particular. First, for determinist and culturalist thinkers, such as Herder (1913) or Fichte (1845), no sense of global British identity should have ever emerged in the United Kingdom. The obvious unity of public opinion at times of crises, particularly during war times, as well as the emergence of a global party system in Great Britain – even though not in the whole kingdom – suggest that elements of civic cohesion have nevertheless appeared over time. Secondly, the British case raises the question of the asymmetric character of the gap between civic and cultural identities in the United Kingdom. Indeed, while the Scots and Welsh have progressively developed specific cultural identities that have been consistently distinct from their British civic identity, most of the English seem to have operated a symbolic superimposition of the unclearly defined territorial levels to which they identify culturally and civically. As shown by Paxman (1999), England (and Wales) seem to constitute a culturally indissociable community for most of the English, while the lexical and cultural appropriation of 'Edin-borough' has upset many a Scot. At the same time, the Union Jack is still waved almost as often as the English flag in football and rugby competitions involving the English team and 'England' is used fairly often by many English people as an equivalent for 'Great Britain' or for 'the United Kingdom'. This asymmetry suggests that the distinction between territorial units of reference for civic and cultural identification may often be the exclusivity of minority groups within a political community. Members of dominant sub-groups, on the contrary, might rationalise their (both social and territorial) civic and cultural areas of identification, be they the English with the United Kingdom, the Russians with the Union Soviet Socialist Republic while it still existed, or the Serbs in former multicultural Yugoslavia.

This raises a significant question in the context of the emergence of a mass European identity. In the process of Europeanisation, will possible groups' self-perceptions of being either dominant or marginal in the integration process affect their sense of European identity, and the rationalisation of their dominant territorial areas of attachment? The Europeans who live in the East and Centre of the continent are regularly upset by the Western tendency to speak of 'Europe' when we mean 'the European Union'. Surely, however, the equal, inter-national origin of the European Union is opposed to the imperial origins of Russia or the

United Kingdom, a country, which has historically been politically, demographically, economically, and culturally dominated by its English sub-part. England still represents 80 per cent of the population and of the wealth of the United Kingdom. In the European Union, on the other hand, the largest country, Germany, represented only 21 per cent of the total population in 2003, down to 17 per cent of the total population of the Union after the enlargement of May 2004. In other words, the demographic and economic weight of Germany in the European Union will be less than that of California in the United States.

If the British situation is different from that of the European Union with regards to the predominance of one of its constituent units, the process of British identity formation and superimposition of identities that refer to different civic and cultural borders in the country is of interest to the European context. Indeed, one can see that the progressive integration of new culturally specific elements into the changing kingdom has been accompanied by an attempt to create both a civic and a cultural mass identity in Britain, and that the civic component seems to have been more efficiently fostered than its cultural counter-part. The dominant cultural model originally proposed by political institutions – essentially that of Englishness – has not always been well received in the non-English parts of the country. However, perceptions of a British cultural identity have also evolved under the pressure of multi-cultural diversification of British society and the redefinition of the English, Welsh, and Scottish identities. In this sense, the process of development of a mass British identity is not unlike my second case study, the United States of America.

American citizenship and the creation of an American identity

While the United Kingdom was built upon progressive imperial extensions of England, the United States emerged, in the late eighteenth century, as a territory seceding from the British empire and a new political project derived from the philosophy of the Enlightenment. Indeed, the new country was not focused on a given pre-established cultural model, but, instead, on a new form of liberal social contract. The emergence of the American national project out of a colonial tax conflict promised that the United States would be a new *ad hoc* political community in search of a definition of its own new cultural and political boundaries, distinctiveness, unity, and, therefore, identity.

The conceptual definition of American citizenship in the Federalist papers (Hamilton *et al.*, 1999) and the American Constitution grounds identity in civil and political rights, rather than on a particular pre-existing cultural character. Laws of acquisition of citizenship confirmed this approach and made of the United States one of the most widely opened countries with regards to immigration in the nineteenth century (Boorstin *et al.*, 1995). As a consequence, a country that was still relatively homogeneous in terms of cultural and ethnic origins in the eighteenth century had become, a hundred years later, a famous 'melting pot' (Boorstin *et al.*, 1995). Under these conditions, not to exclude any sub-part of a changing American polity, the evolution of a mass American identity had to remain more civic, political, and, to some extent, ideological, than 'national', in the sense of German romantic political thinkers and of the new nation-states that had developed in Europe during the mid and late nineteenth century. At the same time, the geographical and cultural organisation of the country helped develop cross-cutting social and cultural identities in addition to a major North/South identity divide. With the progressive resolution of the latter after the 1936 realignment and throughout the twentieth century, and with a civic identity that remained strong and unified, one could not oppose territorially consistent sub-State cultural identities to its national counter-part as in the British case (Colley, 1992).

Two consequences follow from this situation. First, cross-cutting social and ethnic identities became stronger without giving rise to clear sub-territorial cleavages as identified by Lipset and Rokkan (1967) in the context of West European States. Second, there was room for a cultural component of American identity to emerge over time even if it was constructed *ex post*, and needed to integrate the various – and somewhat heterogeneous – ethnic and cultural sub-groups present in the country. These elements and symbols of a shared cultural heritage may lie in the much stronger religiosity of the United States as compared to Europe (Inglehart, 1990, Dalton, 1996) and in the progressive emergence of a 'public morality' in the country over the past 30 years. But this evolving cultural identity has also been constructed through symbols of cultural commonness that emerged from American history, from its dominant groups, and from public memory.

Symbols of cultural identity have included common celebrations, such as the 4th of July, but also Thanksgiving, and in the American transformation and reappropriation of the heritage of some of the minorities that have formed the country. This has led to the creation of a 'national' cuisine using pizza from the Italians (albeit completely different from the Italian pizza itself!), hamburgers and hot dogs from the Germans, coleslaw and cheesecake from Central and East European

Jews and, more recently, chili con carne and fajitas from the Mexicans. The emergence of a national music first started with the creation of Jazz at the beginning of the twentieth century, which was widely inherited from the Black slaves, and used rhythms and musical patterns from African and Caribbean musics, and so on.

Besides the creation of a shared cultural, traditional, and historical heritage, the use of civic symbols to reinforce the political identity of citizens has been more extensive in the United States than anywhere else in the democratic world. The pledge of allegiance, the flag rising in schools and the national motto have all been used quite extensively to garner a strong mass civic identity within the United States (Boorstin *et al.*, 1995). While elections have developed less than anywhere else as a civic icon of mass communication (except, maybe Switzerland), the American State has been progressively 'extended' by physical symbols and images that represent it in the eyes of the public community and, also, of the outside world. The result has been an overall strong level of civic cohesion, primarily based on these civic symbols, despite a clear conscience of the ethnic and cultural diversity of the country (Boorstin *et al.*, 1995).

When compared to most other countries, including the United Kingdom, the institutions of the United States have put very little emphasis on an attempt to forge a top-down American cultural identity during the nineteenth century. This may, in part, explain that the cultural identity that has indeed emerged is perhaps very different from what the founding fathers would have imagined (and probably preferred) it. These institutions, however, have played a major role in generating a very strong sense of civic identity in a nation that could have undoubtedly been deemed as extremely heterogeneous and potentially weak in its foundations. They have predominantly used a large array of top-down symbols of Americanism that were later complemented by bottom-up popular images. As such, the internal fracture that followed the terrorist attacks of 9 September 2001 has probably been assimilated by popular imagination as a new definition of the American collective identity and specificity in a changing global environment.

There is very little doubt that the founding fathers of the European project in the twentieth century considered the United States as their prime – and most similar – reference, despite obvious differences. It is interesting, however, to look at cases of failed identity formation in some European countries, to try and understand better why the American success at inducing the emergence of a new civic identity has not been met with the same success in all other Western democracies.

Distinctiveness and identity in modern Austria

The United Kingdom was born with the territorial integration of Wales, Scotland and Ireland and the imperial extension of England. The United States, on the contrary, was created by the secession of an old British colony and the fusion and federation of its many sub-parts. Modern Austria, however, yet emerged along a completely different scenario. It followed the dissolution of an existing – and fairly old – empire, of which it was once the heart, and which died due to a fatal military failure.

After 1919, the nation-state ideology seduced the winners of the First World War and particularly US President Woodrow Wilson to such an extent that it had a direct effect on the destiny of the former multi-national empires such as the Austro-Hungarian 1867 bi-cephalic state (Fejtö, 1993). The Habsburg empire was not only considered to be a loser of the war, it was held responsible for it, and blamed as the original cause of the conflict, which started with Emperor Franz Josef's military reaction to the murder of an Archduke Franz-Ferdinand in Sarajevo in 1914. Thus, Austria became a small, independent, rather homogeneous and completely new republic, instead of being the epicentre of a declining but wide, powerful, and even legendary multi-ethnic empire of approximately 20 million inhabitants (Fejtö, 1993). The denial of Pan-German claims even made it impossible to compensate the fall of the culturally elitist empire with the prospect of a new integration with Germany.

The overarching identity of the Austrian empire had been primarily based on its civic organisation, its reigning family, its army, its capital – Wien (Vienna) – and its major cross-cultural 'Central-European' heritage to which the Jewish, Hungarian, and Czech populations may well have contributed more, overall, than Germanness (Kundera, 1984). In this context, 'Austria' as a sub-part of the empire had no clear specific identity features of its own before independence. Instead, it was the vibrant but dependent heart of a multi-cultural and truly 'European' empire that significantly outgrew itself. In fact, at the beginning of the twentieth century, while Wien clearly had an identity of its own, Austria clearly had none. Similarly, applying the traditional elements of national identity claims of the nineteenth century (language, religion, ethnic specificity, history, literature) would not have defined the distinctiveness of the new Republic in 1919. Language rendered Austria a claimed sub-part of a larger Germanic world (and was clearly revindicated as such by the Nazis in the 1930s), and the religious background of the Austrian society (a clear counter-reform Catholic majority, with significant Jewish and Vautist minorities) was similar to those of Hungary to the East, Croatia to the South and Slovakia to the North-East. Finally, the general social and cultural background of the population was as diverse in Austria as it was anywhere else in Europe (Fejtö, 1993) and became more so with the severe economic, social, and political crises the country faced in the first few years of its existence.

With this absence of a perceived homogeneous community and cultural distinctiveness of the polity, and with the lack of civic identification of the population with a weakened and rather authoritarian regime after the 1920s, Austria appeared to be a State without self-recognised citizens, and a community without an identity. In these circumstances, it was not surprising, even when one discounts all the frauds, political pressure, and lack of individual liberty, that the referendum held in 1938 on the Anschluss question garnered even greater support in Austria than in Germany with 99.75 per cent of positive votes (Bernstein and Milza, 1994).

After 1945, the situation of Austria became even more ambiguous. In terms of collective identities, the country considered itself to be a victim of the war while it was considered by the rest of the world to be one of the main culprits of the most horrid conflict in the history of the planet. This hiatus, which followed from a gap between popular perceptions and legal reactions, allowed Austria to not question its own role in the atrocities of the war. Officially, only Germany was considered a clear loser and cause of the war, while Austria was de facto considered a legal non-entity during the whole conflict. Austrian borders remained unchanged, and only two Austrians, Kaltenbrunner, and Seyss-Inquart, were condemned at the end of the Nuremberg trials on 13 April 1949. At the same time, however, unlike Germany, Austria technically remained an occupied territory until 1955, while the independence of the Federal Republic of Germany was officially recognised in 1949 (Bernstein and Milza, 1994). Moreover, Austria would not have obtained its independence in the middle of the Cold War without pledging its full allegiance to neutrality, while both halves of Germany ended up positioning themselves in the Eastern and Western blocks in a tense manner which was accepted ultimately. Independence might have participated in the regained economic prosperity of Austria (like Sweden, Finland, or Switzerland, Austria did not contribute financially or humanly to the military effort of the West) but certainly caused it to be considered a relatively negligible diplomatic and international partner, except when a heavily contentious Austrian politician, Kurt Waldheim, headed the United Nations.

As shown by Wodak (1999), for a long period of time, a majority of Austrians ended up lacking a clear sense of positive identification – either culturally or civically – with post-war Austria. No common national heritage could be identified outside of the re-appropriated broader cultural legacy of the Empire. No sense of civic identification took place either, with a State undermined by a rigid party system, under which a fixed permanent SPD/ÖVP coalition deprived the country of the option of political alternation until the pathetic episode of the 1999 elections. Wodak (1999), who bases her study on interviews and discourse analysis analyses this lack of positive definition and perception of an Austrian identity in contemporary Austria (I would add, both culturally and civically). She claims that this explains the emergence of a negative and exclusive Austrian identity founded on the rejection of foreigners by a large part of public opinion and, ultimately, some of the highest levels of open racism, Anti-Semitism, and xenophobia in the Western world (World Values Survey, 1991 results). How else could one understand that the country with the second lowest unemployment rate in the European Union after Luxembourg has been so receptive to extreme-right arguments on foreigners 'taking Austrians' jobs' and once gave 25 per cent of the popular vote to an extreme-right party which, until late 1999, promoted the closure of borders, praised Hitler's social policy, and asked for a withdrawal from the European Union altogether.

Austria has also been characterised by a definitive absence of systematically used national symbols. While no clear acknowledgement of losing the war was endorsed by the masses, part of the political elite expressed a sense of guilt and shame in recent years, which never resulted in official reactions till 2000. This amounted to a lack of top-down symbolic construction by political authorities and suspicion towards any attempt at strengthening a sense of Austrian identity – often equated with patriotism and nationalism. Conversely, the only party that dared to revive symbols of Austrianness, the extreme right FPÖ, did so in openly aggressive and discriminatory ways.

In other words, it seems that as a result of the fear of excessive nationalism, the Austrian authorities paradoxically brought about xenophobia and racism. Fearing that excessive top-down symbolic campaigns of identity-formation would in fact result in greater nationalism, the Austrian authorities failed to help the development of a positive common and distinctive civic and cultural identity. This left aggressive nationalists without competition for the use of national symbols. In turn, this developed into the search for a negative, exclusive, and somewhat aggressive Austrian identity by a large proportion of the mass public (Wodak, 1999). This perception is confirmed on more generic grounds by social psychologists such as Mummendey and Waldzus

(2004), who claim that identitarian prejudices are in fact necessary for individuals to the extent that it allows them to enrich their perception of the world on the basis of their own knowledge. Top-down symbolic and mediatic campaigns allow the elites to try to channel and harmonise the prejudices of citizens. In the absence of positive campaigns, individuals are more vulnerable to the diffusion of more negative prejudices that define one's identity in opposition – and, sometimes, aggressive opposition – to the rest of the world or to specific others. In a sense, the Austrian case mirrors the development of an Israeli national identity, to the extent that Israel was itself founded by European Jews who had been to a large extent forcibly pushed out of the nations in which they had been, at times, integrated for centuries.

Symbols, news, and identity-formation in Israel

The Zionist manifesto (Herzl, 1896) and the other works defining the conceptual logic of Zionism founded the claim for a Jewish State on both the specificity of the Jewish people (Pinsker, 1882, Lazare, 1897) and their lack of security in existing non-Jewish political communities throughout the world (Pinsker, 1882, Nordau, 1897). The desired state would be a home for all willing Jews in the world, Sephardim or Ashkenazi, religious or secular, living in the historical state or in the diaspora. After years of lukewarm hesitation, the Shoah proved too terrible a demonstration of the extreme lack of security of the Jewish people for the international community to keep denying the logic of the Zionist claim. The creation of the state of Israel was approved in November 1947 (UN, 1947).

A first paradox of the new State, however, is that it was originally defined by a non-political attribute, Jewishness, which was not exclusive to Israel (not all Jews were ever bound to live in Israel) and that could be understood in very different ways by different sub-groups of the Jewish people (Jewishness has been interpreted by different individuals as a religious, a cultural, or a social attribute, or any combination of these). The Jewish people was also very heterogeneous in terms of ethnic and cultural attributes with a mixture of Ashkenazi from Central and Eastern Europe, Sephardim from the Mediterranean area, North Africans, and numerous Jews who had remained in Palestine throughout the times of Ottoman occupation not to mention smaller Chinese, Indian, Ethiopian, Yemenite, and Persian minorities among many others (Roth, 1969, Motskin, 1902). Levels of religiosity were equally inconsistent across the Jewish population, from outright secular members of the community, to moderately religious ones, and Hassidic Jews (Roth, 1969). As a result, even before the creation of the State of Israel, nineteenth century Zionism – that is the path for the creation of a new State, in Israel, for the Jewish people – implicitly acknowledged the urgent need for symbols of the new Jewish national quest.

As a result, a flag was adopted right away by the first Zionist Congress in Basel (Herzl, 1896). It featured a 'menorah' (the traditional religious Jewish chandelier, symbol of the first temple) and two olive-tree branches (symbol of peace) all in blue on a white background. In parallel, Ben Yehuda created a new language for the forthcoming new state by modernising and secularising the religious language of the Jews and creating modern Hebrew, now in use in contemporary Israel. Until then, the different Jewish communities across the world used to speak no common language but only different regional languages: mostly German-inspired Yiddish for the Ashkenazi and Spanish-derived Ladino for the Sephardim together with their numerous local languages of adoption. On 14 May 1948, Ben Gurion declared the independence of Israel. The choice of symbols of the first leaders of the new State had a tremendous impact on the definition of a mass cultural identity of the citizens. On the flag, the Magen David replaced the original Menorah, which, as explained earlier was primarily a religious symbol (Ben Gurion, 1951). By contrast, the Magen David represented a secular political symbol dating back to the first Hebrew State of the Ancient times and the political strength and peace of the kingdom of David, the first Jewish King. It did not represent the Jews or the Jewish religion but, instead, properly, the first Jewish State in the sense given by Weber and political scientists to this word (Weber, 1946).

Ever since 1948, the State of Israel tried to mix those of its symbols that belong to the past, and those that clearly look towards the future, in a way that is not dissimilar to the European project. For example, the national anthem, the Ha' Tikvah was soon composed and did not refer to any biblical message. As for the declaration of independence of 14 May 1948, it specifically included a passage on Israel being a secular State, which would always be open to members of all religions (Ben Gurion, 1948). The rejection of a religious identity by the various left and right wing Israeli governments ever since 1948 has implied that national identity has had to find its ground in other possible sources of identification. Attacked by their various neighbours on the very day of the Independence, and facing several wars in its short existence as a state, Israel's common identity was first achieved externally in reference to a common threat (Ben Gurion, 1951, Begin 1981). Elements such as a long military service (three years for men, two for women) became a strong source of citizenship, and signs of civic engagement and of allegiance to the State made its very borders and the defence of its security primary symbols of the Israeli identity.

However, with the evolution and the economic and social progress of the country, patterns of identification changed. Ever since the 1960s, parts of the Israeli media have channelled a stern debate on the role and choices of Israel in its various conflicts with neighbouring countries and with the Palestinians. This debate quickly extended and started to divide the core of the Israeli population (Yehoschua, 1980). The most rightist part of the country insisted on the prevalent and persisting external threat on the country, and the need for internal cohesion and unity without much territorial concession to Palestinians and Arab neighbours. In the 1970s, however, the most leftist part of the country started to question the attitude of Israel towards Palestinian claims, and the attitude of the country towards Lebanon (Katz, 1960, Oz, 1979). This political fracture, relayed by a free and government-challenging press, added to the cultural diversity of the country and weakened the level of civic identity of a small part of the population towards a State, whose policies it challenged. Ever since the beginning of political alternation in the late 1970s, with the first victory of the right-wing Likud party then led by Begin, the radicalising polarisation of the Israeli party system led to an increasing sense of identity defiance towards left and right wing governments alike (Oz, 1979). This was made worse by a system of integral at large proportional representation, which always forces the creation of large, and ideologically heterogeneous government coalitions. At the height of the left–right debates between the hardest-liners within the Likud, such as Netanyahu, and the farthest left Labour leaders such as Peres, in the late 1980s and early 1990s, some left-wing intellectuals actually criticised Likud-led Israel as a regime. They 'refused' to identify with it anymore and rejected the very 'conception' of Israel they attributed to the Likud. In the same way, some radical right-wing citizens could not identify with the image of Israel drawn by Peres and even more centrist Rabin, tragically assassinated in 1994 by a right-wing radical. Throughout the 1990s, many left-wing supporters modified their political approach after the failure of Barak and Clinton's peace efforts at Wye plantation. The distinct evolution of the peace process under Sharon's leadership since 2004 even seemed to displace the lines of fractures within the Israeli society with many Labour and moderate Likud supporting the government's action, and some more radical Likud supporters as well as supporters of nationalist parties and religious parties challenging its legitimacy and perceived attacks on their own conception of Israeliness.

From the Israeli example, we can conclude that specific support for the long-term general direction of the policies of a State may influence the level of identification of citizens with their civic community. Here again, the parallel with the significantly more radical example of post-war Germany and Meinhof *et al.*'s (2000) work comes as an interesting comparison and relevant extension of the impact of this impact of specific support in radically more dramatic circumstances. According to her research, many of the Germans born after the Second World War refused to identify with a country they linked to the horrors of the war and Nazism. Surely, this shows how long-term collective and political attitudes influence mass identity formation and evolution. In the case of Israel, however, the weakening of one of the strongest examples of spontaneous mass civic identity in the world poses identity problems in the Jewish state. While the country used to count on the seemingly fantastic sense of civic identity of its citizens to overcome the remarkably difficult challenges it has faced strategically, politically, socially, and economically, politicians are now protected by bodyguards and separated from the crowd in meetings, a normal situation in Western countries but a new one in Israel. The country still faces a persistent situation of (cold) war with a dozen countries, wide-spread terrorist attacks, but also the absorption in one decade of more than a million new immigrants mostly arrived from the former Soviet Union, that is, about a quarter of is previous population. These new immigrants often came to Israel by right (following the adoption in 1950 of the 'Law of Return' by the Knesset) with hardly any resources, no houses, and no knowledge of Hebrew. Indeed, once again, the maintenance of a strong sense of civic identity has been all the more important for Israel than elements of cultural identity and cohesion has progressively faded. Indeed, the progressive secularisation of the Jewish people both in Israel and in the Diaspora, and the massive arrival of new communities that have not been completely integrated by the Israeli society both challenged the cultural model that had progressively emerged in the pioneer years of 1948–1960. New populations, mostly consisting of North Africans (1960s and 1970s), Ethiopian Beta Israel (1980s), and former residents of the USSR (1990s), changed the face of the Israeli identity over time.

While these challenges may, in part, remind us of the worst fears of pessimists with regards to the Eastern enlargement of the European Union, the attempt by Israeli institutions to foster the emergence of a new national identity that turned towards the past and future and disconnected from a stronger pre-existing religious identity is not without being reminiscent of the choices made by the European founding fathers in their attempts to define Europeanness. This will be more comprehensively commented in Chapter 4 when I address, for example, the design of non-existing monuments on the Euro banknotes.

Comparative synthesis

The Israeli narrative shows us that the evolution of mass identities first and foremost occurs as the result of an evolution of individuals' identities over time. Obviously, generational effects will be significant in terms of the assimilation of new political identities. In the case of Israel, however, we are faced with such a recent phenomenon that it would be impossible to ignore the persistent evolution of individual political identity over a lifetime. Political identity, if it has to do with socialisation, has to do with the continuous socialisation of an individual and not only with his early experiences in life. This confirms Hall's perception that identities are never complete, never finished, but, instead, in perpetual evolution. People's perceptions of the political (and non-political, for that matter) communities change, as the images they associate with them change. Ultimately, the strength and nature of their identities are bound to vary over time. In the long run, as evidenced by the American and Israeli cases, the influence of symbols of or news on their political community can be a major determinant of individual identity reactions.

Similarly, in the American, Austrian, and British cases, we have seen that individual circumstances, such as the other political and social identities of an individual, his political opinions, and probably his personal and family history can influence political identity feelings. It is clear that similar circumstances should be expected to have an influence on the degree of European identity of individuals as well. Obviously, it is far more difficult to study historically the evolution of an individual's identity than mass phenomena, but it is clear that the understanding of individual identity will be essential to the precise grasping of mass evolutions as well. The success of the emergence of a new mass identity following the emergence of a new political community by extension, fusion, or division of existing States is clearly dependent upon institutional outcomes, symbolic campaigns, and the perceived successes and failures of the new community, as well as the way they are portrayed by the mass media. However, it also owes to the individual reactions to changes in his individual political circumstances.

Obviously, the European Union's is in a different situation from all of the four case studies considered here. A European identity can only add up to – and not replace – a pre-existing identity. At the same time, the absence of independence war or Revolution prevented the European project from developing a proposed identity in opposition to a hated particular out-group (even though one could argue that the Second World War constituted a very powerful negative referent). Chapter 4 will develop an analysis of the history of the symbols and institutions of a United Europe. This new narrative will not only answer the study of our 'four lessons from the past', but also be of use to understand one of the independent variables that are used in the second part of this research.

4

With Aforethought? Institutions, Symbols, and the Quest for a New Identity in Europe

After reviewing the importance of institutional input in the fostering of new mass political identities in the United Kingdom, the United States, Austria, and Israel, and before looking at the impact of European institutions and the mass media on the emergence of a new European identity, it seems important to try to characterise – and provide evidence for – what I claim to be the specific attempts of European institutions to foster a new identity. To some extent, the questions of the emergence of symbols of European integration, of what constitutes perceptions of good and bad news on European integration, and of when states start to be part of a global integration process are topics of real substantive importance. They are also as many integral parts of the short but dense history of European integration. In this chapter, I propose to first identify when and how European institutions became concerned with the fostering of a mass identity, and to then propose a history and typology of the symbols used to characterise the European Union from the top.

The context: how European institutions became concerned with identity? Four phases in the history of European integration and public perceptions: 1945–2004[5]

When trying to assess whether or not the institutions of the European Union have tried to wilfully foster and encourage the emergence of a new European identity and how, it is first useful to try and understand how the global perception of European integration may have varied over the past 50 years in Europe. This section claims that it is impossible to understand the reactions of public opinion towards 'Europe' over time without understanding, first, the evolution of the perceptions of what European integration has progressively stood for over the past fifty years. In other words, my first task is to re-read critically the history of European integration over the past fifty years and to analyse the evolution of its political content.

The contention of this analysis, which tries to unify and go beyond several interpretations of the European integration process by political scientists such as Moravcik (1998), Burgess (2000), Gabel (1994), and Dalton (1996), is that since its first steps in 1948, the process of European integration has gone through four distinct phases of development. The first phase, began after the end of the traumatic Second World War. It was a phase of Europeanisation based on international co-operation and designed to favour peace in Europe and avoid the resurgence of the old and bloody nationalisms that had been so omnipresent for a whole century on the European continent. The second phase, started with the signature of the Treaty of Rome on 25 March 1957. It has been a phase of technical integration whereby new policy areas have been progressively devolved to a new 'European' level of government in more and more territorially complex political systems. The third phase that I mentioned began following the first enlargement of the European Communities in 1973 and the first major institutional reforms of the European Communities. It has been a movement of institutionalisation that has been revived before any new enlargement. The fourth phase, which beginning was coincident with the presidency of Jacques Delors at the head of the European Commission in January 1985, has been characterised by European institutions themselves as the creation of a new 'People's Europe'.[6] After the adoption of the Maastricht Treaty in 1992, this approach took a more and more specific character to represent the development of a new democratic project, almost a new 'social contract', for the European Union.

The succession of the four phases of evolution of European integration has not meant that a new stream would annihilate and replace all the previous forms of integration. It has been, indeed, quite the opposite, and each new 'level' of integration has simply added a new dimension, a new ambition, to the previous ones, increasing the globality, complexity and multiple dimensionality of the European project. Figure 4.1 illustrates the evolution described above and some of the most characteristic elements that represented the international, policy, institutional, and citizen-oriented or identity-oriented character of the European project over the last 50 years.

This first section of this chapter on the identity input of European institutions details these four new phases of integration and suggests that these institutions will have expected citizens to develop new,

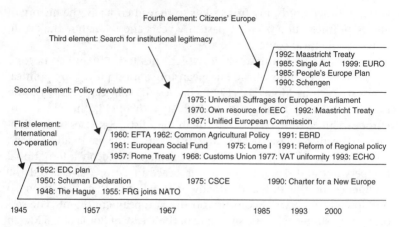

Figure 4.1   A graphic summary of the evolution of European integration after 1945

complex and multi-layered levels of assessment of the European project and of its significance throughout the years. As such, detailing the changing intention of institutions in their characterisation of the European project also results in the proposition of a typology linking perceptions of what European integration is to criteria potentially used by citizens to assess good and bad news on European integration over time.

Let us now propose a more detailed analysis of each of the four phases of development of European public opinion. I concentrate on what they mean, how consistent they are with political science theory, and what they imply in terms of the criteria of support that will be involved, and of the assessment of what 'good' and 'bad' news will be perceived to be.

Phase 1: Europe as an insurance policy against war: cosmopolitanism and anti-nationalism

As far as the first period is concerned, I suggest that the construction of a European Community was first inspired by the ideologies and thoughts of Valéry, Coudenhove-Kalergi, Monnet, Schuman, and the other founding fathers of the European project. These figure heads of the European project primarily presented the need for a united Europe as a consequence of the need for peace in Europe, by and large along the lines that had already been defined by George of Podehřady in 1464.[7] Citizens' reactions to these ideas, from the origins of the European unification process after the end of the Second World War to the mid-1950s, must be characterised as a basis of '*cosmopolitan assessment*' for the European project.

Many political scientists and International Relations theorists have always studied the European project as a typical international agreement. They consider that independent nation-states chose to create a typical – albeit particularly deep – co-operation structure to guarantee peace and development on the European continent (Gautron, 1989). In a way, the European project was first founded upon a certain cosmopolitanism of the participants of the The Hague conference of 1948, whom, from Churchill to Monnet and from Adenauer to De Gasperi believed in the appropriateness of international co-operation to pursue such goals as the achievement of peace and stability in Europe and the world. These politicians' perception of the international situation of the time was such that they thought it particularly indispensable to co-operate with the various partners proposed at the time.

The founding fathers thought that the European project was needed to guarantee peace in Europe, that the partners were trust-worthy enough to give co-operation a chance of success, and that the structure of the proposed European Communities was strong enough to lead Europe on the way to possible peace. At the time, there is also strong evidence to suggest that the perception of European integration by a majority of the European national political elites and an overwhelming majority of the public opinions of the Western European countries was consistent with this 'international' approach to the unification process. A new war was, indeed, feared by many, sometime in the future and likely to involve, again, France and Germany. Elites and masses in the Allied block also shared the perception that a 'Versailles' like solution would be extremely counter-productive, an opinion shared by the Americans after 1945, particularly under the emerging pressure of the Cold War.

It is likely that the Second World War will be remembered in the collective memories of most European societies as the worst long-term trauma they have ever experienced. Its vivid impact on the national consciousness of the West Germans (Meinhof and Galasinski, 2000) and the recurrent painful debate of the French generations on the role of French citizens and of the France of Vichy are but a few examples of this lasting and divisive impact. The Second World War was not only a horrid, murderous, and devastating war (the third for the Germans and the French in less than a century, all against each other, and the cause of over 50 million deaths in 6 years). The conflict also stands apart as a symbol of the dreadful consequences of hatred and nationalism taken to their extreme to result in the voluntary extermination of millions. Thus, it is all but surprising that most European intellectuals and political leaders stood in favour of the project of unifying part or the whole of the

European continent after 1945. This was done, largely, along the cosmopolitan and pacifist lines that had been defined by Paul Valéry, Aristide Briand, and Gustav Stresemann, and was later outlined by Denis de Rougemont at the The Hague meeting of 1948, which truly launched the European project.

There is virtually no empirical data available to study trends in public opinion on Europe in the early 1950s. The little evidence available, however, suggests that indeed, public reactions to the first steps of European integration (the meeting of The Hague in 1948, the creation of the European Community of Steel and Coal (ECSC) on 18 April 1951 and the project of a European Defence Community (EDC) in 1952) had a lot to do with individuals' assessments of whether European unification would guarantee peace on the European continent. Among the winning countries, their willingness to favour an international agreement that would tie France, for example, with its 'historic enemy', Germany was also very significant.

To a large extent, these findings confirm the receptivity of European public opinions to the common political discourse of both supporters and opponents to European unification in the late 1940s and in the 1950s. The Schuman Declaration of 9 May 1950 insists predominantly on the necessity to unify Europe to guarantee peace on the European continent. Peace and reconciliation were also the foremost arguments developed by the most salient supporters of European integration in countries like France and Belgium (Schuman, 1953, Monnet, 1955). At the same time, it is clear that the main opponents to the ECSC and EDC projects were mostly concerned with the danger of an alliance with Germany, and, as far as the EDC was concerned, with the idea of allowing Germany to have again, a national army ahead of the Potsdam schedule. The hopes of peace and the fear of Germany simultaneously seemed to be shared by a majority of the Europeans who were puzzled by this apparent contradiction and hesitated over the extent to which they trusted the process of integration. Simultaneously, many Germans trusted indeed that the European project would annihilate their nationalist heritage and start a new era of cosmopolitan openness for the German nation. Adenauer's thoughts on that matter were almost a caricature (Brugmans, 1970).

For many of the founding fathers of the European project, convincing European public opinion that European integration was the only path to peace and security in Europe was regarded as the most difficult challenge of the time. Many of them were therefore surprised by the maturity and the obvious lack of hostility of the European public towards the Schuman Declaration (Spaak, 1969). The large majority obtained by the Pleven plan when it was presented to the French Assembly on 24–26 October 1950 was also a reason for amazement to many observers (Brugmans, 1970).

Later on, however, the founding fathers faced highly sceptical reactions of several national public opinions to further discussions of the EDC project in the National Assembly. This quite directly led to the final rejection of the EDC plan by the yet predominantly pro-European French National Assembly on 30 August 1954. The failure of the Pleven plan to find support from the public has arguably had a significant impact on the rejection of the project by the French political elites. Adenauer (1965) claimed that while some of the leading French politicians of the time concurred with him on the perception that the EDC was the best way of avoiding any resurgence of German militarism and the creation of a German army (to which he objected), they emphasised that much of French public opinion still thought that a majority of the Germans would 'always be fundamentally nationalist'. The rejection of the EDC by the French National Assembly therefore seemed consistent with the preference, not only of the majority of the French, but probably a majority of the former 'allied' countries, hostile both to the abandonment of their national armies and to a military agreement with the Germans.

Inferences that can be made from the general behaviour of the French public in the 1950s and from the observations made by leading political personalities in the early stages of European unification suggest that phase one of the development of European integration could be characterised as follows:

- It corresponds to a project predominantly perceived to involve international co-operation rather than, as yet, a project of integration into a new supra-national entity. It should be noted that this seems to be in contradiction with the highly federalist perspective of the elite that designed the European project in the aftermath of the war. Indeed, Monnet, Adenauer, and De Gasperi could all be characterised as true 'federalists'.
- At the time, the European project mostly had some ideological and abstract dimensions but only a relatively limited impact in terms of specific policy-making except around the creation of a barrier-free area for steel and coal products.
- For the European elites and the European public – especially in allied countries – two primary elements were at stake in the early stages of European co-operation: the need to guarantee peace in Europe and

the need to decide on a conduct to hold towards Germany. Except in Germany itself, a majority of the European public seemed to believe, ambiguously, that European integration would indeed favour peace, but, at the same time, was built on an excessive trust of Germany. The privileged development of the 'Franco-German axis' in the 1950s and 1960s was probably urged in part by the particularly high levels of such scepticism among the French and German populations, and so was the commonly accepted idea among European elites that European integration would not last if this axis collapsed.

The ambiguous attitude of European public in the first years of European integration had a dual impact on the European project. First, by their implicit general support for the project, the populations of the various European nations made it possible for European integration to continue all together. A clear refusal of the process by any national public opinion, particularly the French, in those early years, would have almost certainly led to an early-aborted integration process. Second, after a few years of original unanimity, by their defiance towards the EDC project, the French public 'froze' the original stream of European integration and forced European politicians to find a new direction for integration after a phase of immobility in the mid 1950s. The Rome Treaty of 25 March 1957 symbolises the evolution of European integration towards a more economic and 'technical' agreement.

Phase 2: Europe as a new policy-maker

As a result, in the second half of the 1950s, the European project had to overcome the EDC crisis by being reinvented with greater 'specificity'. The failure of the Pleven Plan of a EDC in 1954 and the adoption of the Rome Treaty on 25 March 1957 were, indeed, two major steps in the evolution of a very broad and general Europe, progressively replaced by a specific policy-oriented programmatic project. If European citizens started to react to specific policy outcomes thereafter, this evolution of the public perceptions of Europe must now be defined as a time of '*rational assessment*'. Positions on European integration would be primarily linked to the specific policies that have been developed by the European Communities. Such policies were more or less salient across the various countries of the European Communities and include, for example, the Common Agricultural Policy, the progressive abandon of internal trade barriers, and the like.

Amongst the various policy areas targeted by the European Communities, some were of particular importance to individual member-States.

For example, the CAP was particularly salient in France while the end of trade barriers were, at first, better appreciated in the Netherlands, and the creation of European environmental standards in the Federal Republic of Germany. Nevertheless, all countries participated in the greater 'technicality' of the European project following the Rome Treaty.

In a way, as of the late 1950s, European integration ceased to be a sheer international project to become, rather, a new source of 'domestic' policy-making. This seems to correspond to the idea that citizens started to assess the specific policies emerging from the European sphere in various areas.

Obviously, when the process of uniting Europe first began, the perception of its potential policy implications for the general public was minimal. However, the three countries (Denmark, Ireland, and the United Kingdom) which joined the European project in 1973 did so while the policy-making significance of the European Communities had reached a climax, but after most international and peace-related issues had been resolved by the original six founding members. This might make a significant difference to the way public opinion has considered Europe in those countries, as opposed to the six core countries of the ECSC.

Paradoxically, indeed, the second stage of European integration, as started by the Rome Treaty, was far more limited in scope than the first. As far as the question of peace was concerned, West Germany joined NATO in 1955, so that its military situation seemed to be more under control than it was a few years earlier. Simultaneously, the tension of the Cold War had eased – at least provisionally – after Stalin's death on 5 March 1953, so that, by the end of the 1950s, questions of economic development and colonial trouble had become more salient to French, Dutch, Belgian, and European public opinions than the ideals of international co-operation outlined in the late 1940s. The EURATOM Treaty on nuclear co-operation emerged as a symbol of technical co-operation, the newly-created European Economic Community (EEC) gained some regulating powers in terms of competition policy for the first time and, of course, the Common Agricultural Policy was launched in 1962, and has remained of vital interest for many member countries, and particularly France, ever since. Other major policies of interest are regional policy, industry, and so on.

Slowly, the public became more familiar with the policy areas in which European institutions were most powerful. The first detailed and repeated mass opinion survey on European attitudes, Eurobarometer, which started in 1973 after pre-series surveys in 1970 and 1971, shows that ever since the origins of the polling series, European public opinion

Table 4.1 Support of the European public for EU intervention in various policy areas in 2003

Policy area	Differential support for EU intervention
Foreign policy	+30
Environmental policy	+18
Educational policy	+4
Economic policy	0
Immigration policy	−17

Note: Figures are differences in percentage of total respondents
with positive vs negative view of intervention in these policy areas.

Source: Eurobarometer 2003, 60.

has been split into two uneven groups when it comes to assessing the
specific policy outcomes of the European Union. Table 4.1, for example
shows the support of European citizens for EU intervention in five policy areas in 1997. Similar hierarchies could be observed for the European
public at other times since the 1970s. The results highlight the idea that
while European intervention tends to be fairly popular with the
European public across policy areas, it is even more so for the more
'abstract' policies.

Phase two of the evolution of European integration adds, therefore, to
the complexity of the perceptions of the project in the following ways:

- Since the 1970s, Europe has progressively become a specific and
  active source of policy-making as well as an abstract political project
- European policy-making is globally perceived by EU citizens as send-
  ing two contradictory signals: being part of the general process of
  globalisation that is often feared by the most vulnerable parts of the
  European population, and providing Europe with new progressive
  social, cultural and environmental policies, sometimes feared in
  more economically liberal countries, such as the United Kingdom
  and to a lesser extent the Netherlands.

Slowly, however, the European citizenry stopped perceiving the
European project as a simple ideological project and set of policies, and
instead, became familiar with what it represented in terms of new
political institutions. However, while succeeding in becoming a new,
established, level of government, the institutions of the European
Communities faced a new challenge in the 1970s, that is, the need to
gain a clear political legitimacy in the eyes of the European polity.

Indeed, the progressive broadening of the competencies transferred to the European level of government, particularly in terms of foreign and social policies, partly led the public to consider that European institutions had become more important in their daily life.

Phase 3: Strengthening European institutions and the search for popular legitimacy

The third period of integration has begun in the 1970s. It would be best described as a period of development of the *'institutional legitimacy'* of the European institutions. It was logically imposed by the increasing institutionalisation of the European Communities. Indeed, since the beginning of the 1970s (and throughout the 1980s and 1990s), the 'political institutions' of the European Communities started to take such an increasing importance in the life of citizens and countries that their legitimate character started to be questioned as well. As explained in Chapter 2, using the definition of Gibson and Caldeira (1995), the question then became to know whether the European public was starting to develop some 'diffuse support' for European institutions at a time when their policy-making capacity had become salient enough for some of their specific decisions to be contested. Indeed, only diffuse support could provide EU institutions with the necessary levels of political legitimacy, whenever public opinion rejected or disliked some of the specific policy outcomes of the European Communities or have criticisms towards the way a given institution functioned.

According to Gibson and Caldeira (1995), the level of diffuse support of citizens for their institutions can be expected to be related to neither the specific policies made by institutions nor the specific people who form part of these institutions. Instead, citizens express perceptions regarding the *design and functioning* of their political institutions: Are institutions 'fair' in the way they function? Are they democratic, transparent, efficient? Does the design of an institution enable it to make decisions soundly, quickly, and with a guarantee of sufficient public debate? The result of these assessments determines the level of 'diffuse support' that citizens attribute to a given institution, that is, to use Gibson's and Caldeira's expression, a 'reservoir of good will' that will make citizens ready to accept specific policies they dislike without desiring the destruction of the institution that made it. Therefore, it is logical that the member-States and the European Union, in the 1970s, would try and give a margin of legitimacy to the various EU institutions by working on the elements that would be expected to convince citizens that they functioned fairly, transparently, and efficiently while, of course, retaining the subtle equilibrium of national influences they had negotiated with some difficulty over time.

Arguably, it was in the late 1960s and mostly the first part of the 1970s that Europe ceased to be a 'new' political project. This marked the beginning of a period of major institutional reform for Europe which went on in the 1980s and in the 1990s. Throughout these twenty-five years, Europe was enlarged three times and more than doubled in membership. It changed names twice, it adopted the election of the European Parliament by direct universal elections, and it passed four fundamental treaties that completely altered its scope and goals. By then, the European Union had successfully become a new established and integrated level of government defined by specific institutions and decision-making processes.

Throughout these reforms, the European Union has indeed become a fully institutionalised political entity with a comprehensive set of executive, legislative, and judicial institutions. With the exception of studies on US institutions, legitimacy models generally assume that citizens primarily assess the design and functioning of legislative and executive institutions. In the context of the European Union, the sole executive institution is the European Commission and the two legislative bodies are the European Parliament and the Council of Ministers.[8] However, unlike national bodies, European institutions cannot be classified only along *functional* typologies (legislative, executive, judicial) but also show very significant *structural* differences. Indeed, the various institutions of the European Union could be divided into 'integrative' bodies (e.g., the European Parliament and the European Commission) and inter-governmental bodies (e.g., the Council of Ministers). Integrative bodies work as supra-national institutions that take decisions, so to speak, like a 'federal' government (Burgess, 2000), without consideration for the balance of power between infra-federal members. Inter-governmental institutions, on the other hand, make decisions in a co-operative mode with all infra-federal members represented as such within the institution.

The efforts of the EU elites as constitutional authorities, however, have been partly contradicted by the efforts of EU elites as national authorities. Since the acceleration of the institutionalisation of the European Communities, virtually all national governments have extensively used European institutions to take credit for 'good' policy innovations and as an excuse for 'bad' ones. Virtually no European government has been exception, even though, looking at the Nice Summit of December 2000, some countries, such as the United Kingdom, Austria, and Sweden, have shown a particular propensity to play the blame game, while other, like Italy, have seemed relatively non-polemical in their attitude. This has been known by a few political scientists as the 'Uncle Dutch and Aunt Sally' syndrome of European integration (Franklin, 1999). In this context, the 'integrative' institutions have often been blamed more specifically by national governments for all negatively connoted policies. Meanwhile governments tended to take credit for the positively connoted European policies by proposing a glorified image of their own behaviour in the co-operative institutions of the Union such as the Council. At the same time, however, part of the legitimisation phase of integration relied on an attempt to grant some of these integrative institutions – particularly the Parliament and Court of Justice rather than the much-feared Commission – a minimum of power and organisational autonomy that were needed to justify, beyond them, the European project as it stood itself.

The series of bi-annual Eurobarometer surveys on European attitudes give us a relative sense of the success of the attempts by EU elites to legit-imise their institutions. Some studies such as Gibson and Caldeira (1995) also scrutinised the legitimacy of the main judicial institution of the European Union, that is the Court of Justice of the European Communities. Generally speaking, in the 1970s and early 1980s, the new or reformed institutions of the European Communities seemed barely to be trusted by European citizens, with, however, some signifi-cant cross-national differences. Even though the European Parliament was first elected by direct universal suffrage in 1979, only about a quarter[9] of European public opinion trusted it as an institution until 1983. By 1985, the figure was still less than a third. During that time, it would have been impossible to claim that the new democratic body of the European Communities had reached any 'safe' level of political legiti-macy in the perception of the European public. Similarly, the first main reform of the powers of the European Commission was made possible by the Luxembourg Single Act of 1985, which took effect in 1987. This reform reinforced the power and the autonomy of the European Commission vis-à-vis the Council. Strangely enough, the European Commission, which was most often blamed by national governments for the most unpopular outcomes of European integration, was first perceived by European citizens as a far more legitimate body than the democratically elected Parliament. The first time European citizens were asked whether they trusted the European Commission, in 1987, 46 per cent of the respondents said that they did, which was 6 points higher than for the European Parliament in the same survey. The two main reasons for such an acceptance of the European Commission were probably (1) the economic prosperity of 1987 (political science research, for example Stimson *et al.* in 1995 shows us that prosperity tends to increase the perceived legitimacy of all institutions) and (2) Delors's presidency of the European Commission since 7 January 1985. Indeed, Delors was by then one of the most popular European politicians, in more than one country, and, of course, particularly in France and in the most pro-European countries, such as Italy, Germany, Belgium, and Luxembourg.

In the case of both the European Parliament and the European Commission, however, it is clear from Eurobarometer evidence that the legitimacy of the two main integrative institutions of the European Union has slowly but clearly progressed over the past 20 years. This provides the EU institutions with an overall strong level of popular legitimacy with the overall trust in the European Commission, European Union-wide at 46 per cent (against 28 per cent who do not trust the Commission) in 2003. This level of trust and support is even higher for the European Parliament with 54 per cent of citizens trusting the institution in 2003, against 27 per cent who did not. Even more surprisingly, however, according to the Eurobarometer series, the number of countries which actually trust the European Parliament and the European Commission more than their national parliament and government (Figure 4.2). This trend has become more and more common across European Union countries, and while it has been a very regular pattern of public assessment in countries such as Belgium, France, and Italy since the 1990s, it has now reached such countries as the United Kingdom, Finland, Austria or the Netherlands as well. In fact, in 2003, only Denmark still trusted its national institutions more than the EU ones, while Swedes trusted the European Commission more than their national government, but their national parliament slightly more (by one point) than the European one. This pattern is all the more interesting in the view of the fact that while European institutions gained greater political legitimacy in public opinion, national institutions were undermined by several corruption scandals and reached a record low in the 1990s in virtually all EU countries. The legitimacy trends of national and European institutions therefore suggest a possibility for further progress of the legitimacy of European institutions, and a risk of further decline of the perceived legitimacy of national ones, as perfectly illustrated by the French case between 1995 and 2003 (Table 4.2).

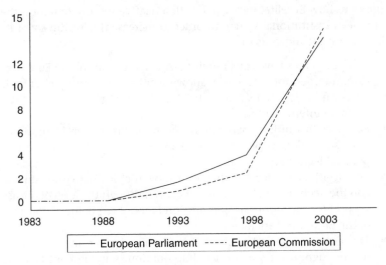

Figure 4.2 The legitimacy of the European Parliament and the European Commission: 1983–2003 (number of member-States where the European Parliament/Commission is trusted more than its national equivalent)

Note: In 1983 and 1988, the number is 0 for both institutions; *when two figures are available for one year, the average of the two is reported in the figure.*

Source: Eurobarometer Survey Series.

Table 4.2 An example of the compared legitimacy scores of national and European institutions in France in 1995 and 1999

Institution	Legitimacy score 1995	Legitimacy score 1999	Legitimacy score 2003	Change 1999/1995	Change 2003/1995
National assembly	45	37	33	−8	−12
European Parliament	48	54	54	+6	+6
National government	42	36	30	−6	−12
European Commission	36	44	50	+8	+14

Source: Eurobarometer Survey Series.

The study of the third phase of development of European integration shows us how EU elites have tried, with a relative success, to reform the European institutional system in order to increase the legitimacy of its institutions. It shows us that:

- European elites have tried to reform the institutions of the European Communities, for example by allowing citizens to directly elect their European representatives from 1979, and granting institutions a little bit more internal autonomy.
- European institutions, particularly European 'integrative' institutions, have succeeded in progressively gaining a relatively solid level of political legitimacy.
- This legitimacy affects both the 'democratic' legislative institution and the 'technocratic' executive one, even though the level of diffuse support for the European Commission is about ten points below that of the European Parliament.
- The 'Uncle Dutch and Aunt Sally' syndrome of government messages has no significant effect on public opinion. On the contrary, the Council has a lower level of diffuse support than the two other major institutions of the European Union.

It is probably thanks to this progressing legitimacy across most European countries, and – at different levels – throughout the European Union, that the leading integrative EU institutions have been able to diversify their areas of influence and to develop, since the mid-1980s, the project of a 'People's Europe', due to re-legitimise, this time, not only EU institutions but the European changing political system as a whole. This project was designed to propose a new European 'social contract' to citizens, to elaborate a new conception of European democracy, and to encourage the development of a new European political identity. Of course, the main texts designed to induce the development of a mass European political identity – the Single Act and the Maastricht Treaty – also included significant stipulations to develop the power and auto-nomy of all major integrative European institutions. The question of political legitimacy remains therefore as relevant as ever while European integration faces the hardest test of all, that is the challenge of designing of a new social contract with its citizens.

Phase 4: European citizenry, European citizenship, and the attempt to foster a new European identity

What I suggest has to be a fourth phase in European integration was therefore, in part, a direct consequence of the attempt to provide EU institutions with greater democratic legitimacy. Indeed, closely following this search for legitimacy of European institutions, these very institutions have tried to promote the European Union as a new citizenship, and Europe as a new political identity. In a way, European leaders have tried to make 'Europe' less of an 'issue' – that is a debatable political outcome – and more of a political system that can be taken for granted, at least in principle. This is not to say that all citizens have become happy with the way Europe is emerging as a new democratic project, and how it is evolving as a political fieldwork. However, the project of developing a EU citizenship and a corresponding identity since the 1980s means that European citizens can assess 'their' political system from the inside, as opposed to an external structure that would be criticised from the outside.

As explained in Chapter 1, in one of the most influential political analyses ever written on a new democratic project, Tocqueville (1835) claimed that American democracy would be guaranteed a long-lived success to the extent that it had already developed a sense of political identification with the nation. The idea that European institutions have consistently worked towards creating a mass European identity ever since the middle of the 1980s, is quite clear whilst reading the various preparatory papers that surrounded the launch of the project of a People's Europe. I believe that institutions developed a new EU citizenship in part so that citizens of the European Union might actually develop a greater sense of identification with the European Union. The European Commission and leaders of several member-States claimed openly their desire to encourage a changing perception of what the European project was, and what it intended to change in the lives of citizens.

According to Jacques Delors, the project of building a new 'People's Europe' was the only way of making European integration survive the turn of the 1980s. With Europe becoming more economically liberal than ever under the influence of such leaders as Margaret Thatcher, the European Community of the mid-1980s was risking losing any 'political' sense and becoming instead primarily a large area of free trade. The Single Act of 28 February 1986 put together the project of a European Single Market that was created in 1993, which was certainly the biggest step ever taken by Europe in terms of economic integration. For this reason, social and cultural measures towards the creation of a 'People's Europe' were deemed necessary to guarantee a 'balance' between the economic and the socio-political aspects of European integration. Programmes of cultural and educational exchange (such as ERASMUS) were developed. The Single Act also launched the first elements of co-operation in the field of foreign policy and other highly 'political' policy areas (Gautron, 1989).

Clearly, all these measures had obvious objectives: to propose a new 'Social Contract' to European citizens, and to develop a new mass European identity rather than let citizens be mere 'consumers' of the economic benefits associated with Europe. The resutls of this campaign on the French public are illustrated by Figure 4.3. Most recent reforms of the European project have been informed by a need to make Europe 'accessible' and aimed at citizens. This means that the past 15 years of European integration have been the most intense in the history of European integration in terms of development of programmes aimed at making European unification a daily reality in the life of citizens. As a result, we come up with a model of public evaluations of European integration based on four components: its international value, its policy outputs, its institutions and its effect on citizens' identities (Figure 4.4).

After having shown the general intent of European institutions to foster a new European identity and allegiance to the EU political system, I want to look at the mechanisms that have been used to achieve such a result. Of course, I mentioned the objective creation of elements of European citizenship. It is also my contention, however, that European institutions tried to use clear and consistently thought campaigns of providing citizens with symbols of their newly emerging political system to reinforce the emergence of this new European identity. The next

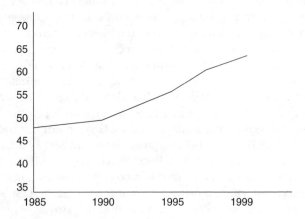

Figure 4.3 Proportion of French citizens mentioning Europe as an aspect of their identity 1985–1999

Source: Eurobarometer Series.

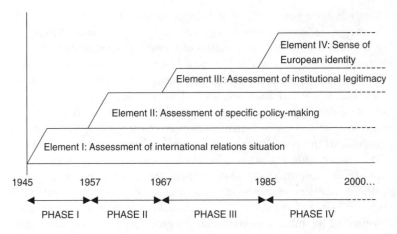

Figure 4.4 Summary model: four determinants in the development of French public opinion towards European integration

section in this chapter analyses the history of Europe using symbols to foster a developing mass European identity.

Understanding the emergence of new symbols of European integration

In this section of the chapter, I first define symbols. I then rephrase my theory of the link between symbols and identity (Chapter 2) to fit the specific case study of the European Union and identify and classify symbols of European integration since the 1950s. Finally, I give evidence of the visibility of certain symbols of European integration to justify the coding strategy adopted for this specific independent variable later on in the book.

What is a symbol?

The word 'symbol' describes a 'physical element' used – for example – to represent a political or social collectivity. This symbol can be an emblem, a flag, a name, an allegory, an anthem, or any other element that could be used to attach a physically apprehensible 'signifier' to a Nation, a State, or any other human collectivity. Indeed, studying the impact of the symbols of a State on mass identity could be described as a 'political' interpretation of the structuralist approach, that is, an adaptation to the world of politics of Saussure's (1974) analysis of the relationship between signifier and signified in the context of linguistics.

Symbols have been used by political entities for a long time, for the purpose of federating the energy of their subjects and citizens. In Chapter 1, I mentioned the creation of a new set of symbols for freshly independent Belgium, and in Chapter 3, we saw how countries such as the United States, the United Kingdom, Austria, and Israel, have made use of symbols to try and assert a specific identity. Since Ancient times, symbols were also expected to convey a specific impression to the outside world and particularly to potential enemies. In the Ancient times, flags or particular anthems or clothes were already used as a means of discrimination between different armies. In feudal societies, emblems were used extensively by monarchs to identify their power and families: tartans in Scotland, banners in Northern Italy, and even flowers and plants in medieval France. Similarly, monarchs' faces were used to recognise coins, a symbol all the more important that the geographical and technological context of the time prevented them from asserting their authority directly to the whole geographic territory of their countries in many cases. In fact, one of the main symbols used throughout history has been the monarchs themselves, who represented their countries on their own. Reputedly claiming that '*L'Etat c'est Moi!*', Louis XIV of France summarised in the most obvious possible way the use of symbols by the guarantors of State and nation unity to give citizens the illusion of the superimposition of an image (the King, a physical, material, person) on an abstract concept (the State). This parallels almost perfectly the construction of a linguistically consistent vocabulary as analysed by Saussure.

From this example, it can be generally considered that a symbol is in fact used to 'personify' a political or social entity and to create a physical image intended to become the allegory of a State in people's minds; the 'image' (or sound etc.) that will represent the collectivity in their conscious or sub-conscious perception. It is, to put it shortly, a first attempt at direct 'identification' between real object and abstract category in itself. In identifying institutionally created symbols of the European Union, I look for all forms of physical objects used to characterise Europe and the European Union or to be associated to them by members of the political community (i.e., European citizens) or outsiders.

The potential role of symbols of the European Union in the creation of a civic and cultural European identity

As explained in Chapter 2, it is easy to understand the logic of the expected impact of symbols on identity formation. Indeed, by trying to force the superimposition of a specific image over a more abstract concept, symbols make it easier for citizens to identify with the political community regardless of their levels of knowledge of the community and of their capacity for abstraction. They identify with the State or nation 'indirectly', through the mediation of a signifier, that is, a symbolic object. Of course, symbols will also influence the specific values and connotations associated with a political project by citizens and foreigners alike.

It is also interesting, however, to link symbols directly to the two components of political identities that have been identified in Chapter 1: civic and cultural. So far, we have already assumed that the importance of the symbol-generating activities of the European Union and the meanings of these symbols are not neutral. More precisely, I have suggested a theory claiming that they might be designed in order to create or reinforce feelings of belonging to a cultural and civic Europe – feelings of European identity – but without specifying which component, if either, has been more specifically targeted.

Asserting the purposeful identity-related character of the genesis of symbols of European integration is not, in itself, easy to demonstrate. To do so, one would need data on the wills and intentions of the main authors of the programmes that have been dedicated to providing the European Union with strong symbols and objects of identity. The purposeful character of generating symbols – not a central element of the argument here, will therefore be merely assumed. Before defining what the main symbols of European integration are that have emerged over the past 50 years, I proceed to demonstrate the potential role of symbols in the strengthening of an emerging identity, and assess more finely their potential messages in the context of this study. Both elements must be clarified before considering the role of symbols in the creation of a new super-national identity.

The intrinsic meaning of political symbols has often been studied by historians, political thinkers, and social scientists alike, from Tacitus (109) to Fejtö (1986). The role of symbols in the construction of identities – that is, the relationship between the intended message and the perception of symbols – however, only became a real issue at the end of the eighteenth century and has been best defined by Cornelius Castoriadis (1975), from a structuralist point of view:

'Every society up to now has attempted to give an answer to a few fundamental questions: Who are we collectively? What are we for one another? Where and in what are we? What do we want; what do we desire; what are we lacking? Society must define its 'identity', its articulation, the world, its relation to the world and to the objects it contains, its needs and its desires. Without the 'answer' to these 'questions', without these 'definitions', there can be no human world, no society, no culture, for everything would be an undifferentiated chaos. The role of imaginary significations is to provide an answer to these questions that, obviously, neither 'reality' nor 'rationality' can provide'.

Some elements relating to the strategic use of symbols in the United States and Israel have been analysed in Chapter 2. To grasp the problem of conflicts of symbols and the hopes that have rested on the definition of new symbols in the most extreme cases, however, it is important to extend the framework of analysis to other punctual case studies. The launching of the French First Republic, in 1792, and the national revolutions of the nineteenth century were occasions when national leaders experienced a cruel need to provide their peoples with concrete symbols that would strengthen their new nations and regimes. Completely new identities would be proposed to whole populations, and the destruction of the imagery of the former powers would lead to the absence of current political symbols and references for the citizens of the new political systems.

In France, for example, following 1789, the *Fleur de Lys* and the head of the king were to be removed from people's minds in revolutionary and post-revolutionary France and to be replaced by new Republican and Revolutionary symbols. Similarly, after the German unification of 1871, inhabitants of the whole of the newly unified Germany would have to be given symbols that would help them to feel German rather than simply Prussian, Bavarian, or Hamburger. And as explained earlier, in the newly created Belgium, in 1830, nationalist demonstrators had forgotten to create a new flag of their own and started to parade the streets of Bruges and Brussels carrying French flags around before creating the new Belgian flag that was soon distributed to demonstrators (Seiler, 1998) to put an end to such a worrying symbolic confusion. Finally, with the Spring revolution of 1848, pro-independence leaders had to work out how the Hungarians would have to be given the impression of belonging to a nation that had not existed as a State since Matthias the Great. It is for such occasions that nationalists and institutions of all kinds had to find new sets of symbols and images for their citizens in a rather short period of time.

One of the necessary elements for the success of symbolic 'operations' is a plausible claim to transcendent legitimacy for the proposed symbols. Old, forgotten flags were reclaimed by historians and writers from several-centuries-old battles and long-dead monarchs and national heroes were resuscitated. Religious symbols also seemed to be particularly useful as, if most subjects were already convinced believers, they would associate their religious ground of identification with the national one. Similarly, the arts emerged as an endless source of national symbolism and development of a national conscience. Every new nation started to celebrate their own (generally mediocre, and since then, often forgotten) modern national poets, writers, musicians, and painters. They related themselves to sometimes obscure artists who lived several centuries earlier, as one of the constants in old and new nations alike is that they must be perceived to be very old in order to feel more legitimate.[10] Older popular cultural figures were also lent, *ex post*, some strong and 'obvious' nationalistic feelings. And sometimes, whole centuries of national history were disregarded in order to focus on more promising episodes of Ancient history that were deemed more glorious. An excellent example is represented by modern Greece, which, from the independence onwards preferred to refer to its Ancient heritage and almost systematically disregarded its medieval, classic, and Romantic history (Alexakis, 1995).

Sometimes, new political systems have tried to emerge outside of the irrational and artificial frame of symbolic politics. The situations of the French Revolutions and Republics, launched in 1792, 1848, and 1871 are very interesting from the point of view of public symbols. Indeed, on all these occasions, the building of a new identity was attempted by political regimes, which pretended to be opposed to the symbolic cults of the past monarchic times. Officially, there was no more person to be adored, no more official religion to divert the citizens from the path of reason, and no more substitution of images, symbols, and affective feelings for a purely enlightened and rational political contract. However, it turned out that the Republic could not survive this symbol-free, rational and transparent political Commonwealth. At the end of the eighteenth century, at a time of poor education, Robespierre had to create, ad hoc, the physical symbols of an alternative brand new deist religion to replace the superstitions of Catholicism – the '*Cult of the Supreme Being*'. In the same way, one century later – and using a pattern which many modern states have followed afterwards – for lack of a king-like figure for the republican citizens to adore, and in order to serve as a real link between them and the Republic, and to raise the patriotic spirits of the French after the defeat of 1871, the Third Republic had to celebrate the cult of the Pantheon. There, '*Les Grands Hommes*' have been celebrated by '*La Patrie Reconnaissante*'.[11] Finally, with the Resistance movement during the Second World War and the launching of the Fourth and Fifth

Republic, new France showed again that it could not do without a set of affective, 'irrational' symbols that would help to create a patriotic and civic feeling amongst the population.

If France is a good historical example of the difficult use of symbols by new political regimes and communities, it is extremely obvious that it is far from being an exception. On the contrary, the Americans, for instance, as explained in Chapter 3, have been even more significant 'consumers' of symbols in the building of their own cultural and civic identity, and so have been most of the newly independent post-communist Central and Eastern European republics, Britain, Asian countries, and many new African States. The use of symbols to achieve peaceful processes of identity formation and legitimisation seems to be mandatory for all modern governments. It appears to be the tribute paid to old images and ceremonials by the modern State, if not the ultimate inalienable link between patriarchal and legal–rational authorities in the Weberian model of State development (Weber, 1946).

As explained earlier, the European Union may, in a way, be in an even more acute position of needing symbols to assert its identity: it has to prove that European identity exists and is compatible with national, regional, and local identities to achieve its modern demo-cratic legitimacy; European institutions also need to fight against the images of bureaucratic, non-democratic, and inhumane organisation that most Euro-sceptics try to attach to them. Hence, the broad and com-prehensive sets of symbols provided by the designers of modern Europe that I analyse in the next few pages. The European project, trapped between the two original ideal-types of legitimate State formation – the nation-State and empires – is, more than any other political project, needing symbols to assert its own originality, it own specificity, and its ethical meaning. That is to say that European institutions have had to take a stance in terms of the criteria of legitimacy that support their political project, by selecting a particular set of symbols of European unity.

The perceptions of this need – and the very clear purpose of European founding fathers in granting the European Communities some specific symbols – are directly illustrated by many declarations made by European officials about the importance of making European citizens conscious of their European identity. In fact, if we consider identifica-tion with symbols as part of a cultural and civic project, we need only remember the words of Jean Monnet, main founding father of the

European unification process:

'Si c'était à refaire, je commencerais par la culture'[12]

I now proceed to introduce the main symbols of Europe and the European Union, typologise their intended meanings, and try to assess the efficiency of European leaders and institutions in designing salient and respected symbols of a uniting Europe. Do people feel the same way on the Day of Europe as they feel during 4 July in the United States or the 14 July in France? Do they feel moved when they listen to Beethoven's Ode to Joy and would they feel moved hearing it together with national anthems at major sport events? Do they like to see a European flag when they travel abroad? Do they feel partly at home in the other countries of the European Union because they see the flag? Do they feel at home in these countries because they do not have to cross border controls to get there, because they do not have to go through customs, and because they do not have to exchange their currency either any more?

Symbols of Europe

Probably no continent was ever attached to so many symbolic representations and images as Europe throughout history. Even more certainly, no other continent has ever used so many symbols to characterise itself. The symbolisation of Europe began as early as the Ancient times. The Greeks were the first ones, indeed, to consider Europe as a consistent entity and to attach the image of the semi-goddess Europa to it (Wintle, 1996).

In a way, however, the symbolic representations of Europe have preceded human attempts to purposefully characterise it. Indeed, the question of European symbolisation was already set up as soon as the notion of a European 'continent' was invented, as Europe – and by corollary, Asia, is the only continent of all to be geographically meaningless (Lewis and Wigen, 1997). It is quite paradoxical, indeed, that the continent that has made the strongest attempts at defining its own 'objective' identity is the only one not to be a continent at all from the point of view of most geographers.[13] Therefore, the problem of the symbols of Europe began when the first Greek geographers tried to draw maps of Europe. Of course, the Northern, Western, and Southern borders of the European continent are generally well perceived (even though the Northern border was, in fact, unclear until the Renaissance period [Black, 1997, Wintle, 1999]), but what about the East? Even now, some geographers hesitate between the Ural Mountains and the Volga River in the North–East while the South–Eastern limits of Europe are even less clear around the Caucasian mountains and the Caspian Sea. The problem of the geographical symbolisation of Europe is, of course, very important with regards to European identity. Indeed, as will be shown by the results of the experiment and the focus groups discussions, when people talk about 'Europe', many actually think of the European Union (at the time of the interviews, 15 countries, mostly in the west of the continent, now 25, still excluding several parts of Europe). Similarly, others can think of the whole western and central parts of the continent (therefore excluding the former USSR), or of 'Europe from the Atlantic to the Ural' (therefore comprising only 'parts' of several countries: 3% of Turkey, 20% of Russia, etc.). Geography apart, of course, many argue on whether Turkey or Russia 'belong' to Europe or should be left out of the natural borders of a European Union that now hopes to ultimately match the borders of 'Europe'.

The difficulty to geographically delineate Europe is well illustrated in the fact that at least six places (there are probably more, but only those whose claims were backed by serious geographical institutes are considered here) currently pretend to be the 'Centre of Europe'! Two can be found in Eastern France, two in Western Germany, one in Southern Poland, and one north-east of Vilnius, in Lithuania! This list does not include the institutional capitals of the European Union (Strasbourg, Brussels, and Luxembourg) and of the Council of Europe (Strasbourg again), or the French–German border, which might all have similar 'symbolic' claims to be the 'real centre' – or at least the real heart – of Europe as well.

Nevertheless, 'natural' geographical symbols, however important and interesting, can hardly be considered to have been, since the origins, purposive symbolic constructions of the European imagery, and in fact, many of the medieval conceptual maps of the world mostly tended to represent shapeless Europe, Asia, and Africa. A lot of other symbols that were used during the Middle Ages and the Renaissance to personify (personification was the most common type of symbol at that time) Europe have been forgotten by Europeans since then. They include Japheth (one of the three sons of Noah), as opposed to his brothers who were used to personify Asia and Africa; Europa, again, or, sometimes, the bull that she rides, and which provided a more evocative and 'reassuring' image during the times of wars and the crusades. Very often, also, Europe was personified by a virgin or a queen, as on many maps of Europe of the Renaissance period (Wintle, 1996).

All these symbols, yet, are those of a religious, spiritual, or abstract Europe, not those of Europe as an institutional power or super-State. They are the justification of a superior-feeling civilisation, and a self-awarded tribute to its leaders and intellectuals. Another set of symbols exists now that target, instead the whole European and non-European populations. Most of these symbols, created by the Council of Europe and the European Communities for their citizens are, on the whole, very recent in the already short history of European institutions. Most of them emerged between the 1970s and the early twenty-first century, consistently with the fourth phase of European integration that was identified in the previous section of this chapter on the four phases of development of the European project.

Surprisingly enough, the first major 'national' symbol of Europe in history was not provided by the European Union itself but by the Council of Europe, the institution (independent from the European Union) that is in charge of cultural co-operation and respect for human rights on the whole European continent. This symbol is the European flag: 'twelve golden stars [forming] a circle against the background of blue sky'.[14] This flag, chosen by the Council of Europe in the 1950s, was adopted only much later by the Council of European leaders (the leading institution of the European Union) in 1972 to symbolise all the European institutions and Europe as a whole. At the same time, the Council of 1972 also approved – as well as the flag I just mentioned, and jointly again with the European Council – the idea of a European anthem, the *Ode to Joy* by Ludwig van Beethoven with the words by Schiller.

However, it was in 1975, at the council of Brussels, that the nine members of the European Economic Community (EEC) chose the first symbol of their institution itself and not of Europe as a whole. This symbol was, somehow, abstract: it was the decision that elections to the European Parliament would now be held at the same time across the member-States of the European Communities under direct universal suffrage. At the time, the idea was mainly backed by the Chancellor of the Federal Republic of Germany, Helmut Schmidt, and the French President Valery Giscard d'Estaing. From 1979, the election of the European Parliament would consist of a direct universal poll that would take place at the same time in all the member-States of the European Community. Later in the history of the making of the European Community, this symbol was also enhanced by the creation of transnational political groups in the European Parliament. Probably in part because of the economic, social and political crises experienced by most European countries and by the European Community in general at that time, no further decisions were taken to provide the Community with new significant symbols in the few years that followed and until 1985.

At that time, as agreed at the Council of Milan, European institutions added to the imagery of the European Communities such symbols as a

European passport and a 'Day of Europe'. The EU passport, common to all EU citizens, with its burgundy colour and information written in all the official languages of the European Union, was considered one of the benchmarks towards the creation of a 'People's Europe' by the Delors administration of the European Commission in the 1980s. Similarly, the Day of Europe, the Schumann day was designed to provide Europe with the closest possible equivalent to its own 'Independence Day', traditional feature of a proud 'liberated' nation. It is celebrated on 9 May, which commemorates the Schumann Declaration of 9 May 1950, when the creation of the ECSC – the first of the three European Communities – was announced. Again, these two symbols of the European Union (then European Communities) were highly significant of the second half of the 1980s. At the time, the European integration process, under the joint push of Jacques Delors (president of the European Commission from 1985 to 1994), Helmut Kohl, and François Mitterrand shifted towards the construction of a 'People's Europe'.

After some slightly more quiet times towards the very end of the 1980s, some new sets of symbols were created during the 1990s and onto the early 2000s. The first is the change of name of the 'European Community' (which had replaced the EEC, ECSC, and EURATOM in 1987) into the 'European Union' with the Maastricht Treaty of 7 February 1992. Under the same treaty, the decision was taken to provide the Union with a single currency, later labelled the Euro.

We see, in Chapter 8, that many EU citizens consider the Euro as one of the most significant symbols of European unity at present. Beyond the topicality of the question, it should be remembered that monetary independence has been a traditional symbol of State sovereignty since the Renaissance, and even announced the creation of West Germany when the Western Deutschmark was launched in 1948. The choice of a name for the new European currency, as well as that of the design of the Euro bank notes and coins in use since 1 January 2002, were made at the Council of Madrid in 1995. Finally, the Amsterdam summit of June 1997 allowed the European Union to choose one more symbol of the external sovereignty of the European Union. Indeed, it was then decided to appoint a 'Mr CFSP' (Common Foreign and Security Policy), currently Javier Solana, who represents the European Council of heads of governments on the international scene.

In spite of a relative crisis in the European integration process, the European leaders have been keen on continuing the effort to provide the European Union with a full set of symbols of its political sovereignty at the turn of the Millennium. The Charter of Fundamental Rights has been widely acknowledged as a symbol of European shared ethical, moral, cultural, and social values, and the joint operational force as a symbol – praised or feared – of a European military independence. Finally, regardless of the failure of the Brussels summit of 2003, EU leaders are still adamant to soon adopt the first Constitution of the European Union. A Constitution is, of course, the symbol of a State, or, at the very least, a sovereign political system *par excellence*, and the draft adopted by the Convention presided by former French president Giscard d'Estaing made a special case of asserting, in its project, the role and nature of the official symbols of this European political system.

Distinguishing categories of symbols of Europe

All those symbols, however, are not equal. In fact, there is a need to consider several ways to differentiate and classify them, which are important to bear in mind since their implications are different for the process of encouraging a European Union identity, and with regards to the likely 'meaning' of the identity thereby stimulated. The two conceptual distinctions that are of the highest importance in this study are a distinction between civic and cultural symbols that matches the identity types presented in Chapter 1, and a classification into co-operative and integrative symbols, following the two broad competing conceptions of European integration.

The distinction that must be made between what can be called 'civic' and 'cultural' symbols of the European Union, mirrors, in a way, the conceptual distinction drawn in Chapter 1. In that sense, on the one hand, it seems logical to call 'civic' such symbols as the election of the European Parliament, the single currency, and the passport since they represent the authority of an institution on matters that are generally under the power of the State. On the other hand, one would naturally tend to deem 'cultural' other symbols such as the anthem, the design of the notes, and the like. They are 'cultural' symbols because they refer to the existence of a shared historical and cultural European heritage that can lead to the definition of a 'European nation', which goes even further than a European civilisation. More specifically, they attempt to convey a particular vision of this shared baggage, which defines the human community of Europeans. A few symbols appear to be a little bit more difficult to fit into either category. The flag and the Day of Europe, for example, could be perceived in so many different ways, and are so intrinsically linked to the global idea of a nation-state in the first place that they have an obvious civic value. However, their very choice characterises the European Union well beyond its strict legal existence. As explained earlier – and as will be detailed more again later – the flag, for example, has been awarded a deeply ethical meaning by European leaders, which clearly makes it an instrument of conveyance of particular cultural meanings. The same can be said of the choice of the Schuman Day.

It is interesting to notice that the chronology of European symbols has showed a certain alternation of cultural and civic symbols. Leaders started with mixed symbols such as the European flag in the Council of Europe when federalist Europeanism emerged a winner out of the The Hague conference of 1948. Then, a first wave of civic symbols were produced in the 1970s, when the European Commission really emerged as a powerful institution. Civic and cultural symbols emerged again to accompany the project of a 'People's Europe' in the mid-1980s, and then with the Maastricht Treaty, the most important renewal of the European institutions since the Rome Treaty. In post-Maastricht Europe, the choice of new cultural symbols became a necessity yet again while Europe underwent a major crisis. Indeed, after the Maastricht debates throughout Europe (Denmark's 'No', France's tiny 'Yes', British rejection of some aspects of the Treaty) the European project was facing a new crisis of identity, a need to legitimise its geographical extent and political scope. But again, after Nice, the institutional crisis of the European Union prompted the multiplication of new civic symbols and in particular the need to officialise the solidity of the European project by giving it a Constitution. In fact, the European Union has constantly needed to produce both kinds of symbols, which most certainly means that it has been looking for both cultural – one could say almost 'national' – and civic or institutional legitimacy.

The second major distinction that needs to be made between what could be called symbols of 'Community' and symbols of 'Unity', however, results in a clearer evolution of the European project in time. Although these very words may be considered to be co-existent and mutually reinforcing symbols in their own right, it must be said that they represent in reality the two opposite legal and political streams of the European project. Community implies the idea of co-operation between the member-States while Union expresses the existence of a single super-national and super-State power. In other words, Community refers to an inter-national organisation, whilst Union refers to an integrated power. Whilst these two components of the European project have often been considered by political scientists such as Moravcik and Burgess to compete in a fairly balanced way for the future of integration, it is interesting to note that their effect has been far from equal in terms of influencing the symbols of the European Union.

Indeed, using the community vs unity distinction, we can say that fundamentally, virtually the only Community symbols of the European Union are the election of the European Parliament (which respects national constituencies and voting systems, and even then, one cannot help noticing that all member-States, by now, have adopted a proportional representation type system for these elections, which was not the case a decade ago) and the design of the Euro coins (which have a national face together with their European one). For instance, despite public beliefs, the European flag is not a community symbol even though many wrongly think the contrary. The number of stars on the flag has never had anything to do with the number of member-States (which is, on the other hand, the case of the flag of the United States). The European flag was adopted by the Council of Europe when it had more than 12 member-States and then by the European Communities when they had only 9. Never referring to twelve as any concrete number, the Council itself simply and abstractly defines it as 'a symbol of perfection, harmony, and entirety' that officials, after the Council compared to the number of months in the year, of constellations in zodiac, or of the Tribes of Israel. So, it is not only non-community oriented, but almost esoteric in its perception and affirmation of unity. The European council of Madrid, in 1995, also refused to give the Euro banknotes a 'national' face and a European one, preferring to make the banknotes the same for all, as an additional proof of their desire to make them a real symbol of unity again.

This insistence shows quite clearly that, while the actual European unification process has always been 'split' between Community and Union tendencies, the main 'fathers' of this process have long been rather determined – at least in symbolic terms – to lead Europe towards Union rather than simple co-operation. This is true even though the latter could have been easier to put in practice and more readily acceptable to most Europeans. Twin jewels in the Crown of the 'Union' victory, the Maastricht Treaty openly renamed the European 'Communities' the 'European Union', and the Constitutional Convention has proposed to retain and officialise 'United in Diversity' as the official motto of the European Union to appear in its forthcoming Constitution. In other words, the authorities of the European Union have definitely decided that they needed to provide ambitious symbols that stressed European unity, rather than its already very-well-perceived diversity.

Europe seen through symbols

Symbols are not neutral. They are designed to provide people with a particular image of Europe (or, for that matter, whichever abstract concept or community is represented by them). The notion of 'unity', although extremely important, does not say everything about the European reality the European founding fathers have tried to promote. Indeed, we also have to go deeper into the substance of the symbols chosen to see which values Europe tries to attribute to itself. Many different interpretations can be made of the intended representation of Europe, as perceived from its symbols. Reading into them implies a needed attempt to interpret the wills of their creators and the perceptions of European citizens. In spite of the inherent challenge of such an exercise, a number of major values can be found at once in the European project, in the justifications given for its necessity, and in some of the main symbols created for contemporary Europe.

The first value to be highly visible in European symbols is that of peace, friendship and harmony. There is no need to quote the words by Schiller in the European anthem to see the point of choosing them as the means to link the idea of a united Europe to the values of peace and friendship. As is well known, and as was discussed more extensively in the previous section of this chapter, peace has been the first value legitimising the project of the construction of a 'United Europe'. It has been emphasised from its first appearance in a letter by George of Poděhřady in 1464, to the The Hague conference of 1948 and beyond. It appears relentlessly in almost every single chapter of the history of treaties on European unification (ECSC, Rome Treaty, Single Act, Maastricht Treaty, negotiations on the enlargement of the European Union towards the East). It would therefore have been very strange not to find this idea in the symbols representing the very institution that has been entrusted with the responsibility to convey and strengthen the idea of peace and mutual-friendliness in Europe. However, what is more interesting is the repeated presence in European symbolism of the notion of 'harmony'. Although derived from the idea of peace, this concept suggests a far deeper perspective. Indeed, if 'friendship' implicitly recognises the predominance of diversity and the need to accommodate it with peaceful relations, 'harmony' transcends diversity to claim the ultimate necessity and superiority of unity with respect to a pre-existing and pre-determined human collectivity. 'Harmony' is no longer a sum, but already a new unit and unity that has become indivisible. It is, in a way, an almost 'mystical' state, which is not divisible into a variety of parts.

Another interesting way to analyse the political and ideological identity that a human collectivity wants to attribute to itself is to study its relations to its own history – here understood in its broadest sense. As was explained earlier, every State or organisation picks some internal references and forgets others when it comes to defining its philosophical, cultural, and ethical heritage. For instance, the United States prefers to refer to Washington, Jefferson and Lincoln, rather than to Monroe; to the 'pioneer' spirit, and the Mayflower rather than to the first immigrants who settled in Southern colonies or even the very strict religious beliefs of the Mayflower landers. France too would rather refer to the Revolution of 1789, Victor Hugo, Descartes and Voltaire than to the Napoleonian Empires, Pascal and Céline.

Somehow, however, the European 'harmony' seems to have few plausible references in human history. At least, European authorities have scarcely drawn parallels to historical situations or 'outstanding' personalities in the choice of their major symbols. There is no 'Pantheon', no massive historical cult of any specific period of the common European history (despite a certain soft spot for Antiquity and the age of Humanism), no mythical battle or sovereign to adore. Europeans can only find marginal references to marginal symbols or personification in the names given to some of the policy programmes of the European Community/European Union from the 1970s onwards, some of which ignore the actual borders of Europe. When such a choice has been made, the acronyms chosen strangely continue to refer to the Ancient Times, Middle Ages, Humanism and the Renaissance, rather than to more proximate periods. Generally (with a few exceptions, however), they also refer to some of the main elements of the shared European heritage, and show a connection with European openness, cross-culturalism, and trans-nationalism.

References to the Ancient times are explicit in programmes such as SOCRATES, the general educational programme of the European Union, which is an example of personification. They are also obvious with EUREKA, TEMPUS, and LINGUA, programmes respectively dedicated to scientific co-operation, educational exchanges with Central and East European countries and learning of languages. All three are also examples of concepts and values, while PETRA (technological programme) refers to a mystic Ancient (non-European) site. Other programmes' acronyms refer to the Middle Ages and the Renaissance. For example, one can remember the ECU (European Currency Unit, which stands as the base of the European Monetary System), which was the currency of Charlemagne's empire, ERASMUS (co-operation between universities), which uses the name of the great philosopher of the Enlightenment, and LEONARDO (Da Vinci), which represents another of the technological programmes of the European Union.

However, the choice of names for programmes of the European Union are relatively minor – while not negligible – symbols. They are linked to the quasi-obligation for administrative efficiency and managing purposes to create meaningful and appealing acronyms for the newly launched programmes of the Community. At the same time, historical references are extremely limited when compared to references to the future.

Moreover, with respect to the study of the symbols of the European Union, it is made extremely obvious that European unification definitely aims at being a construction of the future and must refer to it rather than to any past person, event, or period in the history of European civilisation.

In this respect, it is easy to consider the single currency, for instance, as the archetypical symbol of futuristic Europe. Its name, in spite of the preferences of most Europeans, is not ECU, but EURO, a new name without any reference to anything in the past. It should also be noted that Euro was chosen rather than Euro-mark, franc, liras ... as many politicians wanted, another proof of the preference for symbols of unity rather than community and diversity. But the banknotes also match this choice of the future: unlike almost any other currency in the world, Euro notes will show imaginary, non-existent, monuments rather than anything belonging to the actual 'material' patrimony of the European Union. As mentioned earlier, the same is true of the flag, which does not refer to any historical banner. This contrasts with most European nations, which, when they had to choose flags in the nineteenth century took their inspiration from existing flags: the French one for the Netherlands, Belgium, Italy, or even Germany, the Swedish one for Denmark or Norway.

To sum up this fragile balance between a European shared heritage and a definitive look towards the future rather than the past, one can quote the declaration of the Council of the European Monetary Institute in the fall of 1996 about the design of the future Euro bank notes:

> Le graphisme des Euro symbolise la naissance de la nouvelle Europe unifiée, dépositaire d'un héritage culturel commun ainsi que la vision d'un avenir commun pour le siècle prochain[15]

Ultimately, one of the major ideas that can be consistently detected in the symbols of the European Union relates to the most popular human and political values of Western Europe. I have already mentioned references such as Socrates as a symbol of philosophy, Erasmus as a reference to cosmopolitan humanism, Eureka as an invocation of science, Petra for the human genius in architecture. However, many of the European major symbols (e.g., anthem, flag) make a reference to the Western ideals of openness, tolerance, humanism, human rights, democracy, friendship, peace, and others. All these values reflect the will to create a new period in the understanding of the very concept of democracy and the relations between political institutions and citizens. This is seen in Schiller's text of the Ode to Joy, and in several of the declarations made by European Councils of the Heads of States and Governments after some of the symbols of the European Communities and Union were chosen.

Clearly, the European Union has not been satisfied with trying to project the image of a legitimate and united new nation but has also wanted to claim some legitimacy as a political organisation. It is, after all, a political project, which aims to provide the citizens of the new Europe with a new democracy. It must claim that it will both respect the heritage of a continent used to be at the head of human rights and democracy, and present some aspects of total modernisation and innovative understanding of what democracy is. It must claim to adapt to the expectations of democratic citizens of the third Millennium if it wants to become some form of a European super-State. As a matter of fact, the European Union through the symbols it has provided to itself does not only seek to prove its transcendent necessity from the point of view of post-national legitimacy, but also its revolutionary nature in the forms and practices of political power. This is best illustrated by the 'big deal' made by institutional designers with regards to the perspectives of subsidiarity, direct democracy, and the project of a 'People's Europe'.

Assessing the visibility of symbols of the European Union on mass levels of civic and cultural identity

Before trying to draw a direct connection between European symbols and their effect on the development of a European cultural and civic identity, it seems important to assess the visibility of the main symbols of European integration among European citizens and, to some extent, in the outside world. As was previously mentioned, fewer symbols established by the European Union have been dedicated to legitimacy of its institutions than to the identity feelings of its citizens. Such an imbalance may be explained by how, if European institutions have always been very concerned with their legitimacy and visibility as political institutions, officials probably thought that campaigns to 'give a face' to Europe was more likely to help them to have a greater impact on the citizens than symbols of institutional legitimacy.

Although it has been shown quite clearly by the literature that the campaigns for the elections of the members of the European Parliament are more dedicated to internal issues than to European ones (van der Eijk and Franklin, 1996), Eurobarometer surveys regularly show that a large majority of Europeans in all the countries of the European Union are very attached to the preservation of the mode of election of this most democratic institution of the Union. They perceive very clearly the symbolic importance of voting for Euro-MPs at the same time throughout Europe. In 1994, the citizens of the 'core' of the European Union already thought that European issues were more important than National ones (Table 4.3), whereas in 1989 no country held such views.

Public opinion studies also show very clearly, that a large majority of Europeans identify the Common burgundy passport as a symbol and react favourably to it. They link it to the new power of the European Union (85% of the new bills passed each year in European countries have their origin in Community Law). Table 4.4 illustrates the visibility of the common passport as a symbol of the European Union.

The effects of the single currency as a symbol of the civic legitimacy of the European Union are even more surprising. It seems that many citizens, be they in favour or against the single currency itself, have allowed much more to crystallise on this issue than what it rationally involved in 'technical' terms. A large proportion of European citizens obviously understand and believe that a single currency is linked to a major reinforcement of the united power of European institutions and seals a new step in the process of building a united Europe (Table 4.5). This is true in spite of the numerous attempts of some governments – primarily the British government and the Danish and Swedish governments – to convince their citizens that the Euro did not represent any move towards

Table 4.3 Compared salience of national and European issues in the 1994 European Parliament election decision. European issues more important than national ones

Country	European issues more important than national
Germany	59
France	54
Luxembourg	54
Netherlands	48
Belgium	46

Source: Europinion 1, April 1995.

Table 4.4 Visibility of the European passport

Country	% who have heard of and describe the main features of the common passport
Denmark	92.3
Netherlands	84.6
Luxembourg	76.6
Belgium	76.1
United Kingdom	74.5
Greece	69.8
Ireland	68.9
Spain	63.1
Germany	60.3
Portugal	59.4
France	58.8
Italy	58.3

Source: Flash-Eurobarometer, December 1995.

Table 4.5 Main hopes and fears related to the single European currency

Main hopes	%	Main fears	%
Easier to cross borders	84	Lose control over policy	39
Easier to shop	80	–	–
No exchange costs	77	Bad for the economy	9
Better for currency markets	48	–	–
Bring economic growth	37	–	–
Will create jobs	30	–	–

Source: Eurobarometer 44, Section 4, 1998.

a greater 'political' union but rather an economic technicality. Overall support for the single currency was, at the end of 1995, of 54 per cent versus 37 per cent against. By 2003, however, support had increased to 66 per cent while opposition was going down to 28 per cent (75 and 23% respectively in the Eurozone, according to Eurobarometer 59).

The main explanations given for positive attitudes are related to the deepening of the Single Market and the emergence of a 'People's Europe', with an expected easier life for people who cross borders (84%), a belief that shopping around Europe is made easier (80%), and the disappearance of currency exchange costs (77%). At the same time, justifications relating to internal economic situations are far less important, be they associated with international currency markets (48%), economic growth (37%), or job creation (30%). Most opponents to the Euro were partly blaming it for price increases, while some explained that their nations will lose some of their ability to control economic policy (39%). This argument is, paradoxically, a further proof that Euro-sceptics have heard the same message as people who favour the single currency, and very clearly too. A significant number of people, after the decision to create the single currency, now believe that European institutions are progressively encroaching the power of national governments in deciding the economic policy of European countries for the coming generations. Finally, it is interesting to note how support for the European Monetary Union evolved in the Euro zone between early 1999 and late 2000, that is, through a time of sustained decline of the external value of the Euro. The decline of the Euro on the currency markets then resulted in a relative reduction of the purchasing power of the populations of the Euro-zone in a context of more and more opened economies. However, during this period, support for the Euro indeed increased in six of the eleven countries of the Euro zone, including France and Spain (Table 4.6).

Table 4.6   Support for European Monetary Union in 2003 and 2000

Country	Support 2003	Support 2000	Change 2003−2000
Luxembourg	*83*	*76*	*+7*
Belgium	*81*	*76*	*+5*
Ireland	*79*	*63*	*+16*
Italy	70	81	−11
Spain	70	75	−5
Finland	*70*	*49*	*+21*
Portugal	*69*	*64*	*+5*
France	*68*	*67*	*+1*
European Union	67	58	+9
Austria	*67*	*48*	*+19*
Greece	64	69	−5
Netherlands	62	67	−5
Germany	*60*	*50*	*+10*
Denmark	*52*	*40*	*+12*
Sweden	*41*	*38*	*+3*
United Kingdom	*23*	*22*	*+1*

Note: Countries in italics are those in which support for the Euro has increased between 1999 and 2000 in spite of the drop of the Euro on the currency markets.

Source: Eurobarometers 53 and 51.

The results presented in Tables 4.5 and 4.6 show, beyond specific elements of support for monetary integration, that citizens of European Union are not only aware of the symbols of European integration, but also, and even more importantly, aware of their political and symbolic nature.

Reacting to another of the institutional symbols launched by the Maastricht Treaty, the change of name from 'European Community' to 'European Union', citizens have again shown their approval to this evolution. They perceive, beyond the rhetorical modifications used to describe the European super-State, the increase in its political power and in its influence over the lives of European citizens in years to come. Their reactions to this interpretation of the new name are far from passive. To the disappointment of many Euro-sceptics, the new title seems to be welcomed favourably and willingly by a broad majority of citizens in all member-States including the United Kingdom (Europinion, 1993). One can also note that, for a majority of Europeans, this new name will be the last one. (The treaties first talked of the ECSC, EEC, and EURATOM as separate communities, then of the 'European Communities', then of 'the European Community' after 1987, before introducing the term European Union in 1992.) It is perceived by both the partisans and opponents of such an evolution, that the European Union under its new name will be enabled to have more power than it ever had and will become, in time, a 'real' super-State from the point of view of a majority of European citizens.

Finally, since the symbols of an institution do not necessarily target only the citizens who depend on it, but are also intended to modify the perceptions of people and institutions outside the European Union, it seems appropriate to consider a study conducted a few years ago, in Mexico (Bruter, 1999). It shows that since the establishment of a delegation of the European Commission in Mexico, Mexican journalists have progressively equated it with an 'embassy of the European Union' in general and, at the same time, have accepted the European Union itself as a kind of powerful 'super'-country. This shows very clearly and 'directly' in interviews with local officials, businessmen and journalists, but also 'indirectly' through the numerous awkward errors made in the manner to address the delegation and the head of the delegation in public and in journalistic discourse.

All symbols of the European Union do not benefit from equal levels of visibility and support. For example, as European anthem, EU leaders chose one of the most popular and best-known pieces of classical music that they could possibly find. At the same time, the Day of Europe is only 17 years old and has only 'really' been celebrated for about ten years. Nevertheless, the citizens of 14 countries out of 15 (the only exception being Denmark) support it as a 'good idea' (Table 4.7) In May/ June 1995, this judgement was shared by 61 per cent of the citizens of the European Union, compared to 20 per cent who thought the contrary. In the first year that the Day of Europe was really celebrated and linked to the other major symbols of the European Union (flag, anthem, etc.), positive opinions were seen to rise by five points in two months, while negative ones decreased by two points over the same period. At the same time, we can also note that the two countries in which the most prominent events had been organised that year, France and Italy, had the two highest positive scores in the European Union (75% and 76% versus 10% and 8%).

Another interesting national symbol is the name of the single currency, which was judged positively by 69 per cent just after the Madrid summit when it was chosen. This is despite that when given the choice before the summit, a very large majority of citizens preferred the name ECU and very few supported 'Euro'. This flexibility of public opinion can probably be interpreted as further proof that what people accept in

Table 4.7   Positive attitudes towards the celebration of a 'Day of Europe'

Country	% Supporting	% Opposing
Italy	76	10
France	75	8
Finland	70	8
Luxembourg	69	17
Belgium	62	13
EU as a whole	*61*	*20*
Spain	61	12
Germany (whole)	61	22
Ireland	59	20
Greece	58	12
Portugal	53	9
Netherlands	46	38
United Kingdom	46	39
Sweden	42	38
Austria	41	24
Denmark	32	45

Source: Europinion 5, 1995.

Table 4.8 Knowledge of the name of the new single currency in 1999

Country	% **Spontaneously giving the right name 'Euro'**
France	95
Germany	94
Austria	94
Luxembourg	92
Spain	87
Euro-Zone Average	*87*
Netherlands	87
Belgium	82
Italy	80
EU Average	*78*
Sweden	73
Denmark	69
Finland	67
Portugal	62
Ireland	54
Greece	45
United Kingdom	37

Source: Europinion 14, December 1999.

the name 'Euro' is much more the symbol of what it represents than the aesthetics of the name itself. It is also clear that 87 per cent of the concerned people among the citizens knew the name of the new single currency before it was launched in 1999 (Table 4.8).

Conclusions: European institutions and the attempt to favour the emergence of a mass European identity

In this chapter, we have seen that after three phases when they focused on the pacific virtues, policy attributes, and institutional set-up of the European project, EU leaders started to worry about their role in helping to generate a new European identity that would reinforce and legitimise an increasingly political process. It was shown also that one of the main tools used by institutions to try and help to develop such an identity has been a rapid and systematic effort to provide the European Union with symbols that would enable citizens to characterise more easily (and more positively) their new political system. These symbols have focused more and more on the 'integrative' – rather than communitarian – aspects of the European integration process, and apparently aimed at reinforcing both the civic and cultural identity of European citizens.

In the second part of this book, I now evaluate how these attempts of political institutions – and those sometimes less readily admitted of the mass media – have, indeed, influenced the European identity of citizens and had an impact on the emergence of a new mass European identity.

Part II

Has a Mass European Identity Emerged?

5

Who Feels European? Measurement of European Identity and Differences Across Individuals[16]

The challenge of measuring a European identity

In Part I of this book, we saw that it remains difficult to understand what exactly citizens mean when they claim that, indeed, they 'identify' with a given political community. Because identity can be 'prisoner of language' and therefore difficult to measure and compare across individuals, the goal of this chapter is to propose an operationalisable theory of political identities based on the insights of Chapters 1 and 2.

The only relatively regular measures of European identity used by political scientists till the mid-1990s come from the European Union's semi-annual Eurobarometer surveys. The questions asked by Eurobarometer on European identity have changed over time, and none has been part of the sets of questions asked in every survey of the series.

The items included by the survey designers have first and most notably included the following question: 'In the near future, do you see yourself as: [nationality only; nationality and European; European and nationality; European only]?'[17] However, many scholars agree that this remains a very awkward question when it comes to studying European identity. First, it assumes an arbitrary tension between European and national identities which has now been disproved by many political scientists such as Licata (2000) and Bruter (2003). Second, the very validity of the measure is, to say the least, questionable, and varies with the language of the survey. Indeed, in many cases, it is unclear whether the phrasing measures identity, as suggested by the survey designers, or, instead, a preference or even a mere factual prediction ("probably, in the near future, I will be") with no normative or identitarian connotation.

Third, the measure assumes, perhaps a bit too quickly that respondents all agree on an implicit hierarchy between feeling, say, European and Dutch which would be 'more European' than Dutch and European.

Eurobarometers have also occasionally – and more rarely – asked citizens to directly 'grade' their attachment to their town or village, region, nation, and to Europe on a seven-point scale. This type of question has fewer validity limits than the previous set of questions mentioned. However, this question is precisely the most direct embodiment of Burgess's doubts on whether identity is measurable by self-perception. In other words, and beyond the conceptual problems this entails, one can question whether, using this measure, the answers of different respondents are directly comparable at all, as they might not refer to the same fundamental definitions and conceptions of identity.

From the point of view of this particular study, the third type of problem with the measures provided by Eurobarometer and other mass surveys such as the European Value Study is that they would not allow us to test my conceptual model which relies on a sub-division of political identities into two components. To solve these problems, this chapter now proposes a new framework of analysis for political identities in general and European identity in particular. This will be achieved by providing a series of concrete indicators, grounded in the conceptual framework developed earlier in this book. These indicators will allow us to better understand political identities and to be able to compare more rigorously the way citizens define their political selves.

As explained earlier, the empirical framework of this study is based on the definition of two broad components of political identities: civic and cultural. These two components would be conceptually significant to study any political identity, but become particularly relevant in the case of communities in which identification with the state or political system – which is primarily measured by the civic component – does not correspond to the geographical area of the 'cultural community' with which citizens identify – as measured by the cultural component of identity in this model. This is obviously the case in Europe: institutionally, civic identity will undoubtedly refer to the European Union, while if there is such a thing as a European shared culture, values, and heritage, they will most likely refer to Europe as a whole as it is unlikely that, however it may be defined, a European culture would be perceived to embrace Germany and France but not Switzerland or Monaco. However, a similar gap could also be hypothesised in such polities as India, Belgium, or the United Kingdom – at least for the peripheral nations of Northern Ireland and Scotland.

The civic-cultural distinction opens up new possibilities for sorting out major theoretical paradoxes in the study of European identity and its various components.

The civic and cultural components of a European identity

To some extent, the contradictory findings and hypotheses of political scientists about whether or not such a thing as a European identity might be emerging (see Chapter 2) may be related to contradictory perceptions of what forms political identities assume. The extent to which European identity has emerged (Meinhof, 2003, Bruter, 2003), the positive or negative correlation between European and sub-European identities (Duchesne and Frognier, 1995, Bruter, 2003) might be found to be different depending on the very conception of identity one uses. Similarly, the complexity of political identities as not just simple forms of social identity (Breakwell) may be illustrated by the two dimensions. Cultural identity has a social connotation that 'civic' identity probably does not have (cultural identity referring to common values, language, religion, ethnicity, history, myths, etc., and civic identity referring primarily to a set of relevant institutional contexts that define the individual's values and perceptions of freedom, rights, and obligations as an individual). The distinction between the civic and cultural components of political identities might help us sort out these contradictions and more.

As explained in Chapter 2, my dichotomy between civic and cultural components of political identities relies on the three main perspectives that have been used since the eighteenth century to characterise the foundations of the legitimacy of political communities.

Following this conceptual clarification, we still face significant challenges regarding the definition and measurement of a 'European identity.' The conceptual framework and theoretical model defined earlier was used as the basis of the design of a questionnaire used in the context of a pilot experimental study conducted on 212 respondents in France, Britain, and the Netherlands.

It is first necessary to include some direct (self-perception) measures of citizens' European identity if only to be able to compare the results of the study to those of existing mass surveys, such as Eurobarometer, which include these questions. In fact, if language-dependent measures (in the sense of Burgess) can be confirmed by 'objective' measures of identity with which they covary, it will seem reasonable to use both.

This is the objective of the measurement strategy that is detailed here and a solution to one of the main problems of measuring a European identity. Moreover, this will help us to understand better what most respondents mean when they say that they 'feel European' and, more precisely, to understand whether they identify primarily with the European Union as a relevant institutional context defining them as citizens, or to Europe as a general cultural community or 'civilisation' to which they identify 'socially'. The questions used to measure a European 'general' identity are, therefore, meant to be as direct and general as possible. The two questions chosen are reproduced below from the British questionnaire:

Question 1: In general, would you say that you consider yourself a citizen of Europe? (Please, choose ONE ONLY)

1. Yes, very much.
2. Yes, to some extent.
3. I don't know.
4. Not really.
5. Not at all.

Question 6: On a scale of one to seven, one meaning that you do not identify with Europe at all, and seven meaning that you identify very strongly with Europe, would you say that you ...? (Please, circle ONE NUMBER ONLY)

1. (Do not identify with Europe at all)
2.
3.
4.
5.
6.
7. (Identify very strongly with Europe)

The second of the two questions is followed by controls for other levels of governance (country, region, town/village). These measures of citizens' general European identity only make sense, however, to the extent that they are accompanied by two more specific sets of questions measuring European civic and cultural identity, the correlation of which with general identity measures is carefully analysed.

As explained earlier, the civic identity of citizens has to do with their identification with the European Union as a relevant institutional framework in their life, which defines some of their rights, obligations, and liberties. For this reason, the items chosen to measure civic identity have, in large measure, to do with citizens' identification with the state-like symbols of the European Union (flag, anthem, passport, etc.), and in part with the recognition of the political and institutional relevance of the European Union as a source of definition of their personal citizenship.

The six measures used in my survey to assess citizens' levels of civic identity are outlined below:

Question 2: Since 1985, citizens from all the countries of the European Union have had a common 'European' passport on which both the name of their country and 'European Union' is written. Do you think that this is a good thing? (Please, choose ONE ONLY)

1. Yes, a very good thing.
2. Yes, a rather good thing.
3. It doesn't matter at all.
4. No, a rather bad thing.
5. No, a very bad thing.

Question 4: What would best describe your reaction if you saw someone burning a European flag? (Please, choose ONE ONLY)

1. I would be shocked and hurt.
2. I would be shocked but not hurt.
3. I would not mind.
4. I would be happy.

[control] *Question* 5: What would best describe your reaction if you saw someone burning the Union Jack? (Please, choose ONE ONLY)

1. I would be shocked and hurt.
2. I would be shocked but not hurt.
3. I would not mind.
4. I would be happy.

Question 11: A group of athletes from all the countries of the European Union have proposed that at the Sydney Olympics, whenever an athlete/team from the European Union wins a gold medal, the 'Ode to Joy', the European anthem, should be played after, and in addition to, their national anthem. Do you think that this would be a good idea? (Please, choose ONE ONLY)

1. Yes, a very good idea.
2. Yes, a rather good idea.
3. Neither a good idea nor a bad idea.
4. No, a rather bad idea.
5. No, a very bad idea.

Question 12: When the heads of state/government of a European Union country (such as Queen Elizabeth II, Tony Blair, the French President or the German Chancellor) make a speech on TV, both the national flag and the European one appear behind them. Do you think that this is a good thing? (Please, choose ONE ONLY)

1. Yes, a very good thing.
2. Yes, a rather good thing.
3. Neither a good thing nor a bad thing / It doesn't matter at all.
4. No, a rather bad thing.
5. No, a very bad thing.

Question 13: Does being a 'Citizen of the European Union' mean anything for you? (Please, choose ONE ONLY)

1. Yes, it means a lot.
2. Yes, it means something.
3. No, it does not mean anything.

Question 14: If you answered yes to question 13, would you say that, among other things, it means ...? (Please, choose AS MANY AS APPLY) [civic items only included here]

1.
2. The right to vote in the European Parliament elections.
3. Common institutions.
5. A common European flag, European anthem, European passport.
6. The right to travel to another EU country without passing through customs.
7. The right to travel to another EU ountry without having to show your passport/ID.

As can be seen, the six items try to capture different components of the citizens' levels of civic European identity.

Finally, the last component targeted in this survey has to do with the cultural component of a European identity. By that, I mean literally the perception of citizens that they feel closer to fellow Europeans than to non-Europeans. As explained earlier, this is not assumed to come into conflict with sub-European cultural identities (feeling closer to fellow Swedes than to fellow Europeans, or feeling closer to fellow Parisians than to fellow Europeans), but simply in contradiction to considering the European dimension irrelevant to one's broader cultural identity. Similarly, I do not want to assume anything about the contents and perceived logic of this relative closeness. This is explored in a series of focus group discussions in a related project (Bruter, 2004b). Therefore, I do not presume that cultural identity is based on a perceived common ethnicity, religion, values, or anything else. It could be attributed by respondents to any of this or, indeed, to nothing at all.

Thus, my four measures are limited to assessing the perceived relative closeness of respondents to Europeans and non-Europeans, or the perception that there is such a thing as a shared European heritage in the broadest (and therefore least clearly defined) sense conceivable. The four variables used in the survey are reproduced below:

Question 3: Here is a list of some of the games that will be featured at the next Women's Volley-Ball World Championship in June. Could you say which team you would rather won each of these games? (Please choose ONE team for each of the four games)

A – Ghana vs Denmark
1. Ghana
2. Denmark

B – Italy vs USA
1. Italy
2. USA

C – Spain vs China
1. Spain
2. China

D – Saudi Arabia vs Republic of Ireland
1. Saudi Arabia
2. Republic of Ireland

Question 10: Some say that in spite of their numerous differences, Europeans share a 'common heritage' that makes them slightly closer to one another than they are to, say, Japanese or Chilean people. Do you ...? (Please, choose ONE ONLY)

1. Strongly disagree with this view.
2. Somewhat disagree with this view.
3. Neither agree nor disagree with this view / I don't know.
4. Somewhat agree with this view.
5. Strongly agree with this view.

Question 14: If you answered yes to question 13 [see previous section], would you say that, among other things, it means ...? (Please, choose AS MANY AS APPLY)

1. A shared European heritage.
2. A common European history.
3. Some common ideals.
4. To be a member of the 'European family'.

Question 15: Would you say that you feel closer to fellow Europeans than, say, to Chinese, Russian, or American people? (Please, choose ONE ONLY)

1. Yes, strongly.
2. Yes, to some extent.
3. I don't know.
4. No, not really.
5. No, not at all.

The first of the four questions, using fake sports situations, is obviously the most problematic of all the measures. It is based on the assumption that if citizens feel closer to fellow Europeans than to non-European they will unconsciously be prone to choose the European team against a variety of non-European challengers in games in which they do not have real specific preferences (international women's volleyball is not the most widely followed sport in the world). This assumption can be checked by simple correlation with other variables in the index.

The general definition of the variables targeted and the operationalised items used to measure them is summarised in Table 5.1 and can be checked against the questions outlined above. Table 5.1 represents the basic pattern of what should be measured as part of the general, civic, and cultural European identities of citizens. This pattern and the 'quality' of the indicators proposed now have to be empirically confirmed.

Table 5.1   Conceptual definition and operationalisation of European identity variables

Variable	General identity	Civic identity	Cultural identity
Conceptual summary	Do respondents naturally think of themselves as Europeans?	Do respondents identify with the European Union as a political institution?	Do respondents identify with Europe as a cultural community?
Targeted elements	– Do I feel European? – How strongly do I identify with Europe?	– Does it mean anything for me to be 'citizen' of the European super-State? – Do I identify with the symbols of European political integration? – Do I identify with the civic aspects of European integration?	– Do I identify with Europe as a shared heritage? – Do I think of Europe as a concentric identity level, finding Europeans less close than fellow nationals but closer to me than non-Europeans?

How 'European' are Europeans?

It has been suggested that one of the reasons why political identities should be assessed in opposition to each other is that asking people about their identity outside of a constraining context would just lead to a high skewedness of the answers (i.e., everyone 'probably' feels somehow European, everyone 'probably' feels closer to fellow Europeans than to Africans or Chinese, etc.). With the caveat that once again my sample is, while varied, not representative, my results tend to show the contrary. For 11 of the 12 items considered, the answers are normally distributed with a mean close to the medium possible answer. This is true for the sample of 212 on the whole, for each country sub sample. The only exception has to do with the 'games' measure of cultural identity, which shows a very high skewedness toward high-identity levels. For this reason, the item cannot correlate highly with the other items in the scale and will be dropped later in the analysis. It should be noted, however, that this overwhelming predominance of European 'choice' in fake sports situations suggests a certain underlying European identity in the sample considered.

The next stage of the analysis consists in showing that the conceptual and empirical division of identity into civic and cultural components is proved relevant by the data.

Relevance of the civic–cultural distinction

The relevance of the civic-cultural distinction is best demonstrated by providing a quick factor analysis of the whole sample. In spite of the poor loading of one of the cultural identity items (the games variable), the factor analysis 'correctly' results in a two-factor solution. The results of the factor analysis are reported in Table 5.2. Although it is mostly consistent with the theoretical expectations of my measurement strategy, it sees the fourth cultural item and the two general identity items load, albeit not strongly – on the predominantly civic factor. Apart from this marginal anomaly, the way the items load on the two factors created by the analysis is extremely satisfactory and confirms that the conceptual distinction between civic and cultural identities, at least in the European context, is at once (1) confirmed empirically and (2) well captured by the items chosen. The null hypothesis (that there are no such things as distinct civic and cultural European identities) can clearly be rejected based on this exploratory factor analysis.

To proceed to the measurement of the two variables, and in order to improve the cleanliness of the measures, separate factor analyses are run for cultural and civic identities (general identity, being measured by only two items, cannot lead to factor analysis) with, four and six items entered in the analyses respectively. Moreover, I simultaneously run a global analysis of the whole sample and separate analyses for each country in order to get more refined loading structures. The factor scores are used as dependent variables in the final analysis of the experimental results. In all cases, reliability, measured by the Cronbach's alpha coefficient, reaches acceptable to good levels: 0.60 for cultural identity, 0.65 for general identity (with only two items), and 0.81 for civic identity. In the three countries, the factor analyses of both the civic identity variables and the cultural identity variables all result in one-factor solutions. It is therefore operationally viable to measure separately but consistently the levels of civic and cultural European identities of respondents, using a vast array of measurement items.

Some preliminary findings on respondents' levels of European identity

When it comes to comparing the global levels of civic and cultural identities of the respondents, I create 0–1 indices for each variable. Again the first cultural item is excluded from the index. The 0–1 limits of the index represent the theoretical range of civic and European identities. All

Table 5.2 Factor analyses of civic and cultural identities in the United Kingdom, France, and the Netherlands

	Whole		United Kingdom		France		Netherlands	
Factor analysis for civic identity								
Communalities (extraction)								
Civ. id. 1	0.43		0.55		0.41		0.28	
Civ. id. 2	0.21		0.35		0.20		0.18	
Civ. id. 3	0.56		0.70		0.40		0.46	
Civ. id. 4	0.58		0.57		0.54		0.53	
Civ. id. 5	0.55		0.64		0.48		0.25	
Civ. id. 6	0.48		0.58		0.48		0.22	
Eigenvalue and % variance explained								
Factor 1	3.32	55.4%	3.80	63.3%	3.06	50.9%	3.37	59.0%
Factor 2	0.83	13.8%	0.68	11.2%	0.98	16.5%	0.96	16.7%
Factor 3	0.71	11.9%	0.60	10.0%	0.59	9.8%	0.62	10.3%
Factor matrix								
Civ. id. 1	0.66		0.74		0.64		0.53	
Civ. id. 2	0.46		0.59		0.44		0.38	
Civ. id. 3	0.75		0.84		0.63		0.68	
Civ. id. 4	0.76		0.75		0.73		0.73	
Civ. id. 5	0.74		0.80		0.69		0.50	
Civ. id. 6	0.70		0.76		0.69		0.47	
Factor analysis for cultural identity								
Commonalties (extraction)								
Cult. id. 1	0.13		0.05		0.07		0.21	
Cult. id. 2	0.27		0.37		0.34		0.19	
Cult. id. 3	0.55		0.65		0.60		0.38	
Cult. id. 4	0.34		0.51		0.13		0.30	
Eigenvalue and % variance explained								
Factor 1	1.92	47.8%	2.06	51.5%	1.75	43.7%	1.79	44.7%
Factor 2	0.91	22.8%	0.97	24.5%	0.98	24.6%	0.96	24.2%
Factor 3	0.64	16.1%	0.54	13.6%	0.78	19.5%	0.64	16.01%
Factor matrix								
Cult. id. 1	0.37		0.20		0.26		0.46	
Cult. id. 2	0.52		0.61		0.58		0.43	
Cult. id. 3	0.74		0.81		0.78		0.61	
Cult. id. 4	0.58		0.71		0.37		0.55	

Notes: Extraction method: principal axis; no rotation (all analyses lead to one factor solutions); factors are kept when their eigenvalue is greater than 1.

items are weighed equally in the construction. Consistently with what I said of the univariate distributions of the individual items, the overall distributions are slightly skewed toward high levels of identity (Table 5.3). It is also clear that overall levels of identification with Europe are highest for the French sample and lowest for the Dutch one.

Table 5.3   Mean levels of civic and cultural identities

	Whole	France	United Kingdom	Netherlands
Civic identity	*0.60 (0.22)*	0.70 (0.19)	0.54 (0.23)	0.47 (0.17)
Cultural identity	*0.56 (0.23)*	0.67 (0.19)	0.55 (0.24)	0.45 (0.22)

Notes: Entries are Mean score and Standard Deviation for civic and cultural identities. Variables are scored on a 0 to 1 scale; *N*: 210 (France: 97, Amsterdam: 60, United Kingdom: 55); cultural identity excludes 'Games' variable.

Table 5.4   Break-out of the sample in terms of positive and negative identifiers

	Whole	United Kingdom	France	Netherlands
Civic ID				
Positive	*69.6*	*85.6*	*62.0*	50.0
Negative	30.4	14.4	38.0	50.0
*Cultural ID**				
Positive	*68.1*	*82.5*	*66.0*	46.7
Negative	31.9	17.5	34.0	*53.3*
*Cultural ID***				
Positive	*73.4*	*87.6*	*70.0*	*53.3*
Negative	26.6	12.4	30.0	46.7

Notes: *: Index excludes 'Games' variable; **: Index includes 'Games' variable; entries are percentages of the total sample; 'Negative' represents the proportion of respondents with an index score of 0.5 or lower. 'Positive' are all respondents with a score greater than 0.5; 0.5 is the index score that a respondent would obtain if he chose the 'indifferent' option whenever possible and the 'don't know' option in all remaining cases.

The United Kingdom sample is slightly skewed toward high levels of identity overall, but particularly so in terms of cultural identity. The results can be simplified by comparing the proportion of respondents who fall below and above the theoretical means of the variables (i.e., the score a respondent would have obtained if he chose the indifferent or 'don't know' answer to all identity questions; see Table 5.4). The results, then, show a clearly positive balance of respondents in terms of both cultural and civic identities globally and in each location. In other words, the overall distribution of the sample is clearly skewed towards high levels, and the medians for both civic and cultural identities are definitely in the 'positive' half of the theoretical identity spectra. Civic identity appears to be globally higher than cultural identity if the game variable is excluded from the index. Again, the exception lies in the British sample, in which cultural identity is dominant regardless of the procedure of index construction that is chosen.

Table 5.5 Comparison of the levels of civic and cultural identities of respondents

	Whole	France	Netherlands	United Kingdom
All items				
Predominantly civic identity	*46.9*	56.7	45.0	30.0
Equal	*1.0*	1.0	0.0	2.0
Predominantly cultural identity	*52.2*	42.3	55.0	68.0
Game preferences excluded				
Predominantly civic identity	*55.1*	60.8	53.3	46.0
Equal	*0.5*	0	0.5	0
Predominantly cultural identity	*44.4*	38.1	46.1	54.0

Notes: Method: all items have been converted on 0–1 scales. The means of the converted scores for all civic and all cultural items have then been calculated. Respondents identified as 'predominantly civic' identifiers are those whose civic index score is higher than their cultural index score; the second table uses the same methodology, but the highly skewed 'game preference' variable is excluded from the cultural index.

In terms of comparing levels of civic and cultural identities of citizens, when the two indexed variables are put on a comparable scale, the sample is split almost evenly between respondents having a predominantly civic and a predominantly cultural identity (Table 5.5). Overall, in the total sample, 55.1 per cent of the respondents had a higher level of civic identity, only 44.4 per cent a higher level of cultural identity, and 0.5 percent exactly the same level for the two.

Another interesting element lies in the cross-country comparison of the overall levels of civic and cultural identities of respondents. Indeed, while civic identity is clearly predominant in France and in the Netherlands, cultural identity tends to be more salient in the United Kingdom sample. In spite of the impossibility of generalising results from non-representative samples of respondents, it seems logical to hypothesise that such a difference might come from the self-exclusion of the United Kingdom from some of the main civic components of European integration, such as the European Monetary Union (EMU) and the Schengen agreements on citizen mobility. This hypothesis may be tested using a truly representative sample.

This said, it should be remembered that the correlation between the factor score variables for civic and cultural identities are still highly correlated, with a Pierson *r* of 0.57. This is high enough to confirm that the two variables are largely explained by the same factors and evolve together, but not so high that we should consider them as one single dimension. We may want to remember that, usually, survey analysis shows much higher levels of correlation between such variables as party identification and ideology, which no political scientist would think of collapsing (the correlation is usually 0.6 to 0.7 in the analysis of American National Elections Surveys).

To conclude this first section, I therefore derive from the data that:

- We can clearly differentiate empirically two components of European identity corresponding to my conceptual distinction between: (1) a civic component that makes people identify with the European Union as a significant 'superstate' identity, and (2) a cultural component that makes people identify with Europe in general as an area of shared civilisation and heritage.
- The two dimensions are highly correlated (0.57) but distinct, and each can be measured by an internally consistent and reliable set of variables.
- When people answer non-specific questions about their European identity in general, it is of their civic identity that they think primarily.
- It is also respondents' civic identity that is most developed, except in the case of the British sample, in which Europe means 'technically less' (no EMU, no Schengen agreement) in terms of actual superstate political integration.
- Overall, and in spite of a perfect balance of the stimulus applied, a clear majority of the respondents interviewed have a rather high level of civic and cultural European identities. These factors would nevertheless be difficult to evaluate using traditional Eurobarometer questions.

The relationship between European and sub-European identities: conflict or complement?

I have said that the conceptual framework used here did not prejudice the possible opposition, independence, or positive correlation between European and sub-European identities, unlike the traditional questions sometimes used by Eurobarometer. The second question I intend to answer using the insight of the experimental survey is, therefore, whether people who identify more with Europe tend to identify less with sub-European political levels or if, on the contrary, different political identifications are positively correlated. This is made possible using a series of four similar questions asking respondents to self-position themselves on a scale measuring their level of identity with Europe, their nation, region, and town, city or village. The exact questions and scales can, be found in the appendix.

Two competing hypotheses can be formulated on the emergence of a European identity. The first states that people with weaker national and sub-national identities would be more likely to identify with Europe. This is because Europe represents, in traditional Euro-sceptic discourse, an anti-identitarian structure that tends towards globalisation and the negation of national peculiarities and homogenisation. The second hypothesis states that, far from being contradictory, identities are complementary and that stronger national and regional identifiers should also be stronger European identifiers, since Europe represents a 'positive' identity grounded in the perception of a common civilisation. Here, it is hypothesised that the latter hypothesis is correct and that, indeed, there is no contradiction between political identities but, on the contrary, a positive correlation between the various territorially defined political identities of citizens.

The arbitration between these two theories, which cannot be tested empirically when attention is paid only to the 'hierarchy' of identities of respondents (the only variables targeted by most identity questions in Eurobarometer surveys[18]), is easily provided by simple correlation tables between the four identity variables measured by the questionnaire. These are presented in Table 5.6.

Even though we have to be careful in this analysis because of a possible upward bias due to a construction artefact,[19] it seems quite clear from Table 5.7 that identity levels are, indeed, positively correlated. It is also clear that positive correlations are strongest between closest territorial levels, that is, between European and national identities (0.17, significant at 0.014), national and regional identities (0.17, significant at 0.012), and mostly regional and local identities (0.58, significant at 0.000).

Table 5.6 Correlation table between European, national, regional, and local identities

	European identity	National identity	Regional identity	Local identity
European identity	1.00			
National identity	0.17*	1.00		
Regional identity	0.13	0.17*	1.00	
Local identity	0.07	0.10	0.58**	1.00

Notes: N = 212; *: sig. <0.05; **: sig. <0.01.

Table 5.7   Average levels of European, national, regional, and local identity in each location

	Whole	United Kingdom	France	Netherlands
European	*4.65*	4.46	4.94	4.33
identity	*(1.44)*	(1.53)	(1.27)	(1.57)
National	*5.55*	5.38	5.86	5.20
identity	*(1.53)*	(1.56)	(1.25)	(1.72)
Regional	*4.94*	5.20	4.00	4.15
identity	*(1.27)*	(1.72)	(1.86)	(1.85)
Local	*4.33*	4.92	3.86	4.82
identity	*(1.57)*	(1.69)	(1.89)	(1.87)

Notes: Entries are Mean and Standard Deviation for each category; theoretical range is 1–7.

In absolute terms, while the sample was shown to be quite strongly identifying with Europe, it is made of quite strong identifiers to all four levels of identification on the whole. This is illustrated by Table 5.7, which reports average identification scores for each territorial level for the whole sample and sub-samples in each location. The theoretical range of the scale is from 1 to 7 with a theoretical mean of 4. It is clear that respondents score higher in general for every single level of identification in every single location, with the local identity of the French being the only exception.

Additionally, the cross-country comparison of average identity scores tends to confirm the positive correlation between identities to closest levels of government at the aggregate level. Indeed, the highest average level of European identity (4.94) is reached by the French sample, which also has the highest level of national identity (5.86), while the lowest average level of European identification (4.33) is that of the Dutch sample, which also has the lowest level of national identification (5.20). Incidentally, it should be noted that France has the lowest average levels of regional and local identifications but the highest levels of European and national ones, which tends to dismiss the idea of a strong construction artefact.

Dealing with identity hierarchy, Table 5.8 shows the breakout of the global and national samples by 'rank' of European identity out of the four levels of identification proposed. Here again, if is hard to draw global conclusions, but it should still be noted that overall, respondents ranking Europe as their first identity represent the most numerous category.

Finally, a last very interesting finding is the extremely high level of correlation between the gross score of European identity of respondents and the rank of European identity out of four levels of political identity.

Table 5.8 Rank of European identity out of four possible levels of identification

Rank of European identity (out of 4)	Whole	United Kingdom	France	Netherlands
1	29.0	24.0	34.0	25.0
2	27.5	22.0	35.1	20.0
3	19.8	18.0	15.5	28.3
4	23.7	36.0	15.5	26.7

Notes: Entries are percentages of total sample/country sub-sample. Each column adds up to 100 except for rounding error; the rank of European identity can be held alone or ex aequo with any other level of identification.

For the whole sample, this correlation is −0.57, with a significance level of 0.000. The negative sign is of course perfectly logical (the lower the rank number, the 'higher' the rank – for example, first=1), but mostly, the very high level of correlation means that either variable can be quite safely used as a proxy for the other. This is an important finding from the perspective of using data from mass surveys such as Eurobarometer to further study the emergence of a European identity. This also allows us to argue again quite strongly against the idea of a high artificial bias in the construction of my identity variable. Indeed, were the levels of identity of respondents highly dependent on each respondent's perception of the identity scale, the gross level of European identity and its rank as compared to sub-European identities would obviously be totally uncorrelated.

Overall, the second section of the analysis allows us to draw a certain number of conclusions, enlightening our knowledge of European identity at the individual level. We now know the following:

- Respondents with high levels of subnational identities – particularly of national identity – are more likely to identify with Europe than respondents who have overall weaker levels of political identification. This contradicts traditional Euro-sceptic discourse on the anti-identitary basis of European integration.
- There is great variance in the way citizens 'rank' their European identity as compared to sub-European identities.
- The gross level and rank of European identity, as compared to those of sub-European identities, are highly correlated, meaning that 'relative' levels of European identity can be partly inferred from 'absolute' levels of European identity and vice versa.

The third part of my analysis consists of a study of the distinction between European identity and support for European integration.

Empirically illustrating the independence of European identity from support for European integration

As explained earlier, aside from its mere theoretical interest, the question of the development of a mass European identity is important in that one would hypothesise that it is necessary for the support for and legitimacy of further political development of European integration. It is therefore useful to test the existence of a link between European identity and European integration, but, also (and therefore), of an empirical distinction between the two variables – a distinction that part of the literature refuses (see e.g., Inglehart 1997, Duchesne and Frognier 1995).

In the test of the experimental design, as a precaution, support for European integration is used as a control variable in the multivariate test of the model proposed. From a theoretical point of view, however, political science literature has clearly shown that values and identities precede and constrain attitudes, such as support for a political project, in causal models, and not the contrary (Nie and Andersen, 1974, Hurwitz and Peffley, 1987, Jacoby 1991). Indeed, the main goal of this section is just to support the fact that, not only conceptually, but also empirically, European identity and support for European integration should be considered as two separate variables, which can and should be captured distinctly in survey analysis.

First of all, even though questions on support for European integration and questions on European identity were, respectively, part of the pre-treatment and post-treatment questionnaires, it is important to evaluate their levels of correlation. These correlations are reported in Table 5.9.

While support for European integration is obviously – and expectedly – correlated with all three sorts of European identity, the moderate levels of correlation (from 0.21 to 0.36) clearly show that they should be considered as distinct variables. Of course, correlations would have been higher without an experimental treatment taking place between the administration of the two questionnaires, but it is unlikely that they would have reached high enough levels to prompt a collapse of the variables.

The fact that the highest level of correlation with support for European integration is reached by the general identity variable is probably due to similarities in question framing. Indeed, asking respondents whether they 'feel' European might partly tap into their attitudes towards Europe as well as into their identity *stricto sensu*. In other words, the respondents

Table 5.9 Correlation table between support for European integration and general, civic, and cultural dimensions of European identity

	Support for integration	General identity	Civic identity	Cultural identity
Support for integration	1.00			
General identity	0.36**	1.00		
Civic identity	0.26**	0.68**	1.00	
Cultural identity	0.21**	0.48**	0.58**	1.00

Notes: $N = 210$; **: sig. <0.01; general identity is the mean of the two indicators (see appendix), support for European integration, civic identity, and cultural identity are factor scores.

might have a clear conscience with regard to the 'political' sense of the plainly subjective question, which might not always be true in the case of the 'objective' measures used to construct the civic and cultural identity variables. At the same time, the higher correlation with the civic component of European identity than with its cultural one is explained by common sense. Cultural identity has no direct political implication and applies to 'Europe' in general, not to the European Union.

The next important step of the analysis is to determine whether European identity and support for European integration regress on the same major social and demographic variables. The results of this comparison might be useful in a context of possible instrumentalisation, or to test structural equation models that would include both European identity and support for European integration as endogenous variables. Support for European integration, European civic identity, and European cultural identity are therefore regressed on an identical set of social, demographic, political, and cultural variables. These include indicators of age, sex, media readership, ideological preference, satisfaction with democracy, European experience (life in another country, travel to other countries, knowledge of other languages, family origins), size of the place of origin, and country dummy variables. The comparative results of the regression models are presented in Table 5.10. The first important conclusion that can be drawn from these regression equations is that none explains a significant part of the variance in the dependent variables considered. This variance goes from virtually none ($R^2 = 0.07$) in the cultural identity model to very little ($R^2 = 0.12$) in the support for European integration model. This might be partly explained by the fact that the variance in the variables considered is limited because of the sample. The range of age is relatively small; the ideological distribution is skewed towards the left; the size of locality lacks variance in the

Table 5.10 Regression models of support for European integration, civic identity, and cultural identity on traditional, social, demographic, political, and cultural variables

Variable	Support for integration	Civic identity	Cultural identity
Ideology of media read	0.13*	–	–
Lived in Euro country	0.12*	0.13*	–
Travelled to Euro country	0.13*	–	–
Foreign languages	0.15*	0.22**	0.16*
Sat. with Democracy	0.12*	–	–
Netherlands	−0.17*	–	–
Left right	–	–	0.17**
R^2	0.12	0.09	0.07

Notes: Values are β coefficients; *: sig. <0.10; **: sig. <0.05; N = 212; the only variables entered are those with a significance coefficient lower than 0.10; originally, 14 independent variables were entered in each model.

Netherlands, where a majority of the sample came from the Amsterdam agglomeration; and we do not have any good measure of SES to include in the models.

It is clear that aside from a common core (the positive relationship between polyglots and all three dependent variables), each dependent variable responds to different predictors. Globally, the cultural variables that measure the European 'experience' of respondents are the most consistently influential. Speaking foreign languages and living in another European country make respondents more likely to feel European and more likely to support European integration. Travelling abroad regularly makes them – logically – more likely to perceive the concrete significance of a 'People's Europe' whose citizens can travel without border control (within the Schengen area), and therefore increases their civic identity. Only having some family origins in another European country has no significant effect on any of the three dependent variables considered, probably because of a general lack of variance (only 17.9% of the sample have a family member originating from another European country).

Unsurprisingly enough, support for European integration is the most 'political' of all four dependent variables, and is significantly dependent on such variables as satisfaction with national democracy and the ideological tendency of the newspapers read by the respondents. It is also the only one of the three models for which the Dutch sample has a significantly lower mean score than the other two samples, with the

Dutch dummy having a β coefficient of -0.17. It is more surprising, however, to note that cultural identity is the only one of the three models in which the self-placement of respondents on a left–right scale has a significant – and quite strong – effect. Moreover, the positive sign of the relation means that right-wing respondents are the most likely to have a high level of cultural European identity. This can be explained *a contrario* by the fact that three of the questions on European cultural identity implied a direct or indirect comparison of proximity between the rest of Europe and the rest of the world. In other words, these questions forced respondents to arbitrate between global cosmopolitanism and a European identity defined by a common – and therefore somewhat exclusive – civilisation. Common sense might naturally lead us to expect left-wingers to be on an average more cosmopolitan and right-wingers more likely to oppose a consistent European, Judeo-Christian, Western civilisation to the rest of the world.

This third element of my analysis of the conceptual and empirical nature of European identity enables us to draw the following conclusions:

- European identity, in both its civic and cultural dimensions, is conceptually and empirically distinct from support for European integration, even though the two are obviously correlated.
- Support for European integration and civic and cultural European identities do not show the same statistical relationships with traditional social, demographic, political, and cultural independent variables. All three are influenced by the level of European experience of respondents.
- The moderate but significant correlation between support for European integration and European identity variables suggests that even though they are distinct, the theory suggesting that identities and beliefs determine political attitudes can probably be verified here using structural equation models.

First conclusion on citizens' civic and cultural European identities

In this chapter, I have shown that political identities in general and a European identity in particular could be conceptually divided into two specific components, called civic and cultural, which are implied in citizens' general identity claims. I have demonstrated that the difference between these two components was empirically sustained by a basic factor analysis, and that European identity in general is conceptually and empirically different from support for European integration in spite of the assumptions made by part of the existing political science literature. We have also seen that general, civic, and cultural aspects of a European identity could be captured by a set of 11 direct questions (reported in the Appendix) in mass surveys.

In addition, I have shown that when respondents are asked whether they feel European or not in general, it is, before anything else, of their European civic identity that they think. This is possibly due to the political salience of the question of European integration, but also, maybe, to the relative abstraction, in citizens' minds, of a common European heritage, as opposed to the obvious influence of European integration in citizens' everyday lives.

Other insights from my empirical analysis suggest that European and infra-European identities are not contradictory, that the predominance of civic and cultural components probably varies in a comparative perspective, and that European identity is relatively little correlated to traditional social and demographic indicators. Chapter 6 shows how these two dimensions react to the influence of symbols of European integration and good and bad news on Europe.

6
News, Symbols, and European Identity

The models tested

It is now time to examine whether, and to what extent, the news on Europe conveyed by the media, and the symbols of Europe generated by institutions have the expected impact on the level of European identity of citizens. This chapter also considers whether this effect is the same on the civic and cultural components of European identity. The model tested consequently considers the impact of news on Europe and symbols of the European Union on the general, civic, and cultural aspects of citizens' European identity. The findings are presented both for the whole population studied in the experiment and for each country sample. The chapter then focuses more specifically on the various surprises, shortcomings, and unexplained findings of my results and tries to propose a more critical view of what they might tell us about political persuasion and the potential influence of political institutions, and the mass media on citizens' perceptions and identities. It also discusses the comparative dimension of the models, and the insight added by the cross-national comparisons.

How political institutions and elites influence political identities[20]

It was the main question set by this project to know whether identification with Europe was influenced by messages from the media and the use of symbols by European Union institutions. The results of the experiment are unambiguous. They suggest that it clearly is. The models exploring the impact of news and symbols of Europe on the general, civic, and cultural European identity of citizens are tested using Ordinary Least

Square regression. The measurement of the dependent variables has already been described earlier, and the two experimental independent variables (news and symbols) are both dichotomous (see experimental design). Regression analyses were performed to assess the intensity of the effect of being exposed to good or bad news on Europe and of being exposed or not to symbols of European integration, controlling for any external influence, and particularly for the factors identified above. The regressions were run for the whole sample and again for each national sub-sample. The results are presented in Tables 6.1, 6.2, and 6.3. The tables show that the effects of the two experimental variables are both statistically significant and of clear substantial importance, even when controlling for the pre-test variable (i.e., the level of European identity of respondents before reading the newspaper extracts), and several control variables (only those that had a statistically significant – or nearly significant – effect in the general model or in at least one of the country regressions are included in the tables).

As shown in Tables 6.1, 6.2, and 6.3, the first important finding is that undoubtedly, the mass media, by disseminating good or bad news on Europe and European integration has a strong identity-building power over the citizens of the European Union. All three regressions show that European identity can – and, indeed does – vary over time as a result of

Table 6.1 Regression model of general European identity

Variable	General b (s.e.)	General β	France b (s.e.)	France β	UK b (s.e.)	UK β	Netherlands b (s.e.)	Netherlands β
News	0.82 (0.13)	0.38**	0.70 (0.17)	0.36**	1.13 (0.28)	0.44**	0.74 (0.24)	0.35**
Symbols	0.63 (0.12)	0.29**	0.73 (0.17)	0.38**	0.52 (0.27)	0.20*	0.52 (0.23)	0.24*
Language	0.02 (0.08)	0.02	0.01 (0.13)	0.00	0.10 (0.14)	0.09	−0.25 (0.17)	−0.16
France	0.28 (0.16)	0.13*	—	—	—	—	—	—
Netherlands	−0.07 (0.19)	−0.03	—	—	—	—	—	—
EU. Sup.	0.36 (0.06)	0.32**	0.18 (0.09)	0.18*	0.48 (0.16)	0.37**	0.52 (0.12)	0.48**
Constant	2.77 (0.17)		3.09 (0.26)					
Adj. R²	*0.38*		*0.28*		*0.48*		*0.38*	

Notes: Entries are unstandardised and standardised regression coefficients. Entries in brackets are standard errors; **: sig <0.01; *: sig <0.10; N: Global: 212, France: 97, Netherlands: 60, UK: 55.

Table 6.2 Model of civic European identity

Variable	General b (s.e.)	β	UK b (s.e.)	β	France b (s.e.)	β	Netherlands b (s.e.)	β
News	1.00 (0.11)	0.51**	0.94 (0.23)	0.47**	1.04 (0.16)	0.52**	0.94 (0.20)	0.48**
Symbols	0.63 (0.10)	0.32**	0.41 (0.21)	0.21*	0.81 (0.15)	0.41**	0.45 (0.19)	0.23*
Life in Europe	0.12 (0.09)	0.07	0.12 (0.11)	−0.13	0.05 (0.12)	0.03	0.22 (0.15)	0.16
Languages	0.06 (0.06)	0.04	0.05 (0.21)	0.03	0.11 (0.13)	0.06	0.27 (0.15)	0.18*
Pre-test	0.20 (0.05)	0.20**	0.46 (0.12)	0.46**	0.09 (0.08)	0.09	0.26 (0.10)	0.26**
Constant	−0.94 (0.13)		−0.57 (0.21)		−1.06 (0.24)		−1.31 (0.32)	
Adj. R^2	*0.45*		*0.48*		*0.44*		*0.48*	

Notes: $N = 212$; **: sig. <0.01; *: sig. <0.10.

Table 6.3 Model of cultural European identity

Variable	General b (s.e.)	β	UK b (s.e.)	β	France b (s.e.)	β	Netherlands b (s.e.)	β
News	0.45 (0.11)	0.23**	0.50 (0.24)	0.25*	0.46 (0.15)	0.24**	0.30 (0.22)	0.16
Symbols	1.08 (0.11)	0.55**	0.77 (0.25)	0.39**	1.24 (0.15)	0.63**	0.91 (0.21)	0.48**
Euro. orig	0.09 (0.14)	0.04	0.51 (0.38)	0.17	0.13 (0.19)	0.05	−0.14 (0.29)	−0.05
Languages	0.01 (0.06)	0.01	−0.12 (0.12)	−0.13	−0.04 (0.12)	−0.03	0.12 (0.15)	0.09
Pre-test	0.17 (0.05)	0.18**	0.41 (0.14)	0.40**	(0.08)	0.03	0.26 (0.11)	0.27*
Ideology	0.10 (0.03)	0.18**	0.10 (0.09)	0.14	0.07 (0.04)	0.14*	0.16 (0.08)	0.24*
Constant	−1.16 (0.18)		−0.93 (0.38)		−1.06 (0.27)		−1.36 (0.48)	
Adj. R^2	*0.43*		*0.39*		*0.47*		*0.41*	

Notes: $N = 212$; **: sig. <0.01; *: sig. <0.10.

media communication. In all three models, the regression coefficient – which assesses the influence of the variable on European identity – of news on Europe is statistically significant and unexpectedly high.

Equally strong is the fact that exposure to symbols of European integration is similarly conducive to higher levels of European identity – in its general, civic, and cultural components, for citizens across countries. This confirms the hypothesis formulated earlier in this book that political systems have the power to influence (foster, or, by default, impede) the emergence of new political identities, particularly through the use of symbols and symbolic objects that will allow citizens to 'put a face' on a given political entity of reference.

These two findings combined prove that elite and institutional messages have a very clear impact on citizens' identity, and that the elites – be they political or mediatic, have the power to influence citizens' multiple political identities.

These findings are still reinforced by the relatively low regression coefficient associated with the pre-test variable in all three models. Moreover, all three models show very high levels of variance explained, on the whole, by exposure to news on Europe and symbols of the European Union. The R^2 values of all three models are between 0.38 and 0.45 for a fairly large sample of 212 respondents and limited number of variables entered in the equation. These results are especially encouraging since behavioural models, especially those using experimental designs (Norris *et al.*, 1999, Iyengar *et al.*, 1982), do not generally tend to explain such high levels of variance. Let us now see more precisely what these models tell us about specific effects of media communication and the use of symbols on European identity, addressing each in turn.

Good news, bad news, and European identity

Once again, the finding from Tables 6.1 to 6.3 that exposure to good or bad news on European integration matters in terms of its effects on individuals' European identity is made clearer by Figure 6.1, which shows how European identity progresses as a result of exposure to good news on European integration, or conversely decreases as a result to negative news. Persistent good news on 'Europe', on its achievements and its successes, modifies citizens' perceptions of the unification process and, in turn, clearly influences their likelihood of identifying with Europe. Conversely, being systematically exposed to bad news on European integration, its failures and its threats damages citizens' perception of Europe's record, and, in turn, also makes them less likely to feel part of Europe.

It is also very clear from Figure 6.1, however, that the effect of news is far stronger on the civic component of European identity than on its cultural component. The standardised regression coefficient of the news variable is 0.51 in the civic identity model and only 0.23 in the cultural identity model. The news variable has, by far, the main effect on citizens' civic sense of European identity. This means that what affects citizens' specific support for European integration clearly ends up modifying their perception of being citizens of a European political system and the sense that this system is relevant to their everyday life. It only marginally – if certainly – influences their perceptions of relative closeness to fellow Europeans.

This is an expectable result, given the distinction between the civic and cultural components of European identity. On the whole, news on Europe and the 'record' of the European Union are bound to affect more strongly the part of European identity that has to do with institutions than the part that has to do with perceptions of a shared European heritage. Moreover, while civic identity is more likely to refer to the European Union, cultural identity may, for many refer to a European civilisation at large, who are less likely to be affected by specific news on the European Union. In turn, the strong effect of news in the general identity model confirms that when asked whether they 'feel European', citizens predominantly consider the institutional – rather than the cultural – factor in their answer.

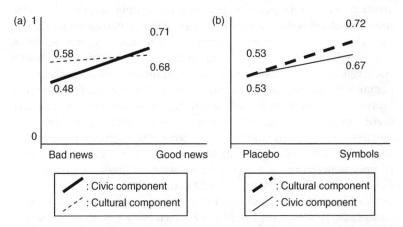

Figure 6.1   Effect of exposure to good vs bad news and symbols of European integration on levels of European identity

Another very interesting finding is related to the comparative analysis of the results or, rather, the overall lack of comparative differences in the way good or bad news influences European identity. One could have expected the news factor to be predominant in polities in which the European question is less salient, and, therefore, citizens' sense of European identity more vulnerable to short-term factors and flexible. However, and in spite of marginal differences, this is not quite the case.

Symbols of European integration and European identity

The results concerning the effect of exposure to symbols of European integration on the European identity of citizens are equally striking. All three models confirm that being consistently exposed to symbols of Europe does, indeed, reinforce a citizen's sense of identification with Europe, consistently with my model, inspired by structuralist theory, and with the hopes of the European elites alike, as shown in Figure 6.1b.

As opposed to the effect of news, however, it is clear that symbols of European unity have a stronger effect on the cultural component of European identity than on its civic component. Symbols are clearly the predominant factor having implications on the cultural component, with a standardised regression coefficient of 0.55 against 0.32 in the civic identity model. On the one hand, symbols of European integration *are* symbols of a political system. A flag, an anthem, a 'national day' all participate in the attempt to develop the European Union along the traditional model of the State, provided with all the traditional symbolic attributes of national political systems. On the other hand, the intended messages of the symbols of the European Union, based on such values as 'peace', 'unity', 'friendship', 'harmony', and the like (Bruter, 1998, European Commission, 1993, European Monetary Institute, 1996) directly stress the desire of European institutions to present 'Europe' as a human community. Indeed, while trying to understand why symbols of European unity seem to affect the cultural rather than civic components of citizens identity, it is interesting to remember that the European flag was not created by the European Communities, but for the Council of Europe, a highly 'cultural' institution, in the 1950s. These findings show how complicated the relationship is between the intended and perceived meaning of the symbols of a political community.

Another interesting finding is that this time, comparative differences in the effect of symbols on European identity are more marked. The effect of symbol exposure seems stronger on the French sample than on the British one, the Dutch sample lying somewhere between the two.

This suggests that differences of political context or socialisation might make people more or less receptive to symbols of European unity.

Nonetheless, the effect of being exposed to symbols of European unity remains surprisingly high on the whole. In terms of the cultural identity of citizens, symbols play a greater role than news on Europe. This shows the importance of symbols and institutionally designed images in the framing of citizens' perceptions of what their political community is, what it 'means' and, ultimately, who it includes.

Discussion and conclusion: opening new research territories

Arising from the main findings presented above is the idea that:

- On the one hand, the media, informing people on the failures and achievements of a political community, will particularly modify the attachment of citizens to this political system and their perceptions of its relevance to them. In other words, good and bad news will primarily affect what has been identified here as a distinct civic component of political identities.
- On the other hand, the institutional formation of mass political symbols has a predominant effect on the identification of citizens to a political community, conceived as a human group. In other words, symbols have a very strong effect on the distinct 'cultural' aspect of political identities.

Civic and cultural components of a European identity primarily reacting to different stimuli, the conceptual and empirical disentangling of European identity into civic and cultural components, and the contrast between the two, therefore, opens the way for further findings.

When civic and cultural identity do not go together ...

First, we saw in Chapter 5 that in the French and Dutch samples in particular, a majority of respondents have a predominantly 'civic' European identity. This means, following the discussion of the two components at the beginning of this paper, that while those participants tend to identify quite strongly with the European Union as a relevant political community and source of political authority, they tend to be less convinced that Europe as a whole shares some cultural and value-based proximity. This might result, in turn, in problems of political legitimacy when the governments of existing member-States will try to convince their polities of the necessity to enlarge the European Union, especially if we give credit to the idea that enlargement of the European Union might pose a risk of slowing down the process of political integration of the Union. In that case, indeed, the civic and cultural components of citizens' European identity would be in tension when assessing the prospect of further enlargement.

By contrast, the balance seems to be reversed in the British case, where a majority of citizens tend to have a predominantly cultural European identity, mostly due to low levels of civic European identity in the British case. This can probably be explained, in large part, by the United Kingdom staying out of two of the main avenues of further European integration in the last 15 years: the Schengen agreements (which symbolically concretised freedom of movement for citizens), and European and Monetary Union, which, across Europe, has been largely perceived as the main direction of further political integration in the 1990s.

An artefact of the experimental design?

It is reassuring to see that these results seem to be largely confirmed using a time-series analysis of Eurobarometer surveys since 1970 in Chapter 7 in which European identity is operationalised as a residualised variable derived from traditional 'support for European integration' questions asked in every Eurobarometer. Nevertheless, the use of an experimental design, which allowed more precise measurement and manipulation, calls for additional information on the robustness of the findings. One of the interesting tests that suggest that the tests are fairly robust is that the news and symbols variables do not only have statistically significant effects for national sub-categories, but also when the sample is split by other basic variables such as gender, age groups, or ideology.

Similarly, while the time elapsed between the two parts of the experiment was relatively short, as compared to the types of lasting identity effects we would ideally like to measure, the findings need to be considered with another element in mind. Indeed, the disproportion between this 'experimental time scale' and real life only matches the other clear disproportion between the stimuli respondents were exposed and the likely effects of being exposed to symbols of European integration on a regular basis in everyday life. The same rationale applies when comparing the three short articles respondents read in the context of the experiment to being exposed to the same eurosceptic or pro-European newspaper every day for years.

Academic and policy-related consequences of the findings of the experimental design

The two hypotheses proposed in the earlier part of this chapter have been largely confirmed by the experimental analysis. The experiment has shown that political communication can affect the political identities of citizens – in both their civic and cultural dimensions – and that the media (using the news) as well as institutions (through symbolic campaigns), have the power to encourage or impede the formation of new mass political identities, such as a European identity.

The consequences of these findings are not negligible. The role of good and bad news on the civic identity of citizens suggests that European integration only has a limited 'reservoir' of political legitimacy. Continuous doubts about the specific outcomes of European integration in some areas could therefore result in a never-emerging identity, which would in turn threaten the whole support for a true political unification of Europe in such countries as the United Kingdom. At the same time, the findings suggest that what we know of perceptions of European integration in some countries (Eichenberg and Dalton, 1993, Bruter, 2000) has already led to the emergence of a strong level of mass European identity in several member-States, as confirmed by times-series analysis. Identification with Europe, to that extent, has probably already largely paved the way to continuing support for European political integration in a majority of European Union countries.

The findings regarding the role of symbols in the development of new political identities are more interesting. The very fact that symbols seem to affect the cultural, more than the civic component of political identities suggests that the use of symbols may help make citizens feel part of a given system. They may also be used to enhance the acceptance of minorities in countries affected by integration problems.

Avenues opened for further research are considerable. A number of controversial debates among political scientists have been or could be partly solved using these results. We know now that there is such a thing as a European identity, which is certainly developed by a significant part of the European polity and is more widely held than has often been supposed. The European identity in particular – and political identities in general – cover two related but distinct components, a civic and a cultural one, each dominant for certain individuals in a pattern that differs by country and presumably over time. We need to understand what explains the dominance of either component for different citizens. While it has been shown by political scientists that European and national identities are not contradictory, it would still be interesting to understand whether either of the two components of European identity is more or less likely to be perceived as contradictory with a sense of national pride and allegiance. This has consequences on the relative perceptions of further political integration and enlargement of the European Union.

Finally, I have shown that political identities in general and European identity in particular can evolve and be influenced by the media messages and the efforts of institutions to provide polities with symbols of their community. A large amount of work still needs to be done in order to understand what have been the effects of different editorial lines of the mass media across European Union countries in terms of the unbalanced formation of a mass European identity in a comparative perspective. Other exciting questions relate to the possible use of symbols by institutions in a national context to try and favour a reinforced identity, integration of minorities, and acceptance of minority groups by dominant parts of the population.

My findings also have clear implications in terms of policy making. They show that the most efficient line in terms of integration policy would probably be the opposite of what is usually chosen in Western countries. Many States choose to try and favour the integration of newcomers by initiating them to the symbols of their new state (the United States, with its highly symbolic and organised process of 'induction' of new citizens is a caricature) and most attempts to fight racism and xenophobia using rational messages. My findings suggest that in an exactly opposite way, symbolic campaigns would be far more efficient at changing citizens' perceptions of who are 'us', while trying to appeal to citizens' reason would generate a greater sense of civic identity – and therefore of political allegiance – among newcomers, hence favouring their integration.

Of course, these results also give European institutions, national governments, and pressure groups some guidelines on how to impede citizens' identification with Europe, or, on the contrary, how to 'win hearts and minds' for European integration (or, indeed, for any emerging state and political community). As explained, what has often been branded as a 'democratic deficit' of the European Union makes it even more necessary to develop a sense of European identity among citizens to give a sense of legitimacy to the European project in a period of intense political integration. Finally, we can also derive from the balance between the civic and cultural components of citizens' European identity implications in terms of the preferences of citizens for further integration or enlargement of the European Union. The civic predominance in my findings, which still needs to be verified with mass surveys, might make it more difficult for governments to 'sell' enlargement to citizens than to promote further European integration. This might even explain some of what we know on Europeans' attitudes towards enlargement, especially if enlargement is perceived as a threat to deeper integration.

More generally, for political science, this study has confirmed that in terms of the emergence and evolution of political identities, as in most questions, there is a need to understand the constant interaction between citizens and institutions. Institutions can influence, in somewhat predictable ways, patterns of political behaviour. However, the way institutional messages are perceived by citizens remains, at times, largely surprising. While the power of symbols, largely understood by structuralist theorists, and the power of the media, common knowledge for political scientists, have been confirmed by this study, these results also contradict simplistic interpretations of these links. They have shown explicitly that the link between the messages elites intend to convey and the way they are received remains largely misunderstood by policymakers and scholars alike.

7
1970–2000 – The Emergence of a Mass European Identity

It has just been shown that, as expected, exposure to symbols of European integration, exposure to positive and negative 'news' on Europe, and, to some extent, the personal experience of European integration of citizens all influence the level of European identity of individuals. These findings are extremely important in that they give us information not known so far regarding the mechanisms of identity change and evolution and the potential role of institutions in mass identity formation. This chapter is precisely concerned with the aggregate level consequences of the findings of Chapter 6 on the progressive emergence of a mass European identity. In other words, if positive news on and symbols of Europe have, as shown in the last few pages, a positive effect on the European identity of citizens, the efforts of EU institutions to generate a full set of symbols for the European political system must have led to a slowly emerging mass European identity, while the type of news received on Europe in the various EU countries must have made this emergence slower or faster across the fifteen member-States. Moreover, a further hypothesis formulated in Chapter 2 suggests that the very membership of the European Union must, in itself, be a factor of increasing identification of citizens with their new political community.

In order to answer these questions, I propose to use the regular surveys of the public opinion of the European Union by Eurobarometer studies since 1970. As discussed in Chapter 5, unfortunately, Eurobarometer surveys only provide occasional and very poor direct measures of the European identity of respondents. These direct measures, as explained before, are flawed conceptually, analytically, and empirically. However, as shown in Appendix 3, I can provide a good residual measure of European identity using the regular Eurobarometer support variables. These measures are validated by the experiment, and allow us to see how a mass European identity has developed, over the past 30 years, in the various member-States of the European Union.

Has a mass European identity emerged? Average scores of European identity in European Union countries since 1970

In fact, as described in Appendix 3, my measure of European identity is justified by the fact that I expect European identity to be that which makes citizens demand European integration when they do not believe that it is actually directly beneficial to them personally, or to their country. I evaluate the level of underlying European identity so defined each year, and in each country, between 1970 and 2000, and I then reassess it on a scale of 0–1 over the whole period to increase the legibility of the results, comparatively, over time and space.

Even though the residual character of the variable prevents my measured levels of European identity to have a clear 'absolute' value, its evolution is a very clear sign of the evolution of European identity across countries and time. The global distribution of the variable shows a global skewedness towards higher levels, with a mean of 0.62 on the 0–1 scale, suggesting rather high levels of European identity over the time period considered. At the same time, the distribution shows a relatively low level of variance with a standard deviation of 0.21, that is, about 35 per cent of the mean. Within country variance is much lower. Given the cross-country variations that will be demonstrated soon, this mostly proves that European identity at the aggregate level does not vary too dramatically over time.

The emergence of a mass European identity across countries

The first series of interesting findings are provided by a comparative analysis of the results. The cross-country comparison shows that the various nations of the European Union have very different mean levels of European identity. Table 7.1 shows how important these variations are, with the average index score of European identity in Italy between 1970 and 2000 being 0.88, and 0.81 in Spain, while the average index score is only 0.19 in Denmark and 0.35 in Great Britain. It is the first finding of this study to show that if a mass European identity has, indeed, progressively emerged, as shown by the 0.62 global average score, it hasn't emerged uniformly everywhere.

Table 7.1 Means and standard deviations of the country samples for the dependent variable

Country	Mean	S.D.	Minimum	Maximum	N
Italy	0.88	0.08	0.56	1	29
Spain	0.81	0.03	0.75	0.88	16
Portugal	0.80	0.06	0.60	0.90	16
Luxembourg	0.75	0.08	0.61	0.90	27
Netherlands	0.73	0.09	0.44	0.90	29
Greece	0.72	0.16	0.47	0.94	20
France	0.69	0.09	0.34	0.83	29
Belgium	0.67	0.07	0.41	0.78	29
Germany	0.65	0.06	0.53	0.79	29
Finland	0.63	0.01	0.62	0.65	6
EU Average	*0.62*	*0.21*	*0*	*1*	*349*
Ireland	0.62	0.13	0.41	0.78	27
Austria	0.56	0.02	0.54	0.57	6
Sweden	0.55	0.02	0.54	0.56	6
North Ireland	0.40	0.17	0.10	0.64	26
UK	0.35	0.14	0.10	0.57	27
Denmark	0.19	0.09	0	0.34	27

Notes: Results on a 0–1 scale; time period: join date to 2000 included; total $N = 349$.

The cross-country variations, however, are not only significant, but also far from randomly distributed geographically. The top nine average scores of European identity are reached quite simply among the six founding member-States of the European Union and the three countries that joined in the 1980s. In a similar way, the lowest six scores are reached in the three countries that joined the European Communities in the 1970s and in the 1990s. This split is far too interesting to be considered a simple coincidence. Referring to the theory of the four phases of European integration I exposed in Chapter 4, it is possible to draw a parallel between the 'spirit of European integration' at the time of joining and the public opinion reactions to an increasingly political European project and, indeed, the European Union as a community of identification. Indeed, the six founding countries of the ECSC promoted a European project that was, as shown in Chapter 4, primarily political and idealistic. In exactly the same way, Greece, Spain, and Portugal, joined the European Communities in the strength of its 'EU identity and citizenship' phase, that is, in the glorious years of the project of a 'People's Europe'. On the contrary, the United Kingdom, Ireland, and Denmark joined the European Economic Community (EEC) in the midst of its policy-making phase, and Sweden, Austria, and Finland, in the crisis years that ran from the Danish first 'nay' to the Maastricht Treaty to the Amsterdam and Nice summits. I suggest that the main character of European integration at a time when a country joined the European Union will, in part, determine the likeliness of its citizens to feel European. In that sense, joining the European Union at a time of political focus of integration could be more favourable to the strengthening of European identity feelings than joining at a time when the European Union is focusing on economic aspects.

Other interpretations of the cross-country variance could be proposed, centred on the geography of the European continent, with the European Rhenan core and south being more likely to identify with the European Union than its northern and western periphery. More consistently with my theory, however, we can note – as is explored in more detail later – that the countries with the lowest levels of European identity on an average are those that have missed out on some of the most significant civic projects and symbols of the European Union: the Schengen agreements (United Kingdom, Ireland) and the Euro (United Kingdom again, Denmark, and Sweden) even though the exact causality is here a little difficult to disentangle.

In a similar way, the comparative analysis of Table 7.1 also shows that variance within countries is very limited in some cases, yet much more important in some political systems such as the United Kingdom (both Great Britain and Northern Ireland), Greece, France, Denmark, and the Netherlands. On the whole, variance in the dependent variable is primarily explained by cross-country differences, but also, to some extent, by variance over time and within country samples. On a scale of 0 to 1, a country like France, Greece, and the Netherlands have known years of very low average European identity (index score of 0.34, 0.47, and 0.44 respectively) as well as years of very high levels of identity (0.83, 0.94, and 0.90 respectively).

The evolution of European identity over time

The second significant question we need to address is whether overall levels of European identity in the various member-States have increased over time. Again, 349 cases and 3 decades are considered in the analysis. There is no need to control, for example, for the economic situation as the residual dependent variable has already been taken this element out. The 349 cases represent 17 countries or political systems across 31 years and 28 time-points.[21]

Two of the hypotheses proposed in this book point out to a progressive increase of mass levels of European identity. The first hypothesis suggests that 'institutional inertia' will lead to regular increases of levels of European identity in a given country as years of membership will make citizens recognise the European Union as a more and more obviously relevant political system in their life, and as their 'experience' of European integration progresses. The second hypothesis posits that the progressive increase in the number of symbols developed by European institutions for their citizens will have an effect on the emerging European identity. As seen in Chapter 4, symbols of European integration have been developed in 'waves' at particular times of European integration, and we may want to look for 'shocks' related to the introduction of particularly significant or numerous new symbols, but the overall expectation is, nonetheless, a progressive increase over time as the symbolic patrimony of the European Union political system has never really ceased to increase.

Figures 7.1–7.16 graphically represent the evolution of aggregate levels of European identity between 1970 and 2000 in the 16 political systems included in my aggregate level study. The first, obvious finding we can derive from this graphic interpretation is quite simple: almost everywhere (the only exceptions are Germany and Luxembourg), a mass European identity has progressively emerged between 1970 and 2000, that is, levels of mass European identity have significantly increased over the past 30 years. Fundamentally, the whole answer to my main research question relies on these 16 graphs as the evidence, even visually, is very strong: over the past 30 years, a European identity has, without doubt, progressed significantly throughout the European Union, be it in the traditionally pro-European member-States such as Italy, Spain, France, and Belgium, or in the least pro-European countries such as the United Kingdom and Denmark.

So discounting for short-term variations, which can probably be accounted for by the imprecision of the measurement, and the permeability of the dependent variable to 'short-term effects' (in the sense used by Campbell *et al.*, 1950), the global evolution of identity scores is clearly pointing 'upwards', which is not so clearly the case when one looks at the time-serial evolution of support for European integration. If we look at the exact figures rather than the general visual impressions, the trend is clearly confirmed.

It is important to consider the only exceptions to the general upward trends of European identity in Europe over the past 30 years. The only clear exception to this pattern is the relative – if limited – decline of levels of European identity over time in Germany. Whether the German sample is considered as a whole or within its sub-parts, it seems that

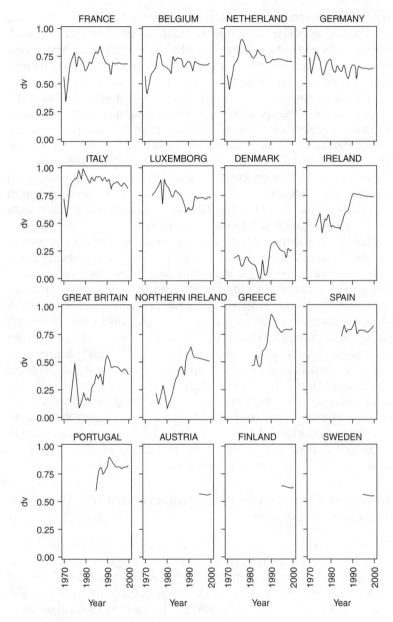

Figures 7.1–7.16 The evolution of mass European identity across the EU: 1970–2000

levels of European identity in Germany have not evolved in the same direction as elsewhere in Europe but have, rather, been stable. Indeed, after progressing in the 1970s and mostly in the 1980s, they have at best stagnated during the 1990s. It is likely that most political scientists who specialise in comparative politics – and particularly in German politics – would agree that the hectic unification process Germany had to go through in the 1990s quite certainly accounts for this fairly exceptional situation. Throughout the decade, Germany had to face a period of economic decline and social tension it had not experienced since 1945. The overall decrease of European identity is, what is more, extremely limited and primarily marked by cyclical short-term variations around a fairly stable level. The trend is very similar to the German case in Luxembourg, but in a very limited way, and starting from such high levels that the evolution is less than noticeable.

Among the other countries studied, the slope seems to be greater among 'recent joiners' than among the original members of the European Union, and particularly among the member-States, which started with very low levels of European identity on the whole. This may be, however, because, as stated in the Chapter 6, their original level of European identity – especially for the 1973 and 1995 waves of joining countries – was much below those of the member-States that founded the European Communities in the 1950s. In fact, I find that to some extent, there is a certain level of convergence between average levels of European identity across the member-States of the European Union. In 1975, two years after the United Kingdom, Ireland, and Denmark, the difference between the aggregate score of European identity in the countries where it was highest and lowest was of 0.80 on a one-point scale. In 2000, and with six more countries in the European Union, this difference was down to 0.55 points between the two extremes.

Institutions and the emerging European identity: aggregate level evidence

There is a second clear pattern shown by the graphs, when the evolution of levels of European identity amongst the European mass public is compared to the timing of the emergence of new symbols of European integration. Indeed, a careful consideration of the years when levels of European identity showed the greatest increases suggests that these increases tend to be particularly substantial in years marking the introduction of further symbols of European integration. Periods of great symbolic significance such as 1972 (adoption of the European flag by the European Communities) and 1986 (launch of the project of a People's Europe, common passport, day of Europe, etc) show very sharp increases of average levels of European identity across member-States.

It may also be that the evolutions of news perceptions are related to the changing level of European identity in the various member-States of the European Union. In a way, the comparative differences illustrated earlier tend to suggest that the countries where the mass media show a traditional defiance towards the European Union such as the United Kingdom, Denmark, and to an extent Germany have relatively lower levels of European identity than the rest of Europe. It also seems that the scandals surrounding a case of corruption in the Santer Commission in the mid-1990s have temporarily stopped the progress of average levels of European identity in most member-States, even though these levels seemed to progress again from 1999 onwards in most member-States. It is, however, very difficult to finely monitor the good and bad news on Europe and on the European Union for individuals exposed to different news and media on a daily basis even though we may suspect that the news variable would probably account for the small 'accidents' and short-term decreases of the levels of mass European identity of the samples considered.

It is important to now provide a more systematic interpretation of the quantitative results that are obtained from the time-series analysis of the dataset. The next section of this chapter presents the results of a multivariate analysis of the time/series model of the influence of institutions on the European identity of citizens. In order to be able to propose such a model, the introduction of major symbols of European integration and of the general connotation of news on Europe in the various European Union countries needs to be achieved. This is done, along the lines described in detail in Appendix 3.

Multivariate times series model

The influence of institutions – in the form of official symbols of the European Union, news on Europe, and institutional inertia – on the level of European identity of citizens across countries and time can then be tested, over the past 30 years and in 17 political systems, using two different designs.

The first design looks at the impact of institutions on the *annual change* in levels of European identity. In this context, what I try to explain is, therefore, a lagged dependent variable used together with lagged independent variables. That means that all the variance previously explained is 'cancelled' by a preliminary control of the dependent variable on its value at $t-1$ and that only the additional (marginal) change in level of European identity from one year to the next will be explained in the model.

The second model explains the *overall level* of European identity of the population of a given country in a given year, controlling, of course, for national effects. This model allows us to use the original independent variables and not their lagged values, which, again, have different theoretical implications.

Three independent variables of interest are introduced in the models and the identity score at time $t-1$ is introduced as a control variable.

News, symbols, and change in European identity

The first model tests the role of institutions in yearly changes in levels of European identity across countries. In other words, it evaluates what proportion of the changes in European identity that can be found each year in each country can be attributed to the role of institutions. In this model, the dependent variable is cleaned for auto-regression effects by control on Y_{t-1} to avoid including effects, which, for each year, had already been accounted for in the earlier years in the analysis. Change in European identity in a given country – that is, operationally, the residuals of the regression of European identity scores at t_0 on European identity scores at t_{-1} – is the new dependent variable, which will be used in the regression analysis.

The variance attributed to previous European identity scores represents 88.3 per cent of the total variance in the dependent variable, which implies that the task of explaining the remaining variance is going to be all the more difficult since not much variance is left. In the analysis, the remaining change in European identity is therefore explained by news on European integration, creation of new symbols, and institutional inertia. The analysis is conducted for the whole sample and, again, within countries, even though there is no particular reason to believe that *change* itself should be affected differently by news, symbols, and time in the European Union in the various member-States.

I first assess the bivariate correlation between the four variables involved in the models (level of identity, symbols, news, and inertia), and then between the lagged variables as they are used in the time serial model (change in identity, new symbolic campaign, news, and consolidation of institutional inertia). The correlation tables are presented in Tables 7.2 and 7.3.

The results of both tables show fairly high levels of correlation between the dependent variable and each of the independent variables

Table 7.2   Correlation table for the variables considered in the visual model

	European identity	Symbols	News	Inertia	Interaction
European identity	1.00				
Symbols	0.22**	1.00			
News	0.59**	0.42**	1.00		
Inertia	0.35**	0.35**	0.16**	1.00	
Interaction	0.51**	0.40**	0.92**	0.13*	1.00

Notes: **: sig <0.01; *: sig <0.05; N = 349.

Table 7.3   Correlation table of variables included in the time-series analysis

	Residualised European identity	Lagged symbols	News	Institutional inertia	Lagged symbols × News
Res. European identity	1.00				
Lagged symbols	0.14**	1.00			
News	0.16**	−0.03	1.00		
Institutional inertia	−0.00	0.05	0.16**	1.00	
Lagged symbols × news	−0.04	0.42**	0.08	0.13**	1.00

Notes: **: sig <0.01 ; *: sig <0.05; N = 349.

included in the model, and also between the independent variables themselves. This might imply a fairly high risk of multicollinearity in the multivariate model tested in this section. The main finding, however, remains the high level of correlation between levels of European identity and symbols of the European Union and news on Europe. These results confirm most clearly the impact of institutions and institutional messages on citizens' political identity. In particular, news on Europe is closely related to the level of European identity of citizens and its short-term changes in each member state.

Indeed, Table 7.3, concerned with the lagged dependent and independent variables – that is, marginal change in national average levels of European identity, numbers of major symbols of the European Union, and of the connotation of the news on Europe presented to citizens shows results that are consistent with the previous table.[22] The levels of correlations between the variables are, this time, far less high, probably because all variables except news and inertia have been cleaned of their common auto-regressive component, either through regression on the previous case (dependent variable) or replacement by the lagged value (symbols). The correlation between the new dependent variable and the lagged symbols and news variables remains statistically significant and of substantial importance (around 0.15, and obviously more if the analysis is conducted within countries).

The next step of the analysis is to include these lagged variables in a multivariate model that will explain, altogether, how much of the change in levels of European identity of European polities can be attributed to institutions, and which mechanisms have the greatest impact on this change. Table 7.4 shows the results of this regression analysis.

The results of table 7.4 are quite compelling. It must be remembered that the analysis is conducted for a global, cross-country, sample, which, naturally (as always in comparative analysis) results in a lower global explanatory power of the model in accounting for the annual changes in average European identity in the 17 political systems considered. In spite of this limited ambition, the model explains a respectable 16 per cent of the change in annual levels of European identity. This is all the more

Table 7.4 Multiple regression analysis of lagged European identity: whole European Union

Variable	β	b (s.e.)
Lagged symbols	0.21**	0.33 (0.09)
News	0.24**	0.92 (0.37)
Institutional inertia	−0.16	−0.01 (0.01)
Lagged of symbols × news	−0.15**	−2.14 (0.95)
Belgium	0.01	0.02(0.26)
Germany	0.07	0.24 (0.27)
Netherlands	−0.01	−0.03 (0.27)
Italy	−0.01	−0.04 (0.28)
Luxembourg	0.04	0.16 (0.27)
Denmark	−0.13	−0.48 (0.29)
Ireland	−0.08	−0.31 (0.31)
Great Britain	−0.04	−0.13 (0.30)
Northern Ireland	−0.02	−0.06 (0.30)
Greece	−0.07	−0.28 (0.36)
Spain	−0.08	−0.37 (0.40)
Portugal	−0.07	−0.32 (0.40)
Austria	−0.06	−0.41 (0.52)
Finland	−0.04	−0.36 (0.52)
Sweden	−0.03	−0.23 (0.52)
Constant		−0.07 (0.11)
R^2	0.16	

Notes: N = 349; **: sig. <0.01; *: sig. <0.10; omitted country for dummies: France.

interesting that none of the country dummies included in the model has a statistically significant effect. This shows that the impact of institutions on changes in European identity is relatively similar across the 15 member-States of the European Union. Even more importantly, both independent variables of interest have statistically significant – and reasonably high – effects on the evolution of European identity in the regression equation. Both news and the introduction of new symbols of the European Union play a very important role in accounting for short-term evolutions of national levels of European identity.

Table 7.5 breaks down the multiple regression analysis and shows the total explanatory power of institutions in the short-term evolution of European identity, year after year, in each country.

These results are telling as they are underlying the high part of the changes in levels of European identity that can be directly attributed to institutions and institutional messages in each country, as opposed to

Table 7.5 R^2 for country specific regression analyses

Country	R^2
Austria	0.99
Sweden	0.92
Finland	0.90
Luxembourg	0.32
Greece	0.21
Germany	0.20
Italy	0.20
France	0.20
Denmark	0.20
Portugal	0.17
Spain	0.16
Belgium	0.13
Ireland	0.10
Great Britain	0.08
Northern Ireland	0.07
Netherlands	0.07

Notes: Artificially high R^2 coefficients in Austria, Sweden and Finland are due to the remarkably low number of cases involved and very low level of degrees of freedom (even though symbols and interactive variables were constant and therefore not included in the equation in all those cases); N varies between 5 (Austria, Finland, Sweden) and 28 (France, Belgium, Germany, Italy, and the Netherlands) depending on the country.

random changes and the effect of various externalities. Obviously, the country-specific equations will be less significant statistically than the equation for the overall model, because of the very low number of cases in each new model (between 5 and 28). In particular, the equations corresponding to countries that have joined the European Union very recently rely on too few cases to be trusted statistically and commented on. For this reason, the Austrian, Finnish, Swedish, and East German samples in particular should be ignored.

Nevertheless – and discounting these four countries – the analysis of R^2 levels for each country equation in Table 7.5 clearly shows that two groups of countries can be compared. The model seems to work out particularly well in such countries as Luxembourg, Greece, France, Germany, Spain, Denmark, and Italy. At the same time, it is not quite as powerful when it comes to explaining identity evolution in countries or regions such as Great Britain, Northern Ireland and the Netherlands. This may be because – as shown in the analysis of the experimental design and uni-variate results – the 'cultural' component of a European identity seemed predominant among the British sample and important amongst the Dutch one. At the same time, the measurement strategy adopted in the time-series analysis clearly suggests a predominantly 'civic' dependent variable.

News, symbols, institutional inertia, and levels of European identity in the 15 member-States

The impact of institutions on European identity is very clearly confirmed when we look at the levels of European identity rather than their change. This is illustrated in Table 7.6. This new table uses average European identity per country per year as the dependent variable, and the number of symbols of the European Union, news on European integration, and institutional inertia as main predictors. Also, the analysis includes controls for year and the sample is split by country.

The results show that the model explaining levels – rather than short-term changes – in European identity is performing much better than the previous one, with an overall R^2 score of 0.43. The explanatory power of institutions in explaining average levels of European identity each year is even more impressive within some specific countries. The model is performing all the better, this time, I include institutional inertia (the expectation that levels of European identity should simply evolve upwards as a general trend, everything else being equal). The model includes controls for the various countries and for the previous level of European identity the previous year. The model performs very well both when the country dummies are included and when they are excluded.

Table 7.6 Time-series multiple regression analysis: dependent variable con-
trolled for year

Variable	Model 1: no country effect		Model 2: country dummies included	
	b (s.e.)	β	b (s.e.)	β
Symbols	−149.6 (74.3)	−0.10**	0.05 (0.01)	0.12**
News	9248.6 (1488.4)	0.66**	1.48 (0.03)	0.39**
Institutional inertia	108.9 (13.07)	0.36**	0.01 (0.01)	0.10*
Interactive	−378.15 (302.0)	−0.13	−0.16 (0.05)	−0.20**
Netherlands			0.51 (0.12)	0.14**
Italy			0.64 (0.12)	0.16**
Luxembourg			0.61 (0.12)	0.16**
Denmark			−2.04 (0.20)	−0.54**
Great Britain			−1.21 (0.21)	−0.32**
North Ireland			−1.21 (0.21)	−0.26**
Constant	−1615.1 (374.8)		0.24 (0.20)	
R^2	0.43		0.79	

Notes: $N = 349$; **: sig. <0.01, *: sig. <0.05; second model: are only included in the table
those dummy variables, which have a statistically significant effect in the equation. All the
dummy variables were included in the equation. Omitted category: France.

Indeed, when country dummies are included, the R^2 progresses impres-
sively from a very high 0.43 to a rare 0.79 (Table 7.6).

Institutions matter through three main types of mechanisms. First,
symbols of the European Union affect positively and importantly the
level of European identity of citizens across countries and time, showing
that the efforts of EU institutions to provide their citizens with a rather
comprehensive set of official symbols of Europe has played a very
important role in allowing a mass European identity to progressively
emerge. Second, news has an even more important effect on the dependent variable, proving that short-term news, over time, has a lasting
impact on the political identity of the citizens of a political community.
Third, institutional inertia also has the expected effect on European
identity, showing that the longer citizens are used to being part of the
European Union, the more European they are likely to feel.

Thirty years of emergence of a mass European identity: comparative evidence

In this chapter, I have answered the second major question of my quest? –
we have seen a mass European identity, and saw that a mass European

identity has progressively started to emerge between the early 1970s and the beginning of the third millennium, and is still progressing.

The trend of the time series is very simple. By and large – and with a few minor exceptions that can be easily explained on the basis of unusual idiosyncratic circumstances, the level of European identity of citizens in the various member-States has generally increased quite regularly, supporting the hypothesis of institutional inertia, which claims that increased length of membership automatically reinforces European identity. However, – and second – institutions have also clearly influenced the European identity of citizens by providing them with more and more symbols of the European Union, which have added to the effect of citizens' membership in the European Union. Third, institutions have also influenced citizens' identification with the European Union indirectly in that the perception of the performance of European integration – as retranscribed by the media in the news on Europe that they convey – also has a very important effect, over time, on European identity. Beyond these clear trends, however – and the suspicion that there is no particular reason why they should not be applicable either to the future or to other new political identities – my analysis of time-series mass survey data points out to some interesting comparative differences.

At first sight, we face a 'predictable' pattern of mass identity levels across countries, in which, on average, Spaniards and Italians tend to identify more with Europe than the Dutch and Brits. In an attempt to unify our perception of comparative differences, I have suggested that historical differences are probably very significant when it comes to interpreting national differences in mass European identity across European Union countries. I proposed earlier in this book a conceptual history of European integration based on four cumulative phases. The first is a phase of international co-operation and pacific project. A second phase keeps the co-operation basis but adds a new policy-making angle. The third phase adds to the first two trends a reinforcement of institutions and institutional legitimacy, and the fourth added to all else – citizenship and identity-building. I suggest that their time of joining the European Union largely explains the differences in average levels of European identity across countries. Indeed, I believe that the fact that countries such as Britain and Denmark joined the EEC in its 'technical' phase has had an impact on citizens' reactions towards the European project, their perception of what it is, and their starting level of political identification with the European Union. Neither country was part of the process of European integration when it was centred on a general (political) cosmopolitan and pacifist ideology, which was the case of the original six member-States, wholly characterised by high levels of European identity on an average. In a similar manner, Spain and Portugal joined the European project at the time when it was mostly centred on the foundation of a People's Europe and was a predominantly political project. As a result, the founding members of the ECSC in 1950 and the three countries that joined the European Communities in the 1980s are topping the list of European identifiers. Similarly, the countries, which joined the project in the 1973 and 1995 waves of enlargement still show a clear deficit of popular European identification.

The question must be raised of what the consequence will be of the time when Central European countries are joining the European Union. This should be after major policy developments, institutionalisation, and the design of a new Social Contract have already been spelt out and implemented. The implementation of the European Social Charter, the adoption of the 'Bill of Rights' of citizens during the Nice Summit, the ratification of the Nice Treaty and – so far – the failure to agree on a European Constitution have not yet symbolised a new step in the process of European integration, but rather, a slightly embarrassing status quo which could, of course, be replaced by the beginning of a fifth phase of constitutionalisation if the negotiations on the Convention's draft turned out successful. Central European citizens may join a more profoundly democratic Europe, or, alternatively, a politically self-restraining European Union, far from the ambitious one that some other countries founded or joined.

This chapter has also allowed us to contradict the large body of literature, which proposes that European identity and support for European integration were empirically – if not conceptually – the same variables. This time-series study enables us to show that a mass European identity has emerged and progressed throughout the European Union over the last 30 years, while support for European integration – and even more perceived benefits from European unification have not, showing a relative decrease, in some countries in the 1990s.

The third broad question this book answers has to do with citizens – how citizens perceive Europe and their own European identity, to try and understand what they 'mean' by it. It is this last important question that Chapter 8 answers.

8
On What it Means to 'Be European': Making Citizens Talk About 'Europe' and 'Europeanness'

In Chapters 6 and 7, I have shown that a European identity has progressively emerged in the European Union over the past 35 years, under the influence of institutions, and in particular of such mechanisms as the news on European integration and symbols of the European Union. This chapter is concerned with citizens' perceptions of these symbols and news, and of citizens' perceptions and understanding of 'Europe', 'Europeanness', and their own 'European identity'. In other words, this chapter tells us what citizens *mean* by feeling increasingly European.

To answer this questions, focus group interviews were organised and used to provide us with better knowledge of citizens' perceptions of the questionnaires used, the stimuli proposed in the experiment, the symbols of the European Union, news of Europe, and of a European identity in general. In fact, referring to the model depicted in Chapter 2, it is clear that the structuralist approach used in this book shows that people's identity derives from people's perceptions of Europe, themselves influenced by the images they form of Europe. The focus groups analysis mostly helps us to understand better what these perceptions are, how images of Europe are formed and interpreted, and how people connect them with an European identity per se.

The design and agenda of the focus groups discussions as well as their technical and quantitative descriptions are described in the appendix. The analysis of the focus groups discussions will be organised according to the five different tasks set for them. These tasks are summarised below:

- The first was to assess the way the questions, stimuli, and organisation and design of the experiment were perceived by respondents.

- The second was to see how people perceive the way they are informed on Europe by various news media.
- The third task was to analyse how people know and perceive the various main symbols of European integration and what they mean for them.
- The fourth task was to establish what direct experience people have of Europe and how it influences their levels of European identity.
- The fifth and last task set for the focus group was to establish what people think of the 'idea' of a European identity. This includes questions such as what it is for them, whether it exists at all, is spread out, what it involves, how it connects with other political identities, and what it means for European citizens.

In all cases, the insights will be drawn from all relevant focus groups across countries, that is, between four and eight focus groups, depending on the category of questions targeted. The real first names and the number and location of the focus group will be used with all quotations.

Talking about the media and Europe: perceptions of the way the media inform us on European integration

The first insight of the focus group allows us to capture respondents' perceptions of the way the media inform them on Europe and European integration. Indeed, the media are the most obvious source of 'images' of Europe. Voluntarily or involuntarily, they affect people's perceptions of what Europe stands for, and it is, for this reason, extremely important for anyone interested in understanding what Europe means to citizens to capture how people perceive the images of Europe conveyed to them by the media. Four of the nine focus groups discussed this question in all three locations.

To introduce the more general topic of how people think the media present and represent Europe, the group organisers started to ask, very briefly, how the respondents perceived the 'sense' of the news presented to them in the newspaper extracts they had just read. With regards to these specific articles, there was no hesitation to call the supposed good news 'positive' and the supposed bad news 'negative'. From there, the participants were asked more general questions about the way the media inform them in general.

Comparative differences were significant. Globally speaking, the respondents judged news on Europe roughly neutral in the Netherlands, neutral to fairly negative in France, and very negative in Britain. About the last case, Paul (United Kingdom, group 1) said that:

> No, no … they always say Europe is shit and all that […] That's what
> you always read, especially in rubbish like the Sun and so on!

He then attributed this negative bias to the Australian ownership of the
largest British media group. He accused the Maxwell group of having an
interest in promoting opposition to the European project:

> They don't even pay taxes in England at all and then they say they
> represent the people! They don't want Europe to be too strong. […]
> Also, you know, they don't want Europe because of their own interest
> too […] especially tax harmonisation and all that: it's not good for
> the rich and it's even worse for the very very rich like them, so they
> try to claim it's bad for the poor to be supported by their readers!

Even in the case of France and the Netherlands, however, many participants noticed that the European Union and its various institutions were
often blamed for what goes wrong with what Ann (Netherlands,
group 1) called the 'legislation on bananas', environmental details and
other tiny questions sometimes addressed by the European Union.

In all cases, the respondents were asked if differences existed, according
to them, in terms of orientation of the information on Europe by any
news organ. In France, the participants claimed that TV tended to be
more negative towards Europe than most newspapers. This remark
might not have arisen outside of a somewhat 'sophisticated' population.
In Britain, major differences were found by the respondents across newspapers, which corresponded to the 'common knowledge' on the question (i.e., particularly Eurosceptic tabloids and *Daily Telegraph*, moderate
Times, and relatively pro-European *Guardian, Independent* and *Financial
Times*). No such difference was spontaneously expressed in France or the
Netherlands, although the question was not asked directly anywhere.

When asked what were the types of good and bad information most
often associated with European integration in the media, the respondents seemed to answer both questions quite easily. Among the negative
images conveyed by the media, the participants mentioned heavy
bureaucracy (Anne-Julie, France, group 2), focus on tiny questions,
internal dissension between member-States, obscure negotiations,
unsatisfactory compromises, and the like (all, several occurrences).
Among the good news, they mentioned in all three countries, economic
development and prosperity, internal co-operation, cultural initiatives,

policy diffusion (Sarah, UK, group 1, albeit not called that way), and others.

Analysing briefly these comments of the participants to the focus group, it seems that the media are perceived to present European integration as a mostly technical project but underline its diplomatic failures. This is confirmed by the policy areas in which participants perceived that the European Union was presented positively or negatively by the media. Areas of negative presentation included competition policy, agricultural policy (only for the French groups) and common foreign policy (particularly emphasised by the British groups). Areas of positive presentation include – still according to the participants – cultural and educational co-operation (particularly emphasised by the Dutch sample), industrial policy, regional development (particularly emphasised by the French sample), and scientific co-operation. The Dutch sample also mentioned environmental policy positively and the French and British samples talked about social legislation.

Therefore, overall, to varying degrees, the focus group perceive that the news given to them by the media on Europe tend to be predominantly negative, particularly in terms of 'political' contents (as opposed to economic). They also thought that this information matters, that people follow it and that, as claimed by Christophe (France, group 2):

[one] cannot think of Europe without thinking of slightly stupid, heavy mechanisms, bogus laws on the size of apples and salmon and so on!

Participants were asked if they often verified the information they are exposed to, using, for example, an alternative source. A few answered in the affirmative, but most answered that they do not. This suggests that the bias mentioned in terms of sense of information is likely to matter with regards to the perceptions of Europe by European citizens.

Talking about symbols of Europe: knowledge and perceptions of the official symbols of European integration

The second theme of discussion for some groups had to do with the symbols of European integration rather than the news and the way the media inform citizens on Europe. As in the previous case, the topic was introduced in relation to the symbols mentioned in the questionnaires or the photographs of symbols of European integration in some of the newspaper extracts. The symbols included in the photographic stimuli included, among other things, the European flag, Euro bank notes, and the European passport. In addition to those, the questionnaires mentioned the European anthem (Beethoven's ninth Symphony *Ode to Joy*), the European 'national festival' (Schuman Day on 9 May), and the elections to the European Parliament.

The participants were asked whether they knew of these symbols before the day of the experiment. No respondent claimed not to know the European flag. The common passport and the synchronised universal suffrage elections to the European Parliament were also known by a clear majority of the members of the focus group. Unlike the case of Britain, in both France and the Netherlands, a majority of the respondents also knew the European anthem and had seen photos of Euro bank notes prior to the experiment.[23] However, in all three cases, very few participants already knew of the Schuman Day. This result was slightly different in France where a non-negligible minority knew of the event, which has benefited from relatively high media coverage and efforts of popularisation by public authorities in the past few years.

Interestingly enough, however, many of the focus group participants expressed doubts as to whether the general public knew much about these symbols, even about the ones they almost all knew (passport, etc). Of course, there would be no sense in taking this information in the first degree (i.e., as an 'expert' indication of the actual knowledge of symbols by the general public). However, this comment tells us something about perceptions of media diffusion of symbols of European integration, perceptions about the salience of these symbols in daily discussions, and probably an unconscious perception that European integration is still, after all, an 'elite' phenomenon.

When the participants knew some of the symbols, they could express surprisingly clearly what images and connotations they associated with them. Emily (United Kingdom, group 2) talked about the European flag. She explained that she perceived it as:

> A more peaceful [...] and positive flag than the Union Jack. Even the colours are softer! [...] You can't think of people going to war with that.

She said that she preferred it to the latter for that reason and that it does not convey any violence or hatred unlike the British flag. About the European anthem, Matthew (United Kingdom, group 2) also explained that he had found it was a good choice, devoid of any narrow political message, unlike the *God Save the Queen*. Most respondents ignored the 'official' symbolism of most of the symbols of the European Union, but among the values and connotations proposed, peace, harmony, co-operation, and others are the elements mentioned most often. The emphasis on co-operation is of particular importance. Indeed, few of the symbols chosen for European institutions and the European Union were designed to represent co-operation between individual States (Bruter, 1998). However, erroneous co-operative interpretations have been quite numerous, in particular in reference to the flag, when the European Communities only had twelve member-States (Bruter, 1998). The focus group discussions showed us that, in fact, these erroneous interpretations have also appeared quite intuitive to many citizens who go on perceiving the State as the main level of political power even in the context of European integration. The European level is then, at most, characterised as an 'anti-national' level by my respondents.

Following this acknowledgement, focus group participants were asked whether they perceived any opposition between symbols of Europe and symbols of their individual State. Interestingly enough, this is one of the themes on which participants were most radically split. In the British sample, group 2 seemed to agree that the 'non-national' symbols of the European Union contrasted with the 'nationalist' symbols of the United Kingdom. Matthew (United Kingdom, group 2) explained that, in his opinion:

> Europe [...] doesn't go against the UK or anything [...] They don't want to destroy it, but when you look at Britain and all our stuff, the anthem and the flag and so on [...] they exclude Europe and everything else because if you think of your country struggling to survive [...] and against enemies and all the rest, you can't imagine Europe.

This is an interesting perception on the 'direction' of a potential exclusion between Europe and the nation-state in terms of symbolic discourse. In Paul's perception, Europe is not, therefore, a threat to the nation-state (if the nation-state accepts Europe, Europe will not exclude the nation-state) but threatened by it, and, as a result, a momentarily interrupted – but important – complement to the United Kingdom.

The discussion on symbols of European integration gives us a certain number of very important elements of information on the way citizens perceive these top-down 'images' of Europe and the European Union. First, we learn that there is a rather good knowledge on the whole of the main symbols of the European Union. Second, we can see that these symbols suggest the formation of subjective images and connotations by citizens who associate them to values of peace, harmony, co-operation, and other elements that represented the first philosophical 'line' of the European project in the first half of the century (Bruter, 2000a). These interpretations and connotations seem 'anti-national' in essence, close to the polar opposite of borders as a political reference. Third, I understand that in spite of their knowledge and interpretation of these symbols, the participants to the focus group expressed doubts about the same being true of the general public. I interpret this comment as an indication of the fragility of the relationship of the participants with symbols of European integration. Slightly forcing the interpretation of participants' comments, the evolution of the focus group discussion on that topic almost gives the impression that they were slightly ashamed of associating positive subjective images with symbols of European integration, particularly in Britain and France.

Talking about their experience of Europe: acquaintance and perceptions of the impact of Europe in citizens' daily life

The next element of the focus group discussion had to do with the perception by citizens of the importance of Europe in their daily life and their own 'personal' experience of European integration as citizens.

The questionnaires given to the participants to the experiment included a series of questions on their daily experience of the European Union. These items aimed at taking a snapshot of citizens' dealing with European integration in everyday life through travelling in the rest of the European Union, living in another EU country, having trans-European families, or speaking more foreign languages. In the focus group discussion, the respondents were, therefore, asked, before anything else, whether they thought that living in or travelling to another European country would make people feel more European, and the same about European origins and speaking foreign languages. The respondents were encouraged to relate the discussion to their own individual experiences and those of people they know. Jonathan (France, group 1), did so in reference to his brother:

> My brother lived in Europe and in the USA [...]. It was so different because it was so complicated, administratively to study in the US, and so easy in England!

At the same time, Christophe (France, group 2) expressed somewhat similar comments on Europe being 'citizens' home' with regards to the

Schengen area:

> I often went through Amsterdam Airport lately [...] from the US [...]
> Every time I arrived and showed my passport, the customs people
> didn't really check my passport and greeted me in French! I felt quite
> moved!!

All these comments showed that European integration is 'felt' by the
respondents (and their families) in the context of travel and life abroad
within – as opposed to without – the European Union. From these
elements, we may guess that living in another country outside of the
European Union might reinforce the sense of European identity of
respondents almost as much as life in another European country (as part
of one's 'European experience' per se).

The groups were then asked whether they expected that the categories
of people who are particularly exposed to the European reality through
travelling and working abroad should feel increasingly more European.
The groups were also asked more directly, if some members had lived
abroad and whether it had made them feel more European. Anne-
Sophie (Netherlands, group 3) explained that:

> When I was in Mainz as an Erasmus student, I felt very European [...].
> We didn't mix up very much with the Germans themselves, because
> many of them lived with their families [...] but we really created a
> group with the other Europeans: I think ... I think the Belgians, the
> Italians, the Spanish, the Swedes, us ... even the Britons: everyone
> felt very 'European', more than when we were at home!

Later, Anne-Sophie formalised her comment further and suggested that
Europeanness can only develop strongly in the context of contact with
fellow Europeans, and even more easily when their similarities are
enlightened by contrast with differences with extra-Europeans (in her
case, in Mainz, she particularly mentioned Americans and Asians). This
may explain, again, the perceived impact of living in a non-European
country as well as – or in reinforcement of – the European experience of
a respondent.

As far as travelling abroad is concerned, the comments of the groups
were a little bit more contradictory. Claire (France, group 3) and Emily
(United Kingdom, group 1) both had positive comments about the
impact of their European travel experience on their European identity.
The former analysed her experience of a seven-week-long 'Interail' trip

through most of Europe (both in and out of the European Union):

> I never thought I could feel so close to Romanians and so on [...]. You
> know, we stopped in Slovakia and the people, there, were really poor
> and so on, and brought up in communism [...] but I really felt closer
> to people there than when I was in Japan or in the USA. [...] Also, you
> know, the food and the languages and so on ... sometimes, you think
> you are back to France when you are in Poland or you feel you are in
> Italy when you are in Romania or you ... you think that Finland and
> Czechoslovakia (sic.) are not unlike because the food and the people
> and the way to go out are really the same. I didn't feel that when I
> travelled anywhere else.

Emily made similar comments, pointing out to similar preoccupations,
interests, and tastes of people throughout Europe. Her comparison
extended even further geographically, since she mentioned countries
like Belarus and Latvia. However, Ann (Netherlands, group 1) regretted
that when she goes to Tuscany, where her parents have a holiday house,
they are still treated like 'foreigners'. She also explained that when they
go to Belgium, she sometimes think that people dislike their Dutch
neighbours even more than they would dislike people who come from
very far away:

> They basically tell us we are all perverse, they hate our football teams
> and even our way of speaking! [...] If we play Brazil, they'll definitely
> support Brazil!

The discussions were then oriented to the impact of speaking foreign
languages in contemporary Europe. Here again, the groups were split
between those who think that speaking foreign languages makes one
feel more 'international' and more integrated in the European Union,
and those who think that it does not make any difference. Various
participants recalled their experiences abroad and in their relationship
with fellow Europeans, mentioning either the relative difficulty ... or
the relative easiness of communicating with people from other
European countries.

Regarding foreign European origins, the few participants who did
have some mostly mentioned their links with family in other European
countries, and their effects in terms of travel, languages, and so on. It is
very difficult to expect citizens to 'know' if this has had any impact on
their own sense of European identity, as it would assume a capacity to

take some distance themselves from the fully internalised conception of how people perceive themselves. If we analyse with some objectivity what was said in the focus group discussions, however, these participants all seem to have developed a fairly strong sense of Europeanness, and several referred to implicit or explicit trans-European 'minority' networks. A good example was that of Anna (Netherlands, group 2), who was born in Opole in Poland and moved to Rotterdam with her family when she was 1. She was 27 at the time of the interview:

> My Dad's brother moved to a fairly poor suburb of Toulouse in France, where there are lots of problems with immigrants [...] but my family settled down really easily. [...] When I go to see them, or family friends who live in Milan and in Münster, I always feel at home! ... We have our own Europe [...] and sometimes it seems to have strengthened much faster than for most people in the EU [...] I would have no problem marrying someone who wanted to live in France or Germany or even Italy if it weren't for the language! ... [...] I love it here, I have many friends, and I have my brother and sisters, but otherwise, I think I could easily feel at home anywhere in Europe!

Judging by my participants' comments, European experience obviously matters. However, respondents did not always perceive directly that European experience is important as such. They either focused on technical consequences of their European experience (easier administrative installation in a foreign – but EU member – country, end of border formalities within Schengen, etc.) or took their European experience to be the revealing factor – as opposed to the consequence – of the impact of European integration for citizens. The stress on symbolic treatment as EU citizens (e.g., the attitude of the customs official towards a French citizen as Schipol) might also tell us more about symbols of Europe than the part of the discussion that was conceived as dealing with 'symbols' by citizens.

Here, the very notion of border – absence of, and remaining ones – is reintroduced at the forefront of the discussion: Europeanness means first and foremost that some physical and symbolic borders have disappeared for citizens (Schengen borders, differences of treatment in other EU countries, etc.) while borders with the rest of the world might have strengthened (fellow European vs non-European students in the Erasmus experience case, comparison of Romania with the United States or Japan, etc.).

This leads to a more general and more direct discussion of the very notion of 'European identity', what it means to citizens, and how salient they take it to be.

Talking about 'European identity': identity within language, identity and borders, identity and citizenship

From talking of the participants' experience of Europe, the discussion was oriented by the organisers towards the last major challenge of the focus group discussion: that is, to understand what participants thought of the very idea of a European identity, of its reality, and of how widespread it is. Ultimately, I intended to capture how significant European identity is in the life of European citizens in general and of the focus group participants in particular and, mostly, to understand what it can mean to citizens.

These questions were approached at the very end of the groups' discussions and all groups were faced with them. They started when the groups' leaders came back to the debriefing elements and reminded the participants that the experiment was, in fact, dedicated to the study of the level of European identity of citizens. The participants were asked, this time, if they thought that the questionnaires' items on European identity did, indeed, measure their level of European identity and what they would understand by these terms.

Some parts of this discussion was actively led by the groups' leaders who were asked, unlike earlier aspects of the discussion, for example, to explicitly ask respondents whether they thought that a European identity and being 'for' Europe were the same thing. No respondent took this line. All perceived quite spontaneously the difference between support for a project and the emergence of a new identity. It was more difficult, however, for the participants to propose a positive definition of what a European identity is. On the whole, the definitions they gave went into two different directions, each approved by a roughly similar proportion of the participants with no clear comparative pattern. Some of the respondents defined a European identity around a set of values like cosmopolitanism, co-operation, cross-national and cross-cultural mixing. For example Adam (United Kingdom, group 3):

> I feel European because there is no sense in struggling against other countries and ... and it just seems stupid, all this money put in armies and military material and everything.

On the other hand, another portion of the participants defined a European identity using a terminology similar to what they would have used to define their own national identity. Peter (Netherlands, group 2) explained that:

> [Feeling European means] to feel close to other Europeans. It's ... that's when you think you could live in another European country and feel 'Ok, that's like home'. [...] It's not necessary that ... it is all the same in Europe but still, when there are some small signs and small stuff ... that ... that all make you think that's all part of the same big society while somewhere else doesn't.

These two radically opposite definitions correspond to two trends in understanding the underlying 'philosophy' of European integration, between globalisation and cultural construction. Surprisingly enough, whether Europe is an anti-national or a meta-national construct divided the focus groups' participants as much as it divides political scientists.

The respondents' direct answer to the question of whether they feel European was predominantly positive, but the focus group discussion allowed us to get a clearer sense of the depth of the answers given by the participants. Few respondents clearly expressed that they had absolutely no sense of European identity. Among the spontaneous non-identifiers, most explained – using different types of discourse – that, in fact, their sense of the differences between Europeans was stronger than their sense of their similarities. Ben (United Kingdom, group 1) explained that he did not feel he had much in common with fellow Europeans or even, for that matter, with Southern Englishmen! In the Dutch focus group, a couple of respondents expressed similar perceptions on a European identity. Ann (Netherlands, group 1) explained that:

> How can we feel European when there is not even enough in common for all of us to feel equally Dutch?

On the other hand, the respondents who expressed a relatively high level of European identity expressed it primarily with regards to a sense of narrowness associated with their national identities and national circles, and a sense of similarities of lives and concerns with fellow Europeans.

They also underlined the 'civic' aspect of European integration and the logic of feeling European when it constitutes a homogeneous political area from the point of view of policy-making, politics and movement.

This was expressed, for example, by Christophe (France, group 2):

> When you know all ... Europe decides so much of our life: you have
> to feel European [...] because we really live in the same 'country'!

This confirms that the perception of the salience of Europe as an area of
civic unity is a major determinant of the level of European identity of
citizens, and that both civic and cultural logics remain significant
when it comes to determining the level of general European identity of
citizens.

To specify their message, however, I asked participants whether their
identity had more to do with 'Europe' in general or with the European
Union in particular. In most cases, and with a few very vocal exceptions,
a majority of the participants claimed that, at the moment, they did not
feel that they had much in common with the populations of Central
and Eastern Europe as yet. Most respondents, however, had no direct
knowledge of Central and Eastern Europe while many of them had vis-
ited at least two other countries of the European Union at some point in
their lives.

The images associated to Europe by respondents varied according to
their main perspective (cultural or civic) of European identity. The traditional values of peace, harmony, co-operation, and others were stronger
among cultural identifiers while civic identifiers were keener on elements like prosperity, free movement, democracy, environmental policy, and, more generally, a set of 'pioneer'-related wordings.

But again, when asked what Europe 'means' to them in less abstract
terms, the predominant and almost unanimous answer in France and
the Netherlands had to do with the modification of physical borders.
Jean (France, group 2) expressed it in very plain terms:

> I spent forty years of my life queuing for hours in the car when we
> were going to see my family from Nice to San Remo, and that was at
> least once a month. We would check if we all had our identity cards,
> and wait patiently and slightly fearfully to see if the customs people
> would check our Ids, ask us to park on the side and search our car, or
> just quickly nod to tell us to go. Now that Europe has become real
> (sic.), the border control point is empty, there is no need to take your
> identity card or to worry about buying too much alcohol [...] but
> even now, I can't drive there without shivering, remembering the
> times when things were so different, and thinking that Europe has
> really gone a long way and changed us (sic.)

Discussion and conclusions

On the whole, the focus group discussions helped us to refine significantly the intermediary steps of the process of formation of a European identity and to understand better what citizens may mean by it. Besides other goals, the focus group were mostly dedicated to a better understanding of the images of Europe and the European Union formed by participants. Another puzzle targeted was the way they are influenced by news on Europe, symbols of the European Union, and their experience of Europe.

I found that in their perceptions of Europe and self-assessment of their European identity, some participants (a majority) appeared predominantly 'civic' while other, but only a minority, were predominantly 'cultural'. The images of Europe held by 'cultural' identifiers had to do with peace, harmony, fading of historical divisions, co-operation between similar people and cultures. The images of Europe held by 'civic' identifiers had to do with borderlessness, circulation of citizens, common civic area, new policy-making, and prosperity. Undoubtedly, all these subjective images, predominantly positive, are those that will be used by citizens to anchor their sense of belonging to this new political community. They will determine the character to be predominantly civic or cultural of their European identity.

Participants were also conscious of some level of communication received from official authorities, through symbolic campaigns and the development of official symbols of European integration formalised by the elite, and from the media, through good and bad news about Europe. They intuitively perceive (and maybe even exaggerate) the impact of these elements of top-down communication and assess their orientation: predominantly negative for the media, with significant cross-national differences, conveying ideal images of harmony, peace and co-operation that echo their own prejudices, in terms of symbols. Interestingly enough, there was an almost general feeling for the participants that while 'they' could be distant and cynical enough to differentiate between disinformation/manipulation and 'the truth', fellow citizens were expected to be too gullible to resist the pressure of positive or negative communicators.

The participants also had the intuition that experiencing Europe would make citizens feel more and more European, and, therefore, that what can be called the 'institutional inertia' of European integration (Bruter, 2003) would develop naturally. Indeed, they thought citizens would become more European while being increasingly exposed to the impact of Europe in their daily life through increased travelling, living abroad, and political salience of the European Union in terms of policy-making and politics. This remains true as a mass-perception even though Arbruster, Rollo, and Meinhof (2003) show us that those who are expected to experience Europe most saliently in their daily lives by living on and around borders do not 'read' symbols of European integration in the way one could expect. In that way, they linked, the individual-level 'European experience' hypothesis to the aggregate level 'institutional inertia' hypothesis using their own personal experience and their perception of the rest of the European citizenry.

Finally, talking about European identity directly, the participants to the focus group in all three countries confirmed its relevance, as a research question, and its intuitive reality for – generally elitist – segments of citizens from the United Kingdom, the Netherlands and France. Finally, the focus group discussions confirmed that the two 'civic' and 'cultural' dimensions of a European identity can be differentiated, and that different respondents may have one slightly predominant dimension, the cultural dimension appearing as slightly predominant, overall, in the British (non-representative) sample and the civic dimension slightly predominant in the two (still not representative) continental samples. In both cases, however, the strengths and weaknesses of respondents' expressed forms of European identity largely had to do with their perceptions of transforming borders within and around the European Union. There was no clear gender or age-related differences in these perceptions of remaining and fading borders, but clearly, the United Kingdom which is still outside of the Schengen area lacked one clear symbol of border deletion, which was perceived, overall, by my Dutch and French participants as *the* best expression and foundation of their modern European identity.

Of course, some of the clear weaknesses of the focus group remain. The technique is somewhat impressionistic, and the unique and unpredictable turn of the discussion in each group as well as the non-representative character of the samples raise questions with regards to the external validity and the generalisability of the findings that have just been identified. Nevertheless, no other technique could help political scientists to understand any better what citizens actually mean when they refer to their political identity in general and to their relative European identity in particular from a 'bottom-up' perspective.

Hopefully, these results will have helped us to face Peter Burgess's paradox of an 'identity prisoner of language' with some new tools. Apart form learning about the way people perceive the way they are informed on Europe, the symbols of the European Union, and their daily experience of European integration, we now know that some level of systemisation can be assumed when comparing individuals' perceptions of European identity and its relationship with physical and symbolic borders. In particular, we have seen that two main components of this identity are referred to by citizens in their answers: a cultural and a civic one, with very different implications for the future of the European project. This impressionistic and limited design will have hopefully helped us to get a better sense of the way to interpret some of the most promising and fundamental questions citizens can be asked when trying to capture and understand their political perceptions, beliefs, and identities.

9
Conclusions: Institutions and the Emergence of a Mass European Identity – Lessons for the Future

This book has shown three important – and yet undiscovered – elements regarding European identity:

- In spite of the sceptical assertions of many journalists and some academics alike, a mass European identity has progressively emerged over the past 30 years, continues to grow, and has already achieved high enough levels not to be ignored by academics commentators, and politicians alike.
- Institutions have played a very important role in the emergence of this new political identity, in particular, by generating symbols of the new European political community, and via the good and bad news conveyed by the media on Europe and on European integration. The European Union has also contributed to the progression of European identity.
- When they explain that they feel European, citizens actually have specific conceptions in mind, particularly a 'civic' conception of their Europeanness, based on the relevance of the European Union as a relevant political system that generates some of their rights, duties, and symbolic civic attributes. To a lesser extent, they also hold a 'cultural' conception of this identity, based on a perceived shared baggage, which may, according to the individual, thought to consist of a variety of historical, cultural, social, or moral attributes.

Beyond these three fundamental findings, however, and at the same time as it answers some unresolved questions, the research presented in this book opens an incredible variety of new puzzles, paradoxes, and challenges regarding the multiple political identities of citizens and their interaction with their political systems. In this last chapter, I first summarise the main findings of this study, and then shift the focus onto some of these remarkably difficult and challenging new questions that will have to be addressed by forthcoming social and human science research.

The role of institutions in influencing identities

The results of the empirical tests that have been performed in this study have all pointed out towards the same conclusion. When it comes to the formation and evolution of political identities, institutions and people both undoubtedly matter. Thanks to a combination of experimental and time-serial evidence, it has been shown that symbolic campaigns are efficient in stimulating the emergence and consolidation of a new political identity. It has been underlined that the way we are informed about the outcomes of a political project has an influence on our propensity to identify with it. It has even been demonstrated clearly that, the very existence, survival, and consolidation of a set of political institutions participates in the generation of its own identity, that is, to the reaction of civic identification of the citizen under its rule with the political community. This, however, should not make us lose sight of the subtle interaction that results from institutions trying to influence increasingly cynical citizens, as is discussed in a few pages.

The design: bridging the gap between individual-level and aggregate-level patterns of identity formation and evolution

The test of the theory and hypotheses presented in Chapter 2 was conducted in three steps throughout this study. The first step consisted of an evaluation of individual-level identity reactions to symbolic and news messages using an experimental design. The second analysis targeted the transposition at the aggregate-level of the model, using a time-serial design assessing and explaining mass levels of European identity in each EU country between 1970 and 2000. The third stage aimed at gathering a more refined evaluation of citizens' perceptions of symbols of Europe, and news on Europe, and a better understanding of the very meaning of European identity and Europeanness for Europeans using comparative focus group discussions.

This relatively complex design enables us to bridge the gap between individual-level and aggregate-level studies of the formation of a new political identity (Chapter 2). It also presents as the interest of 'cancelling out' the respective external and internal validity problems that would have been raised had only either the experimental design or the time-series design been used (Chapter 2). The complex research design also mixes complementary quantitative and qualitative, static and dynamic evidence to better grasp such a complicated object of study as European identity.

As these various tests never ended up contradicting one another, the three-tier research design enables us to reinforce the same line of conclusions. What has been identified at the individual level in the experiment (that news and symbols affect the formation of an individual's political identity) has been confirmed at the mass level and dynamically by the time-series analysis and, again, underlined by groups of respondents who participated in the focus group discussions in different locations (Chapters 6, 7, and 8). Moreover, the various components of the research design each helped to refine specific elements of the overarching research question. The experiment allowed for the development and empirical confirmation of a conceptual framework and measurement strategy for political identities, based on two – civic and cultural – components and an overarching 'spontaneous' dimension (Chapter 5). As a result, we understand better what political identities consist of and how they can be measured. The focus group analysis helped to assess the relationship between the intended and perceived meanings of symbols of European integration and the very meanings of European identity and Europeanness (Chapter 8). Finally, the time-series design was needed to assess the historical progress of the emergence and development of a mass European identity over the past few decades (Chapter 7).

Conceptualisation and measurement: redefining components of political identities

The design of an original questionnaire, specifically dedicated to the measurement of European identity in its spontaneous, civic, and cultural components for the purpose of the experiment, led to the definition of a new conceptual framework and measurement strategy to capture European identity of respondents – or, indeed, political identities in general and their interaction. I proposed to distinguish between an overarching 'spontaneous' measure of identity feelings – that is, a definition of identity 'prisoner of language' and subject to variations of meaning and references – and two substantively defined components: civic and cultural (Chapter 1). Civic identity is conceived as the perception of one's belonging to a given civic community unified by common institutions, rules, and rights. Therefore, European civic identity relates to the perception of belonging to the European Union as an institutional construction and of the status of the European Union as a relevant political system for the citizen. Cultural identity is defined as the feeling of belonging to a culturally meaningful human community, that is, in its simplest expression, the perception of being closer to people within the group than to people outside the group, regardless of the real or imaginary attributes seen to define the human community in question (history, values, language, religion, culture, etc.). In the European context, cultural identity is simply the sense of closeness some citizens feel to fellow Europeans than to non-Europeans.

I also confirmed conceptually and demonstrated empirically the complementarity between various political identities. There is no conceptual reason why there should be any contradiction between a European identity and a national identity. Citizens identifying civically or culturally to Europe can at the same time regard their nation-state as another relevant political system to them and feel closer to fellow nationals, for example, than to other Europeans. In exactly the same way, national identity will not prevent citizens from feeling closer to fellow town persons than to fellow nationals from a different town. Moreover, Chapter 6 empirically shows that the European, national, regional, and local identities of citizens are positively rather than negatively correlated, and that this relation is both statistically significant and substantial across comparative contexts. The empirical results also confirmed categorically that the three components of a European identity have, indeed, a distinct reality of their own, and are also distinct from support for European integration.

Talking about Europe and Europeanness: findings from the focus group analysis

Beyond the quantitative analysis, the focus group discussions provide us with a better understanding of what citizens perceive to be the reality of Europe and of their own European identity. Moreover, they allow us to get a better sense of what respondents think of the way the media inform them about Europe, and what they associate with the symbols of the European Union (Chapter 8). The analysis of the group discussions confirms a suspicion many political scientists have held: that contemporary citizens are rather cynical, which possibly explains, in part, the gap between intended and perceived institutional messages which I comment on below.

The discussions show that citizens tend to associate ideals of peace and cosmopolitanism to the European project, and oppose them to the more 'nationalistic' or exclusive meanings of country-specific imageries. They tend to emphasise the integrative – as opposed to the co-operative – aspects of the main EU symbols. The interviews also show that the various symbols of European integration have very different levels of salience in the eyes of the public, and that the most politically oriented elements of European integration take a dominant symbolic significance in the perception of citizens. In that sense, the focus group participants identify several symbolic elements of the European project to be particularly important in their eyes. This is the case, for example, of the possibility to cross borders within the Schengen area without showing any proof of identification (Chapter 8). It is also the case of the Euro, perceived to be of greater symbolic than technical importance. It confirms the predominantly 'civic' perception of the European project, one which raises hope amongst the most sophisticated respondents that a new way to do politics can be found.

With regards to the outcomes of European integration and the information citizens receive on Europe in their daily lives, respondents express a certain level of cynicism and sophistication when it comes to assessing the reliability of the media on Europe. Apart from being sceptical about the objectivity of the mass media in general, citizens seem to expect Europe to be a topic on which news will be even more biased than average. The greatest level of suspicion was reached in the United Kingdom, even though the other countries considered in the comparative focus group discussions were not exempt from such comments.

Finally, the citizens we talked to have made it very clear what Europeanness and the concept of 'European identity' mean to them. Their comments suggest a perception far closer to the 'civic' dimension defined in Chapter 1 than to the cultural dimension. We also see that 'Europe' and 'European identity' are more often associated – at least in the West and in the current member-States to the European Union rather than to a broader Europe, reaching from the Atlantic Ocean to the Ural. To some extent, the very fact that interviewees described who, according to them, should be 'in' and 'out' of the group confirmed the overall idea that the respondents 'identify' themselves with the European cultural and political community. This is all the more interesting, with a few exceptions, that the respondents also tend to confirm that they do not perceive any contradiction between feeling European and feeling Dutch, French or British or English.

Assessing the aggregate-level emergence of a mass European identity

Finally, the analysis based on an aggregate-level evaluation of the emergence of a European identity and a time-series design results in a series of unprecedented and partly counter-intuitive findings on how a new European identity has emerged and evolved since the 1970s across European Union countries. Without a doubt, a mass European identity has emerged and progressively grown since the 1970s. At the beginning of the third millennium, European identity is already everything but the exception within European public, at least in the 15 'old' member-States. The average level of European identity of citizens across EU member-States has significantly and more or less continuously progressed between 1970 and 2000 in virtually all pre-2004 EU member states and can be expected to progress even further as the European Union is going through the symbolic stage of giving itself its first Constitution.

Second, the time-series analysis confirms the impact of institutions – including political institutions and the mass media – in the emergence of this new European identity. My findings show that the provision of new symbols of European integration has had a clear impact on the consolidation of a European identity every time they have been introduced. This confirms the theory of structuralist political thinkers and the presumption of European authorities that creating a specific European imagery would help in creating a mass European identity. In a similar manner, the analysis confirms beyond doubt that good and bad news on Europe have also had a clear impact on the evolution of mass levels of identification of citizens with Europe. They may account for short term 'accidents' in the evolution of Europeanness as a mass phenomenon without contradicting the relatively regular upwards trend of European identity across EU countries over time in the longer term.

Finally, however, the analysis also shows that levels of European identity are still very different in the various member-States. While the overall levels of citizens' identification with the European Union is now quite extensive in the countries that founded the European Communities as a cosmopolitan and pacific project and those which joined it in the period described in Chapter 4 as a time of 'citizenship construction' (in particular Belgium, Italy, France, and Spain), it is still lower in the countries that originally joined a 'technical' policy-making Europe in the 1970s, or a breathless self-restraining Europe in crisis in the mid 1990s (particularly Austria, Sweden, the United Kingdom, and Denmark). In this book, I propose a theory linking average level of European identity to the dominant 'character' of the European project at the time of joining, and also show empirically that, levels of European identity, while still very different in the 1990s, have tended to converge – at least relatively – over time.

Institutions and political identities: on the ambiguous effects of political communication

This inquiry into the emergence of a new mass political identity would not be complete without underlining that the interaction between top-down institutional attempts to mould a European identity through symbols and communication on political outcomes and the bottom-up reactions of the European public is far from simple. First, several institutional (in a broad sense) players participate in the type of messages that reach citizens from the top, and we know that European institutions, national ones, and the mass media do not always convey the same messages or pursue the same political objectives. Second, it is unclear whether political institutions and social elites can successfully influence the formation of a new political identity *the way they* want through the use and diffusion of worded (news) or non-worded messages.

While elites and institutions try to send particular messages to the public, citizens appropriate these news and symbols to associate sometimes-unpredictable images to the new political community that is being constituted. The whole symbolic and imaginary reality of the European political community is constructed and reconstructed under the perpetual interaction between political elites, the mass media, and variously and complexly socialised generations of citizens, rather than along the clear lines favoured by institutions and elites themselves. It is in this way, as was shown in Chapter 6, that symbols of the European Union have a stronger influence on the cultural identity of citizens (which primarily relates to Europe and not to the European Union[24]) rather than their civic identity, which it was primarily expected to reinforce.

Where to go from there?: First Route – findings on European identity and political identity questions

In the introduction of this book, a claim was made that rather than only being of interest to people specifically involved with research on European identity, the findings of this study, if meaningful at all, would have an impact on a much broader range of research subjects. The first claim was that any findings with regards to this model of European identity formation and evolution would affect the way political scientists can study political and social identities in general. This could even be of interest when dealing with the way policy designers try to approach the integration of new immigrants and ethnic and cultural minorities in democracies.

First and foremost, the model tested here is a model of the effects of political communication on the formation of political identities. As stated in Chapter 3, extensive literature exists on the impact of political communication on political behaviours and attitudes. This research, however, has shown that the findings of authors such as Iyengar *et al.* (1982) could be extended to a deeper and more fundamental category in terms of behavioural analysis: that of political identity. Two elements, here, are of particular interest for political scientists as well as policy designers. First, the confirmation of the role of symbolic campaigns on people's political identification with communities, as derived from Saussure's (1974) and Castoriadis's (1975) theories. Second, the confirmation that different political identities are not necessarily contradictory or perceived as such by citizens.

These findings should encourage the authorities in charge of insuring the integration of new immigrants – that is, that new immigrants will indeed develop a sense of identification with their new country in addition to the pre-existing identities linked to their personal history – to change their approach to some extent. Indeed, what has been shown in terms of symbolic impact on identity formation suggests that such campaigns can be useful, predominantly useful with regards to citizens' cultural sense of identity, while their civic identity – here the predominant target of policy makers – is predominantly affected by news and specific outcomes. Reciprocally, however, symbolic campaigns could have a much stronger effect on the way host populations could welcome the arrival of new waves of immigrants from different countries and regions. Indeed, in order to fight racism and xenophobia, it is cultural identity – largely responsible for individuals' perceptions of the border between in- and out-groups – that is primarily at stake. Cultural identity reacts more strongly to symbols, and yet, tolerance campaigns traditionally insist on 'objective' information instead, which is more likely to have an impact on citizens' civic identity (Bruter, 2005).

In this sense, and with the confirmed perception that identities are not contradictory, this research suggests a need to improve our understanding of such social phenomena as xenophobia, racism, and communitarianism. In Western liberal–democratic and open societies, these issues force us to ask ourselves new questions about what leads to the perception of a minority of individuals that various political identities are contradictory conceptually.

Where to go from there?: Second route – mass European identity and the political legitimacy of European integration

The second claim made in the introduction is that, at the individual level, European identity must have an important impact on support towards further European integration and possibly on other dependent variables of interest such as turnout for European elections, or even electoral behaviour. At the same time, at the aggregate level, the development of a mass European identity is necessary for the political legitimacy of an increasingly political process of European integration.

Again, the time-series analysis proposed has shown that in fact, a European identity has indeed emerged, over the past 30 years. This answers a deep controversy within the sub-field of Europeanists. While authors such as Duchesne and Frognier (1995) claimed that little, in terms of E.I, had European identity had emerged among the mass public – using variables from Eurobarometer, Herrmann and Brewer (2004) claim that one had emerged, but basing their argument on predominantly non-quantitative evidence. This research should add some clear empirical findings to a debate that remained unsolved because of the absence of clear, specific empirical measurement.

Moreover, the individual-level experiment immediately showed that European identity and support for European integration are at the same time correlated (which, in all logic, suggests a causal link from the former to the latter) and distinct. This conceptual and empirical distinction is particularly important, as most authors interested in 'European identity' have indeed simply tended to use support for European integration as an equivalent of identity feelings. It has been shown, here, that the relationship between the two is far more complex than this. This is all the more important when one thinks of European civic identity as what explains citizens' support for European integration in principle, when they disagree with the specific outputs of European integration. This may well explain, in recent year, the emergence of an increasing proportion of Eurobarometer respondents who keep favouring further European integration while believing that it does not, benefit them and their country any more. This is in contrast to an earlier situation when support and perceived benefits were much more strongly correlated. A distinct measure of European identity is therefore necessary as many citizens express doubts about specific European policies and institutional organisation while supporting the principle and progression of integration towards a unified European Union.

This also proves that having specific measures of European identity should be of a great interest for all of those who study European integration, particularly from a behavioural perspective. Indeed, many of the models, which use 'support for European integration' as an independent or a control variable would, in fact, make more sense theoretically if the variable used instead was European identity. In the worst cases, it could even be argued that the identified relationship between support for European integration and the dependent variable of interest is nothing but a spurious relation for models in which European identity has simply been omitted. For example, in the case of turnout in European Parliament elections, it is more logical to expect European identity – rather than support for integration – to have an impact.

It should also be particularly interesting to currently apply the bases of the model to new countries, which have recently joined (or, for some, are still in the process of joining) the European Union. Such countries could help political scientists to get a better sense of the time frame of the articulation between the support for integration and identity in a specific context.

Where to go from there?: Third Route – mass European identity model and comparative analysis

Finally, one of the most interesting findings of the model is, on the whole, the relatively low variation in the ways the model performs across European countries. None of the country dummy variables ended up being statistically significant when entered in the global time-series regression equation, and the overall 'face' analysis of the evolution of mass identity across samples yielded fairly similar pictures of the *process* of identity formation and evolution across case studies. At the same time, the analysis showed that the remaining differences in terms of the overall *levels* of European identity at the end of the 1990s literally split the European Union into two sub-groups. On the higher end of the identity scale, one finds the founding members of the European Union and the countries that joined in the 1980s enlargement waves. On the lower end of the scale, one finds the countries that joined the European Union in the 1970s and 1990s.

In Chapter 9, a theoretical suggestion is made – and remains untested for the purpose of this study – that associates national attitudes towards

European integration to that of four identifiable 'moments' of the history of European integration. These stages are those of international co-operation, policy development, institutional consolidation, and identity formation. Whether the theory is deemed credible or not, the pattern of cross-national differences is by all means too peculiar to be considered a sheer coincidence. It is all the more interesting that it contradicts that part of the literature which suggests that comparative differences are time-related in a linear way and that older means were more European. Beyond my claim that these differences are due to the perceived 'meaning' of European integration at the time, the popular decision was made to join, further systematic study of the impact of joining times on the European attitudes of citizens is needed.

Towards a better understanding of political identity formation and evolution?

Given the little attention traditionally paid by political scientists to political identities in terms of individual-level analysis, and the unreasonable amount of assumptions made by the discipline on the emergence – or absence of – a European identity over the past few decades, the research agenda of this book was unusually dense. The main model tested by this research had to do with the impact of top-down symbolic and substantive messages on individual levels of European identity of citizens, both at the individual level and at the aggregate level. However, it also seemed important – and probably necessary – to address such different questions as: what political identities mean, especially in the unique context of European integration, how to measure them, and whether such a thing as a European identity existed altogether. In this context, the conceptual, theoretical, and empirical components of the present research seemed of equal importance when trying to work out an appropriate research design and agenda.

Nevertheless, it seems that when trying to assess the outcomes and findings of the project, it is, once again, the conceptual dimension, which possibly emerges as the key to any further development of the reflexion started in this volume. In fact, having thought about what political identities and their various components are, and about how they interact, some new conceptual questions become obvious and crucial. Moreover, having shown that there is such a thing as a European identity of EU citizens, that it is both civic and cultural, and that symbolic as well as worded messages influence it, epistemological problems appear more acute than ever. Indeed, if there is such a thing as a

European identity, if it does not contradict the other political identities of citizens, and if it is mostly interpreted by citizens as a 'non-national' identity, then, what is it? In fact, if this European identity can be influenced by symbolic campaigns and the top-down messages sent by the mass media, what does this tell us about identity and its vulnerability to all forms of communication and manipulations? Should we understand, on the basis of the current study, that all aspects of human identity are as fragile as its political aspects? In fact, even within the political dimension, are all levels of political identification as volatile as the European component of our identity?

The answer to both questions is undoubtedly yes. Psychologists have told us on numerous occasions how human perceptions of one's identity can be influenced by such life 'accidents' as a change of work or a new marriage, unemployment or rape, emigration or parenthood. Identity, in its broader sense, has to do with the superimposition between the unique and time-specific perception of who we are, and the idiosyncratic – and, again, time-specific perception we have of what the world – our world – is like. Changes to either dimension are most likely to modify identity feelings – political or not. Similarly, of course, we know how political crisis or conflict will influence any element of one's political identity. This can be the case following a change of regime, a war, or a change in the level of integration of a specific group in a given community. Perceptions that internal or external components of our political community have changed are bound to modify the intensity and shape of the borders we define between 'us' and various out-groups. Therefore, a war, or racist attacks against our community, or even a political crisis will modify our sense of identification with the various political communities to which we feel we belong.

Our identities are also influenced by the way we believe that others perceive us. Racism, anti-Semitism, and xenophobia, all obviously participate in the self-perception of members of a minority. Feeling British but thinking that many other Brits do not perceive me as one of theirs makes the perception and meaning of my very Britishness very different than would be the case if I just feel British and 'typical' from the rest of the community. Have perceptions of what other Europeans feel, mutual trust, and changing history always got such an impact on identities and what is it going to mean for European identity in the coming decades for a European Union that is now more heterogeneous than ever? What will it mean also to perceptions of others, of out-groups outside of Europe. Finally, if multiple identities are compatible and mutually enriching, we must try to understand why some citizens conceive them, instead as incompatible and mutually threatening, and who these particular citizens are.

It is, therefore, the tension between permanent and evolutive components of human identity, which presents the biggest epistemological challenge to our thought. Is any element of our political identities 'fixed'? How do the fixed and evolutive components interact? Finally, how can we interpret, understand, and disentangle the life-cycle and generational components of the emergence of a mass European identity which is bound to deservedly attract enormous attention in a twenty-first century marked by perpetual demands of citizens, across borders, to reinvent citizenship and democracy themselves?

Appendices

Appendix 1: Questionnaires

These are the questionnaires given to respondents before and after their experimental treatment. All the questions designed to measure European identity are in the second questionnaire. The questionnaires were translated in French and Dutch for the relevant samples.

United Kingdom
Questionnaire I

Date:

Respondent Id:

We would like to thank you for your participation in our survey. This survey is totally anonymous and is strictly designed for academic use. It has no commercial, political or media-related purposes whatsoever. On average, the total time spent by respondents on the three parts of the survey is less than half an hour.

Please read each question and all the possible answers very carefully before answering. You might find some questions strange or redundant but we intend to use all of them so, please, answer every one, if possible.

For some questions, you will need to write down the answer. For some others, you must simply circle the answer that best corresponds to your view. Finally, in certain cases, circle all the possibilities that apply to you. We appreciate your efforts to write legibly and are grateful for your time.

Question 1: Please, indicate your age

Age: [   ] year-old.

Question 2: Please, indicate your gender
1. Female
2. Male

Question 3: What village/town/city do you come from?

Town: [   ]

County: [   ]

Question 4: Which of these academic fields best describes your major?
(Please, choose ONE ONLY)

1. Literature, Languages, Philosophy, Education, Human Sciences.
2. Mathematics, Physics, Medicine, Computer Science, Natural Sciences, Sports.
3. Social Sciences, Law, Business, Economics.

Question 5: Which of these socio-professional categories best describes the head of your family? (Please, choose ONE ONLY)

1. Farmer.
2. Factory worker, blue collar.
3. Shop owner, workman, craftsman.
4. Clerk, employee.
5. Middle-management, school-teacher, nurse.
6. Independent worker, professor, medical doctor, senior management, executive.
7. Unemployed.
8. Retired.
9. Other.

Question 6: On a left to right scale, how would you describe yourself? (Please, choose ONE ONLY)

1. Strongly left.
2. Somewhat left.
3. Moderate, slightly leaning to the left.
4. Moderate – impossible to classify.
5. Moderate, slightly leaning to the right.
6. Somewhat right.
7. Strongly right.

Question 7: Which of the following newspapers do you read at least twice a month? (Please, choose ALL that apply)

1. The Times/Sunday Times
2. The Independent/Independent on Sunday
3. The Guardian/Observer
4. The Daily Telegraph/Sunday Telegraph
5. The Sun
6. The Mirror
7. The Daily Mail
8. The Financial Times
9. The Daily Express
10. A local/regional newspaper.
11. Other national newspaper.

Question 8: In general, are you in favour or against the efforts being made to unify Europe? (Please, choose ONE ONLY)

1. Very much in favour.
2. Somewhat in favour.
3. Neither in favour nor against / I don't know.
4. Somewhat against.
5. Very much against.

Question 9: Please, look at these people. No 1 is standing still while No. 7 is running as fast as possible. Which best corresponds to what you would like for the European Union? (Please, choose ONE ONLY)

Question 10: *Generally speaking, do you think that the United Kingdom's membership of the EU has been very positive, somewhat positive, neither positive nor negative, somewhat negative or very negative? (Please, choose ONE ONLY)*

1. Very positive
2. Somewhat positive
3. Neither positive nor negative
4. Somewhat negative
5. Very negative

Question 11: *Have you ever lived in another European country for more than 2 months? (Please, choose ONE ONLY)*

1. No, never.
2. Yes for 2 months to 1 year.
3. Yes, for more than a year.

Question 12: *In the past five years, have you travelled to another European country? (Please, choose ONE ONLY)*

1. Yes, three times or more.
2. Yes, once or twice.
3. No.

Question 13: *In general, would you say that you are satisfied with the way democracy works in the United Kingdom? (Please, choose ONE ONLY) Are you ...?*

1. Very dissatisfied.
2. Somewhat dissatisfied.
3. Neither satisfied nor dissatisfied/I don't know.
4. Somewhat satisfied.
5. Very satisfied.

Question 14: *In general, would you say that you are satisfied with your life? (Please, choose ONE ONLY) Are you ...?*

1. Very satisfied.
2. Somewhat satisfied.
3. Neither satisfied nor dissatisfied / I don't know.
4. Somewhat dissatisfied.
5. Very dissatisfied.

Question 15: Here is a list of the main political parties that compete in major elections in Britain, which would you say you feel closest too? (Please, choose ONE ONLY)

1. Labour
2. Liberal-Democrat
3. Conservative
4. UK Independence Party
5. Green Party
6. Scottish National Party (SNP)
7. Plaid Cymru
8. Ulster Unionist Party (UUP)
9. Sinn Fein
10. Social Democratic & Labour Party Ulster (SDLP)
11. Ulster Democratic Unionist Party (DUP)

Question 16: Did anyone in your family come from another European country?

1. Yes.
2. No.

Question 17: Do you speak any foreign language? (Please, choose ONE ONLY)

1. Yes, 3 or more foreign languages.
2. Yes, 2 foreign languages.
3. Yes, 1 foreign language.
4. No.

United Kingdom
Questionnaire II

Date:

Respondent Id:

Question 1: In general, would you say that you consider yourself a citizen of Europe? (Please, choose ONE ONLY)

6. Yes, very much.
7. Yes, to some extent.
8. I don't know.
9. Not really.
10. Not at all.

Question 2: Since 1985, citizens from all the countries of the European Union have had a common 'European' passport on which both the name of their country and 'European Union' is written. Do you think that this is a good thing? (Please, choose ONE ONLY)

6. Yes, a very good thing.
7. Yes, a rather good thing.
8. It doesn't matter at all.
9. No, a rather bad thing.
10. No, a very bad thing.

Question 3: Here is a list of some of the games that will be featured at the next Women's Volley-Ball World Championship in June. Could you say which team you would rather won each of these games? (Please choose ONE team for each of the four games)

A – Ghana vs Denmark
3. Ghana
4. Denmark

B – Italy vs USA
3. Italy
4. USA

C – Spain vs China
3. Spain
4. China

D – Saudi Arabia vs Republic of Ireland
3. Saudi Arabia
4. Republic of Ireland

Question 4: What would best describe your reaction if you saw someone burning a European flag? (Please, choose ONE ONLY)

5. I would be shocked and hurt.
6. I would be shocked but not hurt.
7. I would not mind.
8. I would be happy.

Question 5: What would best describe your reaction if you saw someone burning the Union Jack? (Please, choose ONE ONLY)

5. I would be shocked and hurt.
6. I would be shocked but not hurt.
7. I would not mind.
8. I would be happy.

Question 6: On a scale of one to seven, one meaning that you do not identify with Europe at all, and seven meaning that you identify very strongly with Europe, would you say that you ...? (Please, circle ONE NUMBER ONLY)

1. (Do not identify with Europe at all)
2.
3.
4.
5.
6.
7. (Identify very strongly with Europe)

Question 7: Applying the same scale as in question 6 to Britain, would you say that you ...? (Please, circle ONE NUMBER ONLY)

1. (Do not identify with Britain at all)
2.
3.
4.
5.
6.
7. (Identify very strongly with Britain)

Question 8: Still applying the same scale as in question 6 to your region, would you say that you ...? (Please, circle ONE NUMBER ONLY)

1. (Do not identify with your region at all)
2.
3.
4.
5.
6.
7. (Identify very strongly with your region)

Question 9: Still applying the same scale as in question 6 to your city/town/ village, would you say that you ...? (Please, circle ONE NUMBER ONLY)

1. (Do not identify with your city/town/village at all)
2.
3.
4.
5.
6.
7. (Identify very strongly with your city/town/village)

Question 10: Some say that in spite of their numerous differences, Europeans share a 'common heritage' that makes them slightly closer to one another than they are to, say, Japanese or Chilean people. Do you ...? (Please, choose ONE ONLY)

6. Strongly disagree with this view.
7. Somewhat disagree with this view.
8. Neither agree nor disagree with this view / I don't know.
9. Somewhat agree with this view.
10. Strongly agree with this view.

Question 11: A group of athletes from all the countries of the European Union have proposed that at the Sydney Olympics, whenever an athlete/team from the European Union wins a gold medal, the 'Ode to Joy', the European anthem, should be played after, and in addition to, their national anthem. Do you think that this would be a good idea? (Please, choose ONE ONLY)

6. Yes, a very good idea.
7. Yes, a rather good idea.
8. Neither a good idea nor a bad idea.
9. No, a rather bad idea.
10. No a very bad idea.

Question 12: When the heads of state/government of a European Union country (such as Queen Elizabeth II, Tony Blair, the French President or the German Chancellor) make a speech on TV, both the national flag and the European one appear behind them. Do you think that this is a good thing? (Please, choose ONE ONLY)

6. Yes, a very good thing.
7. Yes, a rather good thing.
8. Neither a good thing nor a bad thing / It doesn't matter at all.
9. No, a rather bad thing.
10. No, a very bad thing.

Question 13: Does being a 'Citizen of the European Union' mean anything for you? (Please, choose ONE ONLY)

4. Yes, it means a lot.
5. Yes, it means something.
6. No, it does not mean anything.

Question 14: If you answered yes to question 13, would you say that, among other things, it means ...? (Please, choose AS MANY AS APPLY)

1. A shared European heritage.
2. The right to vote in the European Parliament elections.
3. Common institutions.
4. A common European history.
5. A common European flag, European anthem, European passport.
6. The right to travel to another EU country without passing through customs.
7. The right to travel to another EU country without having to show your passport/ID.
8. Some common ideals.
9. To be a member of the 'European family'.

Question 15: Would you say that you feel closer to fellow Europeans than, say, to Chinese, Russian, or American people? (Please, choose ONE ONLY)

1. Yes, strongly.
2. Yes, to some extent.
3. I don't know.
4. No, not really.
5. No, not at all.

Appendix 2: The Experimental Design

General description

The test used is a survey-based, between subjects, comparative experiment. It is intended to measure the effect on individuals of two experimental variables as well as two non-experimental independent variables. The two experimental variables, directly derived from the theory detailed in Chapter 2, are exposure to symbols of European integration and exposure to good/bad news on European integration. The non-experimental independent variables of interest are European experience, in its various components, and country. The surveys also allow us to test for a variety of control variables, such as support for European integration, political preferences, usual media exposure, size of community, etc. The experiment is conducted in parallel in three countries: France, the United Kingdom, and the Netherlands. The total sample is 212 respondents divided in the three national sub-samples.

The Experimental schedule and the pre-test strategy

The experiment is conducted in four steps: (1) a pre-test questionnaire, (2) the administration of the stimulus (in one shot), (3) a post-test questionnaire, (4) focus groups of four to five people with about 15 to 20 per cent of the respondents selected randomly. The total length of the first three steps is about 30 minutes (about seven minutes for each questionnaire and 15 minutes to read the stimulus), and each focus group lasted about 30 minutes.

The first questionnaire is not a real pre-test, mostly because the short time gap between the administration of the pre and post-test questionnaires would present a risk of rationalisation of their answers by the respondents. Instead, a surrogate dependent variable is used in the pre-test according to the theoretical assumptions made in Part I. The surrogate is a measure of the support for European integration of citizens. The theoretical framework justifying this choice is explained in the summary model in Chapter 2, Figure 2.1. It is based, in fact, on the assumption that the correlation between the level of European identity and support for European integration of an individual at a given time must be highly correlated. This expectation will be proven empirically in the next chapter to the extent that the correlation between support for European integration at time t_0 and European identity at time t_1 is high (0.36). The model drawn in Figure 2.1, because of its assumptions in terms of causal relations, justifies this choice of surrogate. Indeed, it implies that the unmeasured support for European integration at time 1 will necessarily be *more highly* correlated with European identity than support for European integration at time 0 since I could summarise the model of

Support for European integration by the following equation:

$$Y'_1 = \beta_1 Y'_0 + \beta_2 Y_1 + u + \epsilon$$

The experimental treatment

The main independent variables of interest in the experiment are the two aspects of the type of experimental treatment received by a respondent. These two aspects are good or bad news on European integration and photographs of symbols of integration or placebo. In fact, the experimental treatment consists of a fifteen-minute exposure to a two-page extract from a fake magazine. Each extract is composed of three news articles presenting either (false) good news or (false) bad news on European integration and of three photographs representing either symbols of European integration or placebos (i.e., photographs not having anything to do with European integration. This creates four possibilities, four 'cells' of treatment, represented in Table A.1, to which respondents were assigned randomly in each location.

The assignment to each group of treatment was totally random and made in such a way that samples would be similar in size for each group in each location, except for mathematical impossibilities (when the total number was not a multiple of 4).

To insure the comparability of the experiment across samples and locations, it was also crucial to design the extracts for each location in such a way that they be as close as possible in terms of expected stimulation effects and, at the same time, fully respect local specificity. The same is true of the choice of photographs included with the various extracts. Finally, it was also important to design the articles in each location so that the good news would be as good as the bad news

Table A.1 Cells of treatment

Images article	Symbols of European integration	Placebo images
Positive	Group 1	Group 2
Negative	Group 3	Group 4

Table A.2 Description of photographs

EU symbols photographs	Neutral placebo photographs
1) Photograph representing European flag	1) Photograph representing politicians
2) Photograph representing EU passport	2) Photograph representing students
3) Photograph representing Euro notes	3) Photograph representing landscape

Table A.3   Contents of news articles by country of experiment

Country	Positive articles	Negative articles
United Kingdom	– Good economic news. Airbus launches A3XX with commands and creates factories and jobs in Britain. – Money for British exchange – New 'Gallery of Europe' in the Millenium Dome financed By EU and free for EU citizens.	– Foreign policy failure in CDR – EU for tuition fees. – EU forbids Sainsbury's expansion in the world.
France	– Good economic news., Euro Airbus launches A3XX with Commands and creates factories and jobs in France. – Progress of inter-university exchange programs. – New 'Gallery of Europe' in Strasbourg financed by EU and free for EU citizens.	– Foreign policy failure in CDR – Reduction of help to inter-university exchange programs. – EU forbids Renault's expansion in the world.
Netherlands	– Former Dutch Prime Minister Successfully appointed to solve Indonesia crisis. – Progress of inter-university exchange programs. – Economic prosperity of the EU.	– Failure of CFSP in human rights violating CDR. – Reduction of help to inter-university exchange programs. – EU blames Netherlands on liberal drug policy.

were bad to respect a symmetry of treatments. The types of photographs and articles used in each case and each location are reported in Tables A.2 and A.3.

The respondents

In the United Kingdom and France, the respondents were all willing to participate in the experiment. In the Netherlands, they were groups recruited through the University of Amsterdam. In the United Kingdom and the Netherlands, the respondents were all students, in France, the sample was a virtually equal mixture of students and others.

In every case, respondents were thanked for their participation with a voucher for a drink in a bar. The actual value of the incentive was low (that is, about €1.50 = $1.50/£ 1.00) but seemed necessary to encourage a sufficient number of people to volunteer and ask them to answer the questionnaires and read the extracts with particular care. The very high reliability of the answers and remarkably low number of missing answers (see Chapter 5) probably had to do, among other things, with the impact of a material incentive on the care for the respondents.

In all cases (whether the respondents were 'captive' or voluntaries), the assistants never mentioned the actual purpose of the design nor its experimental nature at the beginning of the experiment but, instead, mention 'a survey on citizens' perceptions of how the media inform us on Europe'. They also talked of the incentive and explained that the survey had no commercial purpose, and was anonymous. Even though ethical considerations would normally lead us to keep respondents informed of the purpose of a study, it has been generally assumed by political scientists as well as psychologists that mentioning the purpose of an experiment would clearly bias its results. It has also been generally argued and accepted that not mentioning explicitly the exact purpose of a study was ethically acceptable in modern social sciences under some conditions (e.g., Norris *et al.*, 1999, Evans and Norris, 1999). In this case, the purpose mentioned (1) is not untrue, (2) is close enough to the whole truth, (3) is used in a case where the experiment does not seem to have the potential to harm respondents in any remote way, which made us comfortable using it. Moreover, all respondents were informed in detail on what the exact purpose and nature of the design was after the experiment was run and also that the news they had read was false.

When respondents were students, it was attempted to eliminate or diminish the risk of subject bias by only recruiting a limited number of respondents from 'risky' disciplines such as social sciences and humanities, except in the Netherlands. Major was asked in the survey and used as a control variable, however, without being correlated at all with any of the variables of interest. If anything, when the models are run only with the sub-sample of social scientists, the results are slightly less powerful than with the whole sample, which simply transforms the Dutch sample in a 'harder' sample from the point of view of the experimental results.

Experimental process

The experiment was administered to groups of 10 to 20 persons on average. In every case, the experiment was administered by at least one native assistant. All questionnaires and articles were written in the local language to avoid any related bias. An equal proportion of respondents of all cells of treatment were included in each group to avoid the possibility of group effects. To avoid confusions, the questionnaires were printed on four different colour papers and a corresponding mark was put on each fake magazine extract. If respondents asked why they were given questionnaires of different colours, they were told clearly that they were related to the newspaper their extract was from.

Respondents were asked not to talk together during the whole process and were subjected to a very specific timing for each step of the experiment. They were first given six minutes to answer the first questionnaires that were then collected when the extracts were handed out. They had ten minutes to read those before they were collected and the second questionnaires handed in. These were collected after six minutes and the vouchers given to the respondents together with the post-experimental briefing. Timings were calculated using pilots (that are not used) to give enough time to respondents to force them to read the extracts and fill the questionnaires in carefully while avoiding any time of inactivity.

Respondents were not allowed to rush any of the steps and were asked to try to answer all questions as far as possible.

The questionnaires

The questions used to measure the dependent variable are detailed more precisely in Chapter 4. The totality of the post-test questionnaire was dedicated to the measurement of the dependent variable. The two questionnaires are reproduced in Appendix 1. The pre-test questionnaire, however, was designed to measure a certain number of independent and control variables. The variables targeted first included the European experience of respondents (experience of having lived in another European country, travelled to other European countries, having some family from another European country or speaking foreign languages). They also included their pre-test support for European integration, their place of origin, gender, major, the occupation of their head of family, political preferences, ideology, media readership, age, and a few other variables.

The assistants were not allowed to answer about any of the questions asked, or, for that matter, any question about where the articles came from, and so on. A few pilot additional questions were asked in some of the local sub-sample. For example, the French sample asked whether they had ever lived in a non-European country in addition to the traditional question on living in a European country. French and Dutch samples also asked in which country they had lived if they said they had lived abroad. Differences due to translation were kept to a minimum as far as possible.

No major, significant, and unexpected problem was mentioned by any of the assistants regarding the experimental process with all groups. At the end of the experiment, just before the post-experiment debriefing (after, in the Dutch case), the group was asked whether there were any volunteers for a half-hour focus group, for which people would be given a second drink voucher. Except in the Dutch case, the post-experiment debriefing then happened during the focus group.

Focus groups

In every location, two to three focus groups were run with four to eight respondents, each. In each group, roughly the same proportion of people exposed to each stimulus were included, and at least one respondent from each stimulus group. Group discussions normally lasted between 30 and 45 minutes and were animated by one person. The focus groups were used as a complement to the far more 'impersonal' experimental design and were designed to look quite informal and 'free' in spite of a very precise minimum agenda. In addition to a common 'pilot' function leading to a few questions being asked to all groups, the focus groups had three main goals. When three focus groups were available, one was centred on each purpose. When only two focus groups were available, several lines of questions were then asked to a given group.

All focus groups were first asked for their reactions about the questionnaires, photographs, and articles, and if anything was unclear with them. The group was then de-briefed about the articles being fake and asked whether they were credible. The second part of the debriefing – was about the real purpose and principle of the experiment and were then asked for their reactions. Then, commenced the group-specific questions.

The first track of questioning was about symbols of European integration, their role, effect, and the way they were perceived. Participants were asked what symbols of Europe they knew before the experiment. They were asked which symbols they thought people knew in general. They were then asked what the various symbols evoked for them, and how they compared with their national equivalents. Following this, they were asked what they felt when exposed to the various symbols of Europe in real life and whether they thought it had any effect on people in general. The rest of the discussion varied with the participants' answers.

The second perspective had to do with news on European integration. Participants were asked what they thought about the way the various media informed them on Europe, and why. They were asked if they thought the contents of news on Europe had an influence on them, the people they know, or citizens in general. They were also asked to compare the way they are informed on Europe to the way they are informed on other issues. Here again, the contents of the discussion throughout the focus group determined the further directions of the discussion.

The third track was to ask participants what was their personal experience of Europe, the experience of Europe of people they knew, and what they thought of it. People were asked about living in other European countries, travelling to other European countries, meeting with fellow Europeans, noticing similarities and differences. The persons in charge of running the focus groups were asked not to discourage the statement of prejudices or wrong statements about living in Europe and with Europeans since those were of obvious interest to us. The direction of the other questions was prompted by the talk of the participants.

To conclude, the last goal for all groups was to make respondents discuss more widely the notion of European identity. They were asked what they thought it was, if they thought it actually means something, and whether they thought a European identity has indeed emerged, if it is more a 'European' or a 'European Union' identity, if it involves some sub-categories of the population more than others and why. Overall, the main goals of the focus group design were therefore to gain some feedback on the experimental design and material to be sure it captured what was intended; to confront respondents directly with the purpose of the experiment (effect of good/bad news and symbols of European unification on individual-level European identity) after having let them in 'darkness'; to make them discuss the main aspects of the theories developed in this research; to capture any other message the respondents wanted to convey whether it would be used in the analysis.

Focus group discussions were recorded for further analysis and translated literally. Respondents were told that this would be the case. To be reassured about that, we insisted on the exclusive scientific purpose of the study and its anonymous character and 'broke the ice' for the first four or five minutes before beginning to ask truly relevant questions.

Technical details

The United Kingdom experiment, pilot, and focus groups were run between 4 March and 5 April 2000. The Dutch tests were conducted between 13 and

17 April 2000, and the French ones between 18 and 25 April 2000. There were 97 respondents in France, 60 in the Netherlands, and 55 in the United Kingdom, for a total of 212. Three focus groups were run in the United Kingdom, three in France, and two in the Netherlands with a total of 12 participants in the United Kingdom, 13 in the Netherlands and 16 in France. Prior to the first test, a pre-experiment pilot was run in the United Kingdom with four people for comparison of different questions, time measures, and so on. Before all focus groups, people responsible to run them were briefed and given a track sheet of the various questions to include in the discussion even though they were encouraged to let the discussion flow as naturally as possible and not be too keen on a certain order. The contents of the post-experiment debriefing were also explained very specifically. The Dutch focus groups were not taped but noted down literally.

Appendix 3: The Time-Series Analysis Design

This appendix is dedicated to the design of an aggregate-level test of the combined dynamic impact of symbols of European integration, perceptions of Europe, and institutional inertia on the emergence of a mass European identity between 1970 and 2000. The chapter is dedicated to both the design and the measurement problems encountered with this part of the analysis. It is broken down in three sections:

- The design, level of analysis, and data-set used;
- The measurement of the dependent variable;
- An analysis of the univariate distribution of the dependent variable, in both general and comparative terms.

The design of the aggregate-level test and the data used

Chapter 3 introduced and summarised the specific model, which must be tested in this third part of the analysis. Like the individual-level model, the expected pattern of aggregate-level identity formation is dynamic. Unlike it, however, it implies timely fixed, predictable, and generalisable impacts of the three aggregate-level independent variables of interest on mass levels of European identity. In other words, the level of the independent variables ceased to be arbitrary and theoretical to become a measurable historical reality.

Unlike the design of Part II, the first goal is, therefore, to capture a regular, general, and representative trend of the aspects of European public opinion and events over time, which will be needed to proceed to the statistical analysis of the model. Undoubtedly, as far as the public opinion side is concerned, the best of such evaluation is provided by the Eurobarometer European public opinion survey series. Historical and institutional events and predictors will then be easily plugged in the model.

The universe and level of analysis

The model, concerns the whole territory of the European Community/European Union from 1970 (when the first Eurobarometer survey was conducted) to 2000 (when the last Eurobarometer survey that could be used at the time of writing this work was published). It is based on an aggregate-level theory, dynamic, and relying on certain independent variables that will dictate the level of analysis of the study.

Indeed, in the aggregate model I want to test, all relevant independent variables are only conceivable at the aggregate level. However, all three independent variables will certainly assume different values for different national (and occasionally sub-national) sub-samples. Indeed, to start with, the symbols of European integration have not completely emerged at the same time in the whole European sample. As shown in Chapter 9, the Day of Europe or the European passport, for example, were not introduced at the same time across all European countries. Similarly, some symbols such as free border passages for citizens do not apply equally everywhere (the Schengen agreements only apply to 11 of the 15 member-States of the European Union). As far as news and specific perceptions of Europe are concerned, they must be assumed, as explained in Chapter 2, and as shown again in Chapter 7, at least to a certain extent, to be nation-specific. Finally, the level of institutional inertia will be directly dependent on the duration of membership of a given state in the European Union, which varies according to the date of their joining.

All this means that different states should represent different cases. At the same time, because of historical differences, it seems important to separate the cases of East and West Germany because of significant differences in institutional inertia and average scores of support for European integration. It also appears to be useful to differentiate between Great Britain and Northern Ireland because of significantly different scores of support for European integration and economic and political situations. That means that the unit of analysis will be based on 17 national (or, in 4 cases, sub-national) systems.

The second component is temporal. The number of Eurobarometer surveys to be run in the course of one year has varied over time between one (or nought) and three. Eurobarometer surveys have normally been administered once a year in the early 1970s, and then either twice or thrice a year thereafter. Not all the relevant questions needed to derive levels of European identity have been available in every survey, but they were always available at least once a year over the time period concerned (except for 1972 and 1974 in which there was no Eurobarometer survey organised). It is therefore logical to use years as the natural time point and basis for the unit of analysis. Moreover, this allows us to use the mean scores for the various Eurobarometer published in one year and, therefore, limit the problems that are linked to the use of a well-known reliability problem of Eurobarometer surveys, especially in countries like Portugal and Greece. Countries will be entered as new cases from when the first Eurobarometer survey was available with results for them or when they joined the European project, whichever came later, until and including 2000. This means that the final level of analysis of the test will have to be a given country at a given time. The number of cases in the final analysis will have to be countries × time points available with a measure of the dependent variable. That means that:

- Unit of analysis = Political system × year
- Number of cases = 349

The dataset

As explained above, Eurobarometer surveys are administered twice a year in the whole European Union since 1970. Some questions are asked regularly – particularly questions over respondents' support for European integration and various political, social and demographic control variables. Other questions, on the other hand, including the very few questions ever asked to (imperfectly) measure the European identity of respondents, have only been asked occasionally, and, in any case, not often enough to allow for a test of their evolution over time with a sufficient number of time points.

The first challenge in the design of the test is, therefore, to find a satisfactory and reliable measurement strategy for the dependent variable, of which I do not have any direct measure. The artificially created measure must be available with enough time points for a comprehensive test of the hypotheses. A second important element is the transformation of the original individual-level data into aggregate level time-series trends to fit the unit of analysis of this section. I build a test for an aggregate-level model while the data I have are primarily gathered for individual-level analysis and my dependent variable intrinsically an individual level element. I therefore need to bridge the gap between these individual-level elements and the aggregate level research design and theory tested by this part of the research. That also means that the test needs to be operationalised in several very distinct albeit quite simple steps.

First, I needed to find a way to measure the average level of European identity at a given time in a given country, through the aggregation of individual-level measures. Then, I shall have to code the values of the three independent variables of interest for each case. Then, only, I shall be able to proceed with the actual statistical analysis of my model of European identity. A fourth possible independent variable, following the reasons proposed in Part II, is an interaction between the symbols and news variables. There are two possible strategies of derivation of the dependent variable, both of which deserve to be considered carefully, given the absence of direct measure of the variable in the database used. The first strategy to try to assess the level of European identity of individual respondents and, then, to aggregate it, would imply the creation of a satisfactory instrumental variable that will be used as a surrogate of European identity.

For the test of the experimental design, I used support for European integration as a surrogate for pre-test European identity, in spite of clear conceptual and empirical differences between the two variables. I also showed in Chapter 5 that a certain number of independent social, demographic, and political predictors are correlated with the individuals' level of European identity. These predictors, however, did not explain much variance in European identity. Moreover, it would be problematic to create an instrument of European identity on the basis of the results of the experiment. Indeed, the sample I used was not representative on at least two grounds. First of all, only three countries were included in the experimental analysis, which does not account for possible comparative differences. Second of all, even the French, Dutch, and British sample were obviously not representative of the general population of their countries, so that the results cannot be generalised to create instrumental variables. The second possible strategy, and the one which will be used in this analysis, implies the residualisation on various predictors of support for European integration, consistently with the model depicted in Chapter 6 and the insights of Chapter 2. In Chapter 2, the global 'map' proposed made European identity an independent variable that partly caused support for European integration. Support for European integration was, therefore, a function of European identity and of some other social, demographic, and political factors partly time-specific and partly fixed for a given individual. It is therefore clear, reasoning backwards, that if I can 'clean' support for European integration of the influence of these 'irrelevant' factors (for the purpose of a study on identity), I will theoretically obtain an acceptable measure of the level of European identity of a given individual. In the second section of this chapter, I shall determine the most appropriate way to residualise support for

European integration for that purpose. In the other three sections of the chapter, I shall determine the coding strategies for the three independent variables of interest in the model.

Determining average levels of European identity: a residual model

The first step of the analysis is to create a unified index of support for European integration using the data available in the cumulative file and later Eurobarometer. As explained in the previous section, the choice made here is to approximate the dependent variable through a residualisation of an index of support for European integration on various individual-level and aggregate-level predictors.

The index of support for European integration is the mean of the only two questions on that matter asked in every Eurobarometer survey since 1970. One measures how favourable a respondent feels towards European unification and the second assesses how beneficial this unification process has been until the time of the interview according to the respondent. The two variables are rescaled on a 0–4 scale with roughly similar standard deviations and are simply mean-indexed.

The index of these two variables constitutes the operational measure of support for European integration that I will have to 'clean' of the effect of irrelevant predictors of support for European integration to obtain my approximate measure of European identity. Those will then be averaged by case (country × time-point) to create the dependent variable used in this analysis.

I use two sorts of predictors in the regression that will help us to approximate the average level of European identity of citizens of a given country at a given time: individual-level predictors and aggregate-level predictors. The residualisation is built in two steps with these two series of predictors. I start with the individual-level predictors and will only go on with the aggregate level predictors after aggregating the data (since the same values will be applicable to all the respondents that will be merged in a given case).

The first step of residualisation is on the individual-level predictors of support. These largely include predictors of self-interest and various social, demographic, and political predictors, which should not have any particular relevance in the European identity models tested in Chapter 6. The demographic and social predictors of support for European integration include age, income, gender, education, social class, religiosity, social class, and size of community. The political predictors include ideology, satisfaction with democracy, anticipation of future situation, fear of war, and index of post-materialism. The basis for using all of them can be found in the existing literature, including Duchesne and Frognier (1995), Eichenberg and Richard (1993), Gabel (1994), Bruter (2000a), etc.

Of course, some of those predictors should be expected to have an impact on European identity. This is the case, for example, of education, if only through the impact of speaking foreign languages, as evidenced in Chapter 6. We may expect better educated people to have a greater sense of the shared historical and artistic heritage of Europeans, a higher propensity to think more abstractly about the idealistic elements of the European project, and so on. However, given the format of operationalisation of the dependent variable I have to take this 'cautious' approach that will lead to the cleanest possible measurement of the dependent variable. The downside, obviously, is that it will deprive us of some legitimate variance in the dependent variable of interest, therefore undermining the empirical potential of the model that is tested in Chapter 8. This first regression of support for European integration on a reduced set of independent predictors has a limited R^2 of 0.06 on the whole. The regression results are reported in Table A.4. Given the nature of the model (and the fact that it does not include any aggregate-level independent variable as yet, and particularly not country dummy variables or year), this result is far from negligible. Overall, the social predictors are better than the political ones except for ideology. The unstandardised residuals are kept and then aggregated within each case of the aggregate-level analysis, that is for a sample defined by a country of residence and a year of interview (using, of course, the necessary weights).

The aggregation leads to a new sample of 349 cases with an aggregate average residual for each of them, which represents the starting measure of European identity. Sixteen countries are represented in the dataset (Great Britain and Northern Ireland are differentiated as their scores are significantly different over time). Scores are attributed for every year between either 1970 or the time when a country joined the European Communities (whichever came later) and 2000. No results were available for 1972 and 1974. Results represent the average of the various Eurobarometers published in the same year. After aggregation, the next step consists of a second phase of residualisation through the regression of the averaged residuals on aggregate-level independent predictors of support for European integration. Those are derived from existing scholarly work but will exclude, of course, time and place, which determine the cases of the sample.

One of the main theories that relate support for European integration with aggregate-level independent variables is derived from Franklin and Wlezien (1997). The two authors showed that overall, the evolution of support for European integration over time has been strongly correlated with that of the

Table A.4 Approximation of European identity by residualisation: step 1: regression of support for European integration

Variable	b (s.e.)	β
Ideology (self placement)	0.02 (0.00)	0.05***
Satisfaction with democracy	−0.12 (0.00)	−0.08***
Anticipation of future year sit	−0.13 (0.00)	−0.05***
Evaluation of war risks	−0.07 (0.01)	−0.02***
Religiosity	−0.08 (0.00)	−0.04***
Age	0.01 (0.00)	0.02***
Sex	−0.14 (0.00)	−0.06***
Income	−0.07 (0.00)	0.06***
Education	0.05 (0.00)	0.13***
Size of community	−0.05 (0.00)	−0.04***
Post-materialism	0.02 (0.00)	0.01***
Social class	0.08 (0.00)	0.03***
Constant	3.38 (0.02)	
R^2	*0.06*	

Notes: N = 452187; ***: sig. <0.001; **: sig. <0.01; *: sig. <0.05.

economic situation, as measured by the misery index. There seems to be, however, no theoretical reasons why the economic situation should have an impact on the level of European identity (as opposed to support for integration) of European citizens. On the contrary, the hierarchy, mentioned in Chapter 1, between identity, values and beliefs, attitudes, and behaviours, suggests that the economic situation should only affect lower-order attributes of one's political stances, rather than their identity. It seems important, therefore, in the second step of the construction of the dependent variable, to regress the first step residuals on the economic situation of the year for the country of interest. Like Franklin and Wlezien, and for the same reasons, the objective economic situation of the country will be operationalised by the misery index, that is, the sum of the inflation rate and the average unemployment rate of the year.

As a reminder, one of the main reasons to use this form of operationalisation of the economic situation with regards to economic theory is its reliance on the Philips curve. This curve, used in the 1970s to predict the effect of economic policy, then heavily criticised by a majority of economists, and was finally used again after a significant re-interpretation of its bases by Friedman. The curve presents economic policy as the arbitration between two possible priorities: lower inflation or higher growth (or lower unemployment). Public authorities will choose a point of preference on the given indifference curve. The 'level' of the curve itself is representative of the overall economic situation of the country at the time considered. The statistics used are the OECD ones to respect the methodological consistency of the sources throughout times and countries (national statistics offices have used different calculation systems for inflation and unemployment over times and locations).

The regression of the individual-level constructed aggregated residuals on the misery index show some clear but not overwhelming effect of the economy on support for European integration, as illustrated by Table A.5. The misery index explained about 5 per cent of the variance in the residualised dependent variable.

The results of this second step of the residualisation process may be partly explained by the amount of variance in misery indices that is simply related to country differences as shown by Table A.6. This shows when the regression is carried out within – and not across – countries, with results boosted to a level of about 0.20. The levels of variance of the two variables are also so different that it creates a statistical artefact bound to reduce the empirically observed explanatory power of the misery index over the period. The important element, however, is that at this point, we have a dependent variable that has been cleaned for all

Table A.5   Second step of the residualisation of the aggregate dependent variable

Variable	b (s.e.)	β
Misery index	2123.4** (43.8)	20.21
Constant	1575.4** (467.5)	
R^2	0.05	

Notes: $N = 349$; **: sig.<0.01; *: sig.<0.05.

Table A.6   Coding of the 'symbols' variable

Symbol	Value = 0	Value = 1
European flag	All countries until 1972	All countries from 1973
Direct elections of Euro. Parl.	All countries until 1978	All countries from 1979
European anthem	All countries until 1984	All countries from 1985
European passport	All countries until 1984	All countries from 1985
Day of Europe	All countries until 1984	All countries from 1985
No customs control	All countries until 1992	All countries from 1993
Schengen agreement	All countries until 1994 Italy until 1996 UK, Ireland, Greece, Sweden, Denmark, Finland as yet	France, Belgium, Netherlands, Germany, Luxembourg, Spain, Portugal, Austria from 1995 Italy from 1997
Euro	All countries until 1998 Greece until 1999 UK, Sweden, Denmark as yet	France, Belgium, Netherlands, Italy, Germany, Luxembourg, Spain, Portugal, Ireland, Finland, Austria from 1999 Greece from 2000

Notes: The total score for the variable 'symbols' is the sum of individual scores for each of the variables included in Table 8.2. For example, in the case of France in 1994, the score for the variable will be 6, that is: 1 for flag, 1 for European Parliament, 1 for anthem, 1 for passport, 1 for Day of Europe, 1 for the absence of customs control, 0 for Schengen and 0 for the Euro. The score of the same country will be 7 in 1995 (1 for Schengen instead of 0), but still 6 for the UK.

short-term effects and can be used in my aggregate-level evolutionary model of the emergence of a European identity over the past 30 years.

The dependent variable is finally recoded linearly on a scale of 0 to 1 to increase the direct readability of the results. On the whole, about 25 per cent of the original variance in support for European integration has been excluded by the residualisation process.

Using a residualised variable: problems and solutions

By nature, using an indirect measure for any form of variable will always cause a certain number of validity concerns. I have tried to address the main among these doubts as transparently as possible. Another series of problems, however, arises from the use of the imperfect variable in any form of model. In the present case, my indirect measure of European identity is derived from direct measures of support for European integration. The measure has been aggregated, and 'cleaned' for number of polluting effects, but what about the remaining independent variables, in the model, which might be estimated in a biased way in the next step of the analysis? In this case, an estimate will be wrong if one attributes to a given dependent variable an explanatory effect on European identity, which should, indeed, be a direct effect of the variable measuring support for European integration per se. To determine whether this is likely to be the case, I need to refer to the enlarged model of Chapter 2, presented in Figure 2.2, where European identity is also modelled endogenously in relation to support for European integration.

Coding of symbols of European integration

We have seen, through the brief historical and analytic interpretation of the emergence of symbols of the European Union in Chapter 4 how symbols of integration have appeared and progressed as markers of a new civic and cultural reality. It is now easier to propose a coding strategy for symbols of European integration in my aggregate-level model of the emergence of a mass European identity over the past 30 years. My coding strategy consists of including only those symbols that have been shown to have a strong purposive component and a high level of visibility within the European Union. Is considered a visible symbol one, which is seemingly known by about half of the European Union population.

It is difficult to code the impact of these new symbols, which should have a 'graphic' effect in the model. There are, at least, four major problems to consider prior to the coding of the 'symbols' variable. The first problem is that while the 'graphic' effect should be symbolised by a steep short increase in the average level of European identity of respondents, the effect of new symbols should have a persistent effect over years after its introduction. Another problem is the dating of the expected effects of the introduction of symbols. Should symbols have an effect once the decision to introduce them is taken, or when the symbol is actually introduced, or, finally, after a short time-gap for citizens who are sure to be exposed to the symbols mentioned, which would still need to be precisely evaluated? The third problem is related to the relative weight of the various symbols included in the model. Should they all have the same impact or an impact that depends on their estimated salience on the European population in a given country? The European passport, for example, has only touched directly the small part of the European population (less than a quarter in some countries) that actually owns a passport. At the same time, the Day of Europe is obviously less salient and less well-known, as a symbol, than the European flag. Should they be coded differently, and if yes, how to hierarchise them and to operationalise differences of salience?

The choice of the symbols that will be included in the model follows what was said in Chapter 4. The symbols considered will therefore comprise the election of the European Parliament through direct universal suffrage, the adoption of the European flag by the European Communities, the European passport, the adoption of the Day of Europe, the removal of customs, the removal of border control within the Schengen area, and the adoption of the European anthem. In terms of dating the effect of symbols effects, I chose the introduction date as the date of start effect of the new symbols. This seemed to be the least unnatural choice for two reasons. First, using the date of official symbol's adoption would not correspond to any reality in terms of popular perceptions (why should the 1975 decision on the election of the European Parliament through universal suffrage influence citizens' images of Europe, rather than the application of the decision itself). Second, it would be impossible to calculate theoretically a natural time gap between symbols' introductions and their effects on citizens' perceptions, even though there is probably such a gap. Moreover, the time frame of case delimitation is already vague enough (by year) to 'absorb' a large part of the likely gap. The third problem – that of the relative importance of the different symbols introduced in the model – is far more difficult to solve. Obviously, it is quite intuitive to presume that some symbols of the European Union are 'major' symbols while other are 'minor' symbols. Placing various symbols in these two categories, assuming that these are, indeed 'categories' rather than a continuum of symbolic salience, and finally relating a coding strategy to the principle of categories would all be highly arbitrary steps. Moreover, basing a coding of symbols on their 'salience' for the European citizenry would, in itself, pose a problem of endogeneity to the extent that receptivity to the symbols has been shown to be an indicator of identity (see Chapter 6). Finally, any differentiated coding strategy would probably be suspected a priori of being self-serving and used to improve the power of the model artificially. For all those reasons, it was decided not to quantitatively differentiate between the various symbols of the European Union. The score of a given case for the 'symbols' variables is therefore the sum of the scores of each variables, as summarised in Table A.6.

Coding institutional inertia

The second independent variable of interest is institutional inertia. This is much easier to operationalise. The only problem is to determine a starting point. For the first member-countries of the European Communities, should the 'year 0' be that of the Schuman Declaration (1950), the Rome Treaty (1957), or something else? Obviously, this choice has no impact on within country time-serial analysis, but has some effect when it comes to cross-national analysis. The choice made, here, is that of the Schuman Declaration as a starting point for European integration. In the case of newcomers – as in the case of symbols, analysed above – should the starting point be the decision to accept one more country in the Union or the actual joining time? To insure consistency between operationalisation strategies, the choice made here is to start the count of a country as participating in European integration from the date of membership (1973 for the United Kingdom, Denmark, and Ireland, 1981 for Greece, 1986 for Spain and Portugal, 1995 for Austria, Sweden, and Finland).

Institutional inertia is then operationalised as the total number of years of participation in the European integration process. For example, in 1976, Italy has a score of 27 and Denmark a score of 4, while Portugal and Spain are not yet in the sample. The operationalisation of inertia will imply some light degree of multicollinearity with the 'symbols' variable since the two are chronological by construction (for a given country, for both variables, we can say that $X_t \geq X_{t-1}$). Given this coding strategy, the first group of countries to have founded the ECSC in 1950 start with an institutional inertia 'bonus' of 23 as compared to the first joiners of 1973. Of course, it should be reminded that countries are only included in the dataset once they have joined the European Communities/European Union and that East Germany is considered a separate entity after its absorption in 1990. Northern Ireland is also considered a separate entity all throughout the time period considered.

Coding news on Europe

Finally, still following the discussion of Chapter 4, on the four times of development of mass perceptions of European integration, we can come up with an overall typology of aspects and components of assessment of European integration by citizens. This typology will be of use when trying to figure out what can lead citizens to assess the specific outcomes of European integration at a given time as positive or negative. Table A.7 summarises it.

In spite of this typology, however, we still have a choice to operationalise the good/bad news variable using either objective or subjective measurement strategies. I first consider possible objective measurement strategies and the difficulties they present before proposing an alternative subjective strategy.

Throughout the second half of the twentieth century, public opinion, across Western European countries, has evolved in its perceptions of what 'Europe' is.

Table A.7 A typology of perceived aspects and specific assessment of European integration by citizens

Type of assessment	Associated criteria	Theoretical predictor	Examples of good/bad news
Cosmopolitan Assessment	– Does European integration help to provide peace? – Can we trust fellow European partners?	Post-materialism (Inglehart, Dalton)	– German commitment to Europe in 1990. – War in Yugoslavia.
Policy Assessment	– Is the policy-making of the European Union positive on the whole? – Does the European Union cover areas of policy-making overlooked by other levels of government?	Rational Choice (Downs, Gabel)	– Socrates reinforced. Mad cow crisis.
Legitimacy Assessment	– Do European institutions follow reasonably fair and transparent decision-making processes on the whole? – If a specific outcome of European policy-making is negative, should we scrap the institutions that made it?	Legitimacy (Caldeira–Gibson)	– Modernisation of EP. – Corruption scandal of EC.
Citizen Assessment	– Do citizens get positive attributes of citizenship through belonging to the European Union? – Does the European Union serve its citizens?	Citizenship (Meehan)	– Schengen. – The 'cucumber policy'.

Public attitudes towards the European project cannot be assimilated to mere attitudes towards an international agreement like the North American Free Trade Agreement, with attitudes towards given policies or with attitudes towards new political institutions. Public opinion in Europe is obviously sensitive to the four elements of opinion formation identified, but citizens have probably ended up merging the four aspects of their assessment of the European integration process, perceiving it as a global political project, which makes it even more difficult to find a unified way of coding good and bad news on Europe according to the lines defined above.

Another fairly clear problem has to do with the difficulty in coding the salience of various news on Europe and finding out a reasonable threshold of what constitutes salient enough news on Europe in a comparative perspective. If I base my analysis on this approach, we may consider some of the main aspects on which the achievements and failures of European integration will have been judged over time. In the first period of European integration – as defined in the analysis of the evolution of perceptions of the European project, successes and failures of European integration would be judged primarily according to the expected impact of European integration on the prospects of peace and security in Europe. Those European citizens who did not believe in the peaceful intents of Germany in the 1950s for example, would consider as 'bad news' the Pleven plan of a European Defence Community. Similarly, the successes of the European communities to garner financing for reconstruction and later on to unify their steel and coal market with clear efficiency will have been perceived as a general success of integration by European citizens as a whole. With the beginning of the second period, specific policies became more central to the evolution of European integration, and the process of unification may be expected to have been assessed more explicitly according to their policy outcomes. First of all, the European Communities inaugurated new policy areas that had been neglected by many national governments in Western Europe until then, such as the environment. Environment legislation may have been perceived as a good news on Europe by those favouring what Inglehart has called 'post-materialist' issues (Inglehart, 1970), giving illusory grounds to the otherwise unsustainable theoretical claim of the author that support for European integration is just one of the many faces of post-materialism. On the other hand, those opposed to environmental concerns will have judged this intrusion of Europe in a new area of policy-making negatively. However, cunjunctural and structural economic policy at large remained the main area of expansion of European integration and the sustained level of economic growth with moderate inflation and low unemployment of the 1960s must have been perceived as global socio-tropic good news on European integration. The groups and regions that benefited most from the economic, agricultural, and industrial policy of the European Communities must have felt even more positive towards European integration. These include first the main beneficiaries of structural funds such as Northern France, Corsica, and Southern Italy at first, Scotland, and Ireland from 1973, then Greece, Portugal and Spain after their accession in 1981 and 1986, and finally Eastern Germany. It is also the case, however, of some professional categories such as meat producers, wheat producers and electronic components companies. In the third period, when institutional legitimisation started to become a real issue, as illustrated as the third section of Table A.8, the record of given institutions, and the institutional design, transparency, and legitimacy must have become significant elements of the assessment of

European integration by citizens. In this context, clear elements of democratisa-
tion, such as the announcement of the election of the European Parliament
under direct universal vote must have been globally perceived as good news on
Europe. At the same time, recent scandals on corruption in the European
Commission must have sounded as bad news on Europe for all citizens. This may
have damaged the legitimacy of European institutions in general and of the
European Commission in particular. Still in very recent times, I can identify a few
non-equivocal good and bad news. Failure to develop a common foreign policy in
the Yugoslavian multi-faceted crisis will have been perceived as bad and so will the
inability of European authorities to master quickly the several food scandals it was
faced with. On the other hand, given the trend of economic thought and the presentation of the media, the recent new successes of the Euro will have been perceived as positive by virtually everyone in the 12 countries of the 'Euro-zone'. In
the same way, the successes of Airbus have definitely become political issues, at
least in France, Germany, Spain, Italy and Britain, and, as shown by mass public
opinion surveys, news on cultural and social mobility (student exchange programmes, cultural initiatives, etc.) are virtually always welcomed as good.

As far as salience is concerned, it seems important to consider that European
news are not the dominant topic of interest of European citizens so that only very
salient news must have made a significant impression on the public of a given
country at a given time. Also, one could legitimately ask whether or not highly
salient and lowly salient news should be given the same importance in the coding. Another difficulty is to decide when news is, indeed, news. Occasionally,
related topics become 'news' a few days apart (e.g., in November 2000, the BSE
crisis in France, and then the BSE crisis in Germany and Spain the week after).
Also, sometimes, news develops across a certain period of time and only becomes

Table A.8 Average good/bad news index score per country

Country	Mean	Min.	Max.
Great Britain	−0.21	−0.41	0.15
Northern Ireland	−0.20	−0.41	0.15
Sweden	−0.18	−0.43	−0.01
Denmark	−0.10	−0.28	0.09
Netherlands	−0.08	−0.27	0.32
Germany	−0.01	−0.22	0.28
Luxembourg	−0.01	−0.46	0.49
Finland	0.03	−0.15	0.19
Austria	0.04	−0.10	0.21
Belgium	0.11	−0.28	0.39
France	0.12	−0.03	0.44
Ireland	0.24	−0.04	0.57
Italy	0.33	0.16	0.61
Greece	0.33	0.07	0.63
Spain	0.34	0.11	0.54
Portugal	0.38	−0.24	0.63

Notes: Theoretical scale: −1 to 1; $N = 349$.

salient piece of news some time after the first breakthrough. To stick with the mad cow disease example, the original BSE crisis in the United Kingdom only became a salient and traumatic news issue a few weeks after the original problem was, indeed, discovered. Any empirical model taking into account the influence of news involves the same complication.

With all those problems, objective coding of all good and bad news on Europe in the various countries of the European Union would be extremely difficult and arbitrary. Another possibility would be to ask experts what is their perspective on the balance between good and bad news in a given year of the European project. However, this would assume that experts would remember perfectly well the perceptions of good and bad news in a given country as long ago as in 1970, for example. This appears to be, again, an improbable, impractical way of assessing the balance of actual good and bad news on Europe in a given year. Again, a measurement strategy must be used which accommodates the arbitrariness of the perception, the focus, specifically, on perceptions as opposed to actual 'objective' good and bad news themselves (because, as explained in Chapter 3, what is 'good news' for someone could be 'bad news' for someone else, and it would be impossible to identify clearly how this would work). Therefore, it seems simpler to use directly a combination of perceptions of the way the media present the annual record of European institutions according to respondents themselves. Such a measure is given to us directly by quite an important number of Eurobarometer surveys. The respondents are first asked if they have read or heard about the European Parliament, the European Commission, and their actions over the past 12 months in the media. They are then asked if they felt the information gathered in the media tended to be quite positive, quite negative, or neither positive nor negative on the whole. The questions I proposed to use are then normally phrased as follows:

If you have heard or read about the European Parliament [Commission] and its actions in the past twelve months, did you think that on the whole, what you heard or read made you feel: quite positive, quite negative, or neither positive nor negative about it?

The proposed variable to be used as a good/bad news index is the mean of the Parliament and Commission variables, where each variable score per year per country is the difference between the percentages of positive and negative perceptions for the given sample. Those two items are far from perfect from the point of view of my analysis. Here are some of the main problems encountered with the strategy and the main reasons why it is argued, here, that they are still a reasonably good way to measure the concepts targeted. The first problem is a fairly clear validity problem. Very often indeed, we might expect the answer of a given respondent to measure their own support for the European institution targeted rather than how they interpreted the news conveyed to them by the media. As a matter of fact, it is likely that the original survey designers expected to capture this feeling towards European institutions as opposed to their perception of how the media presented them, with, I would argue, strong validity problems yet again. Moreover, the focus on two specific institutions and not, for example, on the Council might give a misleading representation of perceptions regarding the European Union as a whole. However, as explained above, it is quite clear that the pre-existing opinions of respondents will of course have an impact on the way news will be perceived. This matches the relationship, previously mentioned, between specific and diffuse support. A strong Euro-sceptic will undoubtedly feel alienated by what will be perceived as good news by many a Euro-enthusiast. One may even reinterpret obviously 'good' news as a piece of political propaganda. At the same time, the question is focused clearly enough on the media to be understood by the respondents. Indeed, it is clear from the analysis of the actual data that respondents' answers are influenced by news on Europe. The effects of major successes, such as the signature of the Single Act, and major scandals, such as the ESB ('mad cow') disease scandal are directly reflected in the respondents' answers. As for the focus on institutions, it is argued here that they are the two institutions respondents traditionally associate most closely with the European Union. Albeit far from a perfect summary of perceptions of news on the European Union as a whole, it is expected that the index will probably be a truly acceptable rough estimate of it. Second, the questions have not been asked in every Eurobarometer, breaking my time line. This implies a need to 'recreate' the missing scores of media evaluation to complete the time-series analysis. In one of the cases as well, the question was only asked for one of the two institutions concerned. Missing values are a constant problem in data analysis and the number of missing cases here is relatively small, even though the time-series design makes them truly problematic in that case. Traditional ways of replacing missing values by valid scores include creating instruments and replacing by the mean of the distribution. In this case, the suggested solution is to replace the missing value by the mean of the nearest available values before and after the year targeted as the patterns of available scores show some level of continuity and smoothness throughout the time periods concerned. Third, missing values for individuals' answers to these questions are not negligible (often between 5 and 20% of the whole sample) as some respondents claim not to have heard about the institutions concerned over the past 12 months. It is posited here that this does not threaten the overall validity of the measure, as people who do not read or hear news about European integration should only be marginally influenced by them in terms of their levels of European identity anyway.

As an additional test of the measurement strategy chosen and assessment of the first validity doubts mentioned earlier, I propose to assess the degree of direct correlation between the specific news assessment variables and the original 'support for European integration variable' used and residualised to obtain my aggregate level constructed dependent variable. If the superimposition is too high, then, we should have doubts about the validity of the variable, and also about the risk of artificially added explanatory power in the model – that is a risk of linear dependency created by the measurement strategy. However, the analysis shows that this particular correlation, while real is not at all overwhelming (0.24). This is an encouragement to proceed with the strategy and assess the univariate distribution of the variable. The average news score per country are reported in Table A.8.

The results of Table A.8 are quite interesting. They confirm that the average news score vary according to the level of euro-enthusiasm of the countries concerned, but, at the same time, that news interpretation scores are more tightly linked to years than to countries, proving some overarching cross-national pattern of evaluation. This is true regardless of the overall level of enthusiasm of the countries studied towards European integration. Indeed, as shown by the range of values for each country, virtually all countries have got both known years of overall negative (only three exceptions) and positive (only one exception) evaluation of how the media present Europe to them.

Notes

1. This interesting paradox about the conceptual nature of identity was developed by philosopher Peter Burgess in a conference on European identity held at the European University Institute in Florence, 9–10 June 2000.
2. It is important to remember that the laws normally apply to everyone within the territory of a given state. Therefore, citizenship will entail rights and duties that define the 'legal identity' of the political community, rather than the rules of the land.
3. This section is inspired by an application to a research grant to the Economic and Social Research Council (ESRC) of June 2000. Grant reference: R000223463.
4. This section is inspired by a conference given at the European University Institute, Florence, Italy, 9–11 June 2000.
5. This section largely represents an application to the greater context of European public opinion formation of the contribution of the author ('French public opinion and Europe') to S. Stern-Gillet and M.T. Lunati, 2000. *Perspectives on Europe*. London: Edwin Mellen Press.
6. It is interesting to note that the French text talks of a 'Europe des Citoyens': a 'Citizens' Europe', thus reinforcing the idea of the desire to create a new political identity.
7. The Bohemian King sent a letter to all fellow European monarchs in 1464 proposing the creation of a unified political community in Europe to avoid and manage potential economic and territorial conflicts. His proposal did not receive much support from other sovereigns.
8. The Council of Ministers is often confused for an 'executive' institution of the European Union, probably because of its composition: the Council is indeed made of representatives of national executives and has the size of a traditional national cabinet. The Council, however, has not got the traditional powers of executive institutions (such as the power of initiative, held exclusively by the European Commission) and has the traditional function of any legislative institution in a democracy: that of passing the 'laws' of the European Union. It should also be noted that while the Council of Ministers has the 'physical' size of a traditional cabinet, it truly has the 'virtual' size of a traditional legislature given voting quotas on all policy aspects that use a qualified majority. The Council is very similar in spirit with the higher chambers of federal states where the federate units – rather than the population – are officially represented, except that it acts as the main legislative institution in the European Union architecture while most federal higher chambers have a secondary role.
9. Note that for all the analysis of levels of legitimacy that follows, answers to questions on the trust of political institutions were coded in three categories: (1) trust, (2) indifferent/don't know, (3) do not trust. The proportion of indifferent answers is often quite high.

10. In this context, it is of particular interest to remember the extremely dramatic first sentence of De Gaulle's *Mémoires*: 'La France vient du fond des âges' ('France comes from the end of the ages').

11. 'Aux Grands Hommes, la Patrie Reconnaissante' ('to the Great Men, the Grateful Fatherland') is the message written on the Pantheon, monument created by Republican France to celebrate its 'heroes'.

12. 'If I was to start again, I would start with culture'.

13. Lewis and Wigen define continents as geographical masses delimited naturally (normally by seas or straights), which is, obviously, not the case of Europe and Asia, separated from each other by doubtful and artificial borders.

14. One of the heraldic descriptions of the European flag, considered for the draft of the new European Constitution.

15. The design of the Euros symbolises the birth of the new united Europe, inheriting a common cultural legacy as well as the vision of a common future for the coming century.

16. This chapter is largely inspired by a conference paper presented at the European University Institute, Florence, 9–11 June 2000.

17. For example, Eurobarometer 54, 2001.

18. Eurobarometer traditionally asks respondents whether they feel '[British] only, [British] and European; European and British, or European only'. This implies a conflict between the possible identities of respondents.

19. The respondents are asked to position themselves on a one to seven scale on which only the two extremes are labelled as 'do not identify at all' and 'identify very strongly.' Their answers might therefore be slightly influenced by each respondent's perception of the meaning of the scale, that is, what a three or a five mean, and whether a respondent 'goes for the extremes' easily or not. This would create artificial internal consistency between the four answers of a given respondent. This problem, although limited in terms of quantitative effect, is quite usual whenever arbitrary scales are used, for example to ask experts to evaluate the ideological profiles of political parties or when respondents are asked to position their own preference and those of the main parties' to test spatial hypotheses. Because 'absolute levels' are not interesting then, one can avoid bias by dividing all answers by the mean of the values chosen by a given respondent. This solution, however, would make it totally impossible here to test the hypothesis of positive correlation between identity levels since it would precisely kill the variance in terms of overall identity levels between 'strong' and 'weak' identifiers, implicitly assuming that this difference is a pure scale artefact. Further tests will help us argue against this criticism.

20. This section is partly based on Bruter, 2003 (see bibliography).

21. As explained earlier, there is no data available for 1972 and 1974.

22. Of course, 'change in institutional inertia' would not be a variable but just a constant, as institutional inertia simply and mathematically increases by one every year.

23. The experiment and focus group discussions took place in 2001, before the launch of the Euro as a 'physical' currency.

24. See Chapter 1.

Bibliography

Abeles, Marc, Bellier, Irene, and McDonald, Marion. 1993. 'Approche anthropologique de la Commission Européenne'. Unpublished Report. Paris: LAIOS.

Adenauer, Konrad. 1965. *Mémoires, 1945–1953*. Paris: Hachette.

Akin, Benjamin. 1964. *State and Nation*. London: L. Hutchinson.

Alexakis, Vassilis. 1995. *La Langue Maternelle*. Paris: Gallimard.

Anderson, Benedict. 1991. *Imagined Communities: Reflections on the Origin and Spread of Nationalism*. London: Verso.

Arbruster, Rollo and Meinhof, Ulrike. 2003. 'Introduction' in Meinhof, Ulrike H., ed. *Bordering European Identities*. Special Issue. *Journal of Ethnic and Migration Studies. 29.5.*

Bates, Robert, Levi, Margaret, and Weingast, Barry. 1997. *Analytic Narratives*. Princeton: Princeton University Press.

Bellamy, Richard. 2000. 'Citizenship beyond the Nation-State: The Case of Europe' in Noel O'Sullivan, ed. *Political Theory in Transition*. London: Routledge.

Ben Gurion, David. 1951. 'The Call of the Spirit of Israel'. Address to the Knesset.

Bernstein, Serge and Milza, Pierre. 1994. *Histoire de l'Europe* (five volumes). Paris: Hatier.

Black, Jeremy. 1997. *Maps and History: Constructing Images of the Past*. New Haven: Yale University Press.

Boorstin, Daniel, Brooks Mather, and Boorstin, Ruth Frankel. 1995. *A History of the United States*. Needham: Prentice Hall.

Bourdieu, Pierre. 1991. *Language and Symbolic Power*. Harvard: Harvard University Press.

Breakwell, Glynis. 2004. 'Identity Change in the Context of the Growing Influence of European Union Institutions'. In R. Herrmann, T. Risse, M. Brewer, eds. *Transnational Identities*. Oxford: Rowman and Littlefield.

Brugmans, Henri. 1970. *L'idée Européenne 1920–1970*. Bruges: De Tempel.

Bruter, Michael. 2005 (forthcoming). 'Institutions and Identity: Towards a Reformulation of Integration and Tolerance Policies'. In Hieroniymi, Otto, ed. Special Issue on Identity and Integration. *Refugee Survey Quarterly*. UNHCR.

Bruter, Michael. 2004a. 'Measuring European Identity: Civic and Cultural Components'. In R. Herrmann, T. Risse, and M. Brewer. eds. *Transnational Identities*. Oxford: Rowman and Littlefield.

Bruter, Michael. 2004b. 'On What Citizens Mean by Feeling "European": Perceptions of News, Symbols, and Borderless-ness'. *Journal of Ethnic and Migration Studies*. Vol. 30.1 (January): 21–41.

Bruter, Michael. 2003. 'Winning Hearts and Minds for Europe: The Impact of News and Symbols on Civic and Cultural European Identity'. *Comparative Political Studies*. Vol. 36.10 (December): 1148–1179.

Bruter, Michael. 2000a. 'French Public Opinion and European Integration'. In T. Lunati and S. Stern-Gillet, eds. *Historical, Economic, Social, and Political Aspects of European Integration*. London: Edwin Mellen.

212   *Bibliography*

Bruter, Michael. 2000b. 'Urbanity and Support for European Integration'. *Research Papers Series*. Hull: Centre for European Union Studies.

Bruter, Michael. 1999. 'Diplomacy without a State: The External Delegations of the European Commission'. *Journal of European Public Policy*. Vol. 6.2: 183–205.

Bruter, Michael. 1998. 'The Symbols of European Integration'. Washington, DC: Centre for German and European Studies.

Bruter, Michael and Deloye, Yves, eds. 2006 (forthcoming). *Encyclopedia of European Parliament Elections*. Basingstoke: Palgrave-MacMillan.

Burgess, Michael. 2000. *Federalism and the European Union*. London: Routledge.

Butler, David and Stokes, David. 1974. *Political Change in Britain*. London: MacMillan.

Caldeira, Gregory and James Gibson. 1995. 'The Legitimacy of the Court of Justice in the European Union: Models of Institutional Support'. *American Political Science Review*. Vol. 89.2 (June): 356–376.

Campbell, Angus, Converse, Philip, Miller, Arthur, and Stokes, David. 1960. *The American Voter*. New York: Wiley.

Castano, Emanuele. 2004. 'Entitativity and Multiple Identities'. In R. Herrmann, T. Risse, and M. Brewer, eds. *Transnational Identities*. Oxford: Rowman and Littlefield.

Castoriadis, Constantin. 1975. *L'Institution Imaginaire de la Société*. Paris: Seuil.

Churchill, Winston. 1995. *Discours Choisis*. Paris: Poche.

Colley, Linda. 1992. *Britons: Forging the Nation: 1707–1837*. New Haven: Yale University Press.

Coudenhove-Kalergi, Richard. 1924. *Pan-Europa*. Wein: Pan-Europa.

Dalton, Russell. 1996. *Citizen Politics: Public Opinion and Political Parties in Advanced Western Democracies*. Chatham: Chatham House.

Delors, Jacques. 1992. '1992: a Pivotal Year'. Address. Brussels: EC.

Deloye, Yves. 1997. *Sociologie Historique du Politique*. Paris: La Découverte.

Deth, Jan (van) and Scarbrough, Elinor. 1995. 'The Concept of Values'. In Jan W. Van Deth and Elinor Scarbrough, eds. *The Impact of Values*. Oxford: Oxford University Press.

Downs, Anthony. 1957. *An Economic Theory of Democracy*. New York: Harper.

Duchesne, Sophie and Andre-Paul, Frognier. 1995. 'Is There a European Identity?' In Oskar Niedermayer and Richard Sinnott, eds. *Public Opinion and Internationalized Governance*, Oxford: Oxford University Press.

Eichenberg, Richard and Dalton, Russell. 1993. 'Europeans and the European Community; The Dynamics of Public Support for European Integration'. *International Organization*. Vol. 47: 507–534.

Eijk (van der), Cees and Franklin, Mark, eds. 1996. *Choosing Europe*. Ann Arbor: Michigan University Press.

Ester, Peter, Halman, Loek, and de Moor, Ruud, eds. 1993. *The Individualizing Society: Value Change in Europe and North America*. Tilburg, Netherlands: Tilburg University Press.

European Communities. 1992. *Treaty on the European Union*. Luxembourg: Publication Office.

European Monetary Institute. 1996. *Press Releases*. Frankfurt: Press office of the EMI.

Evans, Geoffrey and Norris, Pippa, eds. 1999. *Critical Elections: British Parties and Voters in Long-Term Perspective*. London: Sage.

Feldman, Stanley. 1988. 'Structure and Consistency in Public Opinion: The Role of Core Beliefs and Values'. *American Journal of Political Science*. Vol. 32.2. (May): 416–440.

Fejtő, François. 1993. *Histoire de la Destruction de l'Autriche-Hongrie: Requiem pour un Empire*. Paris: Seuil.

Fichte, Johann Gottlieb. 1845. *Samtliche Werke*. Berlin: Veit Franklin.

Franklin, Mark. 1999. 'Borrowing from Peter to Pay Paul: European Union Politics as a Multi-Level Game against Voters'. Paper presented for the 1999 meeting of the *American Political Science Association*, Atlanta.

Franklin, Mark and Wlezien, Christopher. 1997. 'The Responsive Public: Issue Salience, Policy Change, and Preferences for European Unification'. *Journal of Theortical Politics*. Vol. 9: 247–263.

Franklin, Mark and Wlezien, Christopher, eds. 1992. *Electoral Change*. Cambridge: Cambridge University Press.

Gabel, Matthew. 1994. 'Understanding the Public Constraint on European Integration: Affective Sentiments, Utilitarian Evaluations, and Public Support for European Integration'. PhD Thesis. University of Rochester.

Gautron, Jean-Claude. 1989. *Organisations Européennes: Droit Européen*. Paris: Dalloz.

Gellner, Ernest. 1983. *Nations and Nationalism*. Ithaca: Cornell University Press.

Greenstein, F. 1965. *Children and Politics*. New Haven: Yale University Press.

Guild, Elspeth. 1996. 'The Legal Framework of Citizenship of the European Union'. In David Cesarani and Mary Fulbrook, eds. *Citizenship, Nationality and Migration in Europe*. London: Routledge.

Habermas, Jürgen. 1992. 'Citizenship and National Identity: Some Reflections on the Future of Europe'. *Praxis International*. Vol. 12.1 (April): 1–19.

Hall, Stuart. 1991. 'Old and New Loyalties'. In King, Anthony, ed. *Culture, Globalisation, and the World System*. Basingstoke: Palgrave-Macmillan.

Hamilton, Alexander, Madison, James, and Jay, John. [1999 edn]. *The Federalist Papers*. New York: Mentor.

Herder, Johann Gottfried (von). 1817–1913. *Works*. Berlin: Weidmannsche Buchhandlung.

Herrmann, Richard and Brewer, Marilyn. 2004. 'Identities and Institutions: Becoming European in the EU'. In R. Herrmann, T. Risse, and M. Brewer, eds. *Transnational Identities*. Oxford: Rowman and Littlefield.

Herzl, Theodor. 1960. *The Jewish State*. New York: Herzl Press (first published 1896).

Hix, Simon. 2005. *The Political System of the European Union*. Basingstoke: Palgrave Macmillan.

Hooghe, Liesbeth. 1997. 'Serving "Europe" – Political Orientations of Senior Commission Officials'. *European Integration Online Papers*. Vol. 1.8. (http://eiop.or.at/eiop/texte/1997–008a.htm).

Howe, Peter. 1995. 'A Community of Europeans: The Requisite Underpinnings'. *Journal of Common Market Studies*. Vol. 33.1: 27–46.

Hurwitz, Jon and Peffley, Mark. 1987. 'How are Foreign Policy Attitudes Structured?: A Hierarchical Model.' *American Political Science Review*. Vol. 81.4: 1099–1120.

Inglehart, Ronald. 1997. *Modernization and Postmodernization: Cultural, Economic, and Political Change in 43 Societies*. Princeton: Princeton University Press.

Inglehart, Ronald. 1990. *Culture Shift in Advanced Industrial Society*. Princeton: Princeton University Press.

Inglehart, Ronald. 1971. 'The Silent Revolution'. *American Political Science Review*. Vol. 65.4. (December): 991–1017.

Iyengar, Shanto, Peters, Mark, and Kinder, Donald. 1982. 'Experimental Demonstrations of the "Not-So-Minimal" Consequences of Television News Programs'. *The American Political Science Review*. Vol. 76.4. (December): 848–858.

Jacoby, William. 1991. 'Ideological Identification and Issue Attitudes'. *American Journal of Political Science*. Vol. 35.1: 178–205.

Katz, Daniel. 1960. 'The Functional Approach to the Study of Attitudes'. *Public Opinion Quarterly*. Vol. 24.2: 163–204.

Kymlicka, William. 1995. *Multicultural Citizenship: A Liberal Theory of Minority Rights*. Oxford: Clarendon Press.

Kundera, Milan. 1984. 'The Tragedy of Central Europe'. In Gale Stokes, ed. (1991): *From Stalinism to Pluralism*. Oxford: Oxford University Press.

Laclau, Ernesto, ed. 1994. *The Making of Political Identities*. London: Verso.

Laffan, Brigitte. 2004. 'The European Union and its Institutions as Identity Builders'. In R. Herrmann, T. Risse, and M. Brewer, eds. *Transnational Identities*. Oxford: Rowman and Littlefield.

Lazare, Bernard. 1897. 'Le nationalisme juif', Conference to the Association des Étudiants Israélites, le 6 mars 1897.

Leca, Jean. 1992. *La Citoyenneté dans tous ses Etats*. Paris: L'Harmattan.

Lewis, Martin and Wigen, Karen. 1997. *The Myth of Continents: A Critique of Meta-Geography*. Berkeley: University of California Press.

Licata, Laurent. 2000. 'National and European Identities: Complementary or Antagonistic'. Paper presented at the ID-NET conference, European University Institute, Florence: 9–10 June 2000.

Lipset, Seymour Martin and Rokkan, Stein. 1967. *Party Systems and Voters Alignments*. Cambridge: Cambridge University Press.

McKuen, Michael, Erikson, Robert, and Stimson, James. 1989. 'Macropartisanship.' *The American Political Science Review*. Vol. 83.4. (December): 1125–1142.

McKuen, Michael, Erikson, Robert, and Stimson, James. 1992. 'Peasants or Bankers? The American Electorate, and the U.S. Economy.' *American Political Science Review*. Vol. 86.3. (September): 597–611.

McLean, Mairi and Howorth, Jolyon eds. 1992. *Europeans on Europe: Transnational Visions of a New Continent*. London: MacMillan.

Meehan, Elizabeth. 1993. *Citizenship and the European Community*. London: Sage Publications.

Meinhof, Ulrike and Richardson, Kay. 1999. *Worlds in Common? Television Discourse in a Changing Europe*. Routledge: London and New York, p. 187.

Meinhof, Ulrike and Galasinski, Dariusz. 2000. 'Photography, Memory, and the Construction of Identities on the Former East–West Border'. *Discourse Studies*. Vol. 2.3: 323–353.

Miller, David. 2000. *Citizenship and National Identity*. Oxford: Polity Press.

Mokre, Monika, Weiss, Gilbert, and Bauböck, Rainer, eds. 2003. *Europas Identitäten. Mythen, Konstrukte, Konflikte*. Frankfurt: Campus Verlag.

Monnet, Jean. 1978. *Mémoires*. Garden City: Doubleday.

Monnet, Jean. 1955. *Les Etats-Unis d'Europe ont Commencé*. Paris: Laffont.

Moravcsik, Andrew. 1998. *The Choice for Europe: Social Purpose and State Formation from Messina to Maastricht*. Ithaca: Cornell University Press.

Müftüler-Bac, Meltem. 1997. *Turkey's Relations with a Changing Europe*. Manchester University Press: Manchester.

Mummendey, Amelie and Waldzus, Sven. 2004. 'National Differences and European Plurality: Discrimination or Tolerance between European Countries'. In R. Herrmann, T. Risse, and M. Brewer, eds. *Transnational Identities*. Oxford: Rowman and Littlefield.

Nie, Norman and Andersen, Kristi. 1974. 'Mass Belief Systems Revisited: Political Change and Attitude Structure'. *Journal of Politics*. Vol. 36.3: 540–591.

Nordau, Max. 1897. Address at the First Zionist Congress. Basel: 29 August.

Norris, Pippa, ed. 1999. *On Message: Communicating the Campaign*. London: Sage.

Oz, Amos. 1979. *Under this Blazing Light*. Cambridge: Cambridge University Press.

Parekh, Bikhu. 2000. *The Future of Multi-Ethnic Britain*. Report. London: Runnymede Trust.

Pastoureau, Michel and Schmidt, Michel. 1990. *L'Europe: Mémoire et Emblèmes*. Paris: L'Epargne.

Pattie, Charles, Seyd, Patrick, and Whiteley, Paul. 2004. *Citizenship in Britain*. Cambridge: Cambridge University Press.

Paxman, Jeremy. 1999. *The English*. London: Penguin.

Petőfi, Sandor. 1871. *Poésies*. Paris: Lacroix.

Pinsker, Leon. 1882. 'Auto-emancipation' (Pamphlet).

Renan, Joseph Ernest. 1882. 'Discours de la Sorbonne' in *Discours et Conferences* Discourse pronounced at La Sorbonne University on 11 March.

Rochard, Bertrand. 2003. *L'Europe des Commissaires: Reflexions sur l'Identité Européenne*. Bruxelles: Bruylant.

Roth, Cecil. 1969. *A Short History of the Jewish People*. (Revised Edition). Hartmore House.

Rougemont, Denis de. 1965. *The Meaning of Europe*. London: Sidgewick and Jackson.

Rousseau, Jean Baptiste. 1762. *Le Contract Social*. Genève: Rey.

Saussure (de), Ferdinand. 1974. *Cours de Linguistique Generale*. Edited by Bailly, C. London: Fontana.

Seiler, Daniel-Louis. 1998. *La Vie politique des Européens: introduction aux pratiques démocratiques dans les pays de l'Union Européenne*. Paris: Collection U.

Seiler, Daniel-Louis. 1982. *Politique (la) Comparée*. Paris: Collection U.

Schuman, Robert. 1963. *Pour l'Europe*. Paris: Nagel.

Shore, Cris. 1993. 'Inventing the "People's Europe": Critical Approaches to European Community "Cultural Policy". *Man*, New Series. Vol. 28.4. (December): 779–800.

Shore, Cris and Black, Annabel. 1992. 'The European Communities: And the Construction of Europe.' *Anthropology Today*. Vol. 8.3. (June): 10–11.

Spaak, Paul-Henri. 1969. *Combats Inachevés*. Paris: Fayard.

Stimson, James and MacKuen, Michael, and Erikson, Robert. 1995. 'Dynamic Representation'. *The American Political Science Review*. Vol. 89.3 (September): 543–565.

Tacitus, 109. *Annals*. (1872 Edition). London: Whittaker.

Taylor, Charles. 2004. *Modern Social Imaginaries*. Durham: Duke University Press.

Tiesse, Merse. 1999. *La Création des Identités Nationales en Europe du XVIIIeme au XXeme siècles*. Paris: Seuil.

Tocqueville (de), Alexis. 1835. *Democratie en Amerique*. Paris: Gosselin.

Valéry, Paul. 1962. *History and Politics*. New York: Bollingen Foundation.

Waever, Ole. 1995. 'Identity, Integration, and Security: Solving the Sovereignty Puzzle in E.U. Studies'. *Journal of International Affairs*. Vol. 48: 389–431.

Weber, Max. 1946. *Selected Works*. Oxford: Oxford University Press.

Wiener, Antje. 1998. *European Citizenship Practice: Building Institutions of a Non-State*. Boulder: Westview Press.

Wintle, Michael. 2000. 'Europe's Eastern Border: Arbitrary beyond Description?' *De Weerspannigheid van de Feiten*. Amsterdam.

Wintle, Michael, ed. 1996. *Culture and Identity in Europe*. London: Avebury.

Wodak, Ruth. 2004. 'National and Transnational: European and other Identities Constructed in Interviews with EU Officials'. In R. Herrmann, T. Risse, and M. Brewer, eds. *Transnational Identities*. Oxford: Rowman and Littlefield.

Wodak, Ruth. 1999. *Nationale und Kulturelle Identitaten Osterreichs: Theorie, Methoden*. Wien: IFK.

Index

217

218   *Index*

220 *Index*